International Monetary Fund and Its Responsibilities

International Monetary Fund and Its Responsibilities

V.K. Mathur

CYBER TECH PUBLICATIONS
4264/3, Ansari Road, Daryaganj, New Delhi-110002 (India)
Ph.: 011-23244078, 011-43559448 Fax: 011-23280028
E-Mail: cyberpublicationsdelhi@yahoo.com
Website: www.cybertechpublications.com

INTERNATIONAL MONETARY FUND AND ITS RESPONSIBILITIES

V.K. Mathur

First Edition 2010

Asian Offset Printers

Published by :

G.S. Rawat for **Cyber Tech Publications**
4264/3, Ansari Road, Daryaganj, New Delhi-110002 (India)
Ph.: 011-23244078, 011-43559448 Fax: 011-23280028
E-Mail: cyberpublicationsdelhi@yahoo.com
Website: www.cybertechpublications.com

Preface

Recent years have seen calls for increased accountability in the International Monetary Fund (IMF). The IMF has recently taken some modest steps in the areas of evaluation and audit, but the organization is generally perceived to be lacking in its adaptation to the new policy and governance frameworks demanded by increasing globalization. In relations across the Executive Board, IMF staff, the governments it serves, and civil society, the Fund has avoided its proper share of responsibility for failed policy prescriptions and has little incentive to adapt or improve its operations.

Developing or strengthening a poverty reduction strategy is on the agenda of about 70 low-income countries, as a requirement for receiving debt relief under the enhanced HIPC (Heavily Indebted Poor Countries) Initiative and concessional assistance from the World Bank and International Monetary Fund (IMF).

The International Monetary Fund (IMF), the World Bank, and the General Agreement on Tariffs and Trade (GATT) gathered at Bretton Woods, New Hampshire, to examine critically the creation of these multilateral economic institutions, their adaptations over the last five decades, and their capacity to respond to current and future planetary challenges. The Bretton Woods – GATT System: Retrospect and Prospect after Fifty Years brings together over twenty of the most insightful papers produced for the Bretton Woods Revisited conference, which was convened by the Institute for Agriculture and Trade Policy.

This book would not have been possible without the help, encouragement, and support of a number of individuals.

—Author

CONTENTS

1

Introduction

The International Monetary Fund (IMF) is an international organization that oversees the global financial system by observing exchange rates and balance of payments, as well as offering financial and technical assistance when requested. Its headquarters are located in Washington, D.C..

BACKGROUND

Data Dissemination Systems: In 1995, the International Monetary Fund (IMF) began work on data dissemination standards with the view of guiding IMF member countries to disseminate their economic and financial data to the public. The International Monetary and Financial Committee (IMFC) endorsed the guidelines for the dissemination standards and they were split into two tiers: The General Data Dissemination System (GDDS) and the Special Data Dissemination Standard (SDDS).

The IMF executive board approved the SDDS and GDDS in 1996 and 1997 respectively and subsequent amendments were published in a revised "Guide to the General Data Dissemination System". The system is aimed primarily at statisticians and aims to improve many aspects of statistical systems in a country. It is also part of the World Bank Millennium Development Goals and Poverty Reduction Strategic Papers.

The IMF established a system and standard to guide members in the dissemination to the public of their economic and financial data. Currently there are two such systems:

General Data Dissemination System (GDDS) and its superset Special Data Dissemination System (SDDS) for those member countries having or seeking access to international capital markets.

The primary objective of the GDDS is to encourage IMF member countries to build a framework to improve data quality and increase statistical capacity building. This will involve the preparation of metadata describing current statistical collection practices and setting improvement plans. Upon building a framework, a country can evaluate statistical needs, set priorities in improving the timeliness, transparency, reliability and accessibility of financial and economic data. Some countries initialy used the GDDS, but lately upgraded to SDDS.

MEANING OF IMF

The International Monetary Fund (IMF) is an international organization that provides financial assistance and advice to member countries. This article will discuss the main functions of the organization, which has become an enduring institution integral to the creation of financial markets worldwide and to the growth of developing countries.

The IMF was born at the end of World War II, out of the Bretton Woods Conference in 1945. The Fund was created out of a need to prevent economic crises like the Great Depression. With its sister organization, the World Bank, the IMF is the largest public lender of funds in the world. It is a specialized agency of the United Nations and is run by its 184 member states. Membership is open to any country that conducts foreign policy and accepts the statutes of the Fund.

NATURE OF WORK

The IMF is responsible for the creation and maintenance of the international monetary system, the system by which international payments among countries take place. It thus strives to provide a systematic mechanism for foreign exchange transactions in order to foster investment and promote balanced global economic trade. To achieve these goals, the IMF focuses and advises on the macroeconomic policies of a country, which affect its exchange rate and its government's budget, money and credit management. The IMF will also appraise a country's financial sector and its regulatory policies, as well as structural policies within the macroeconomy that relate to the labor market and employment. In addition, as a fund, it may offer financial assistance to nations in need of correcting balance of payments discrepancies. The IMF is thus entrusted with nurturing economic growth and maintaining high levels of employment within countries.

FUNCTIONING

The IMF gets its money from quota subscriptions paid by member states. The size of each quota is determined by how much each government can pay according to the size of its economy. The quota in turn determines the weight each country has within the IMF-and hence its voting rights-as well as how much financing it can receive from the IMF.

Twenty-five percent of each country's quota is paid in the form of special drawing rights (SDRs), which are a claim on the freely usable currencies of IMF members. Before SDRs, the Bretton Woods system had been based on a fixed exchange rate, and it was feared that there would not be enough reserves to finance global economic growth. Therefore, in 1968, the IMF created the SDRs, which is a kind of international reserve asset. It was created to supplement the international reserves of the time, which were gold and the U.S. dollar. The SDR is not a currency; it is a unit of account by which member states can exchange with one another in order to settle international accounts. The SDR can also be used in exchange for other freely-traded currencies of IMF members. A country may do this when it has a deficit and needs more foreign currency to pay its international obligations.

The SDR's value lies in the fact that member states commit to honor their obligations to use and accept SDRs. Each member country is assigned a certain amount of SDRs based on how much the country contributes to the Fund (which is based on the size of the country's economy). However, the need for SDRs lessened when major economies dropped the fixed exchange rate and opted for floating rates instead. The IMF does all of its accounting in SDRs, and commercial banks accept SDR denominated accounts. The value of the SDR is adjusted daily against a basket of currencies, which currently includes the U.S. dollar, the Japanese yen, the euro, and the British pound.

The larger the country, the larger its contribution; thus the U.S. contributes about 18% of total quotas while the Seychelles Islands contribute a modest 0.004%. If called upon by the IMF, a country can pay the rest of its quota in its local currency. The IMF may also borrow funds, if necessary, under two separate agreements with member countries. In total, it has SDR 212 billion (USD 290 billion) in quotas and SDR 34 billion (USD 46 billion) available to borrow.

THE FIVE THINGS THAT MOVE THE CURRENCY MARKET

The IMF offers its assistance in the form of surveillance, which it conducts on a yearly basis for individual countries, regions and the global economy as a whole. However, a country may ask for financial assistance if it finds itself in an economic crisis, whether caused by a sudden shock to its economy or poor macroeconomic planning. A financial crisis will result in severe devaluation of the country's currency or a major depletion of the nation's foreign reserves. In return for the IMF's help, a country is usually required to embark on an IMF-monitored economic reform program, otherwise known as Structural Adjustment Policies (SAPs).

There are three more widely implemented facilities by which the IMF can lend its money. A stand-by agreement offers financing of a short-term balance of payments, usually between 12 to 18 months. The extended fund facility (EFF) is a medium-term arrangement by which countries can borrow a certain amount of money, typically over a three to four-year period. The EFF aims to address structural problems within the macroeconomy that are causing chronic balance of payment inequities. The structural problems are addressed through financial and tax sector reform and the privatization of public enterprises. The third main facility offered by the IMF is known as the poverty reduction and growth facility (PRGF). As the name implies, it aims to reduce poverty in the poorest of member countries while laying the foundations for economic development. Loans are administered with especially low interest rates.

The IMF also offers technical assistance to transitional economies, such as the former Soviet Republics, in the changeover from centrally planned to market run economies. The IMF also offers emergency funds to collapsed economies, as it did for Korea during the 1997 financial crisis in Asia. The funds were injected into Korea's foreign reserves in order to boost the local currency, thereby helping the country avoid a damaging devaluation. Emergency funds can also be loaned to countries that have faced economic crisis as a result of a natural disaster.

All facilities of the IMF aim to create sustainable development within a country and try to create policies that will be accepted by the local populations. However, the IMF is not an aid agency, so all loans are given on the condition that the country implement the SAPs and make it a priority to pay back what it has borrowed. Currently, all countries that are under IMF programs are developing, transitional and emerging market countries (countries that have faced financial crisis).

VARIED OPINIONS

Because the IMF lends its money with "strings attached" in the form of its SAPs, many people and organizations are vehemently opposed to the Fund's activities. Opposition groups claim that structural adjustment is an undemocratic and inhumane means of loaning funds to countries facing economic failure. Debtor countries to the IMF are often faced with having to put financial concerns ahead of social ones. Thus, by being required to open up their economies to foreign investment, to privatize public enterprises, and to cut government spending, these countries suffer an inability to properly fund their education and health programs. Moreover, foreign corporations often exploit the situation by taking advantage of local cheap labor while showing no regard for the environment. The oppositional groups say that locally cultivated programs, with a more grassroots approach towards development, would provide greater relief to these economies. Critics of the IMF say that, as it stands now, the IMF is only deepening the rift between the wealthy and the poor nations of the world. Indeed, it seems that many countries cannot end the spiral of debt and devaluation. Mexico, which sparked the infamous "debt crisis" of 1982 when it announced it was on the verge of defaulting on all its debts in the wake of low international oil prices and high interest rates in the international financial markets, has yet to show its ability to end its need for the IMF and its structural adjustment policies. Is it because these policies have not been able to address the root of the problem? Could more grassroots solutions be the answer? These questions are not easy. There are, however, some cases where the IMF goes in and exits once it has helped solve problems. Egypt is an example of a country that embarked upon an IMF structural adjustment program and was able to finish with it.

Providing assistance with development is an ever-evolving and dynamic endeavor. While the international system aims to create a balanced global economy, it should strive to address local needs and solutions. On the other hand, we cannot ignore the benefits that can be achieved by learning from others.

THE WORLD BANK AND IMF

Created after World War II to help avoid Great Depression-like economic disasters, the World Bank and the IMF are the world's largest public lenders, with the Bank managing a total portfolio of $200 billion and the Fund supplying member governments with money to overcome short-term credit crunches. But the Bank and the Fund are also the world's biggest loan sharks.

When the Bank and the Fund lend money to debtor countries, the money comes with strings attached. These strings come in the form of policy prescriptions called "structural adjustment policies." These policies-or SAPs, as they are sometimes called-require debtor governments to open their economies to penetration by foreign corporations, allowing access to the country's workers and environment at bargain basement prices.

Structural adjustment policies mean across-the-board privatization of public utilities and publicly owned industries. They mean the slashing of government budgets, leading to cutbacks in spending on health care and education. They mean focusing resources on growing export crops for industrial countries rather than supporting family farms and growing food for local communities. And, as their imposition in country after country in Latin America, Africa, and Asia has shown, they lead to deeper inequality and environmental destruction.

For decades people in the Third World have protested the way the IMF and World Bank undemocratically impose such policies on their countries. In just the last year, those protests have spread to the power centers of the developed world. In April, some 20,000 people gathered in Washington, DC during the institutions' spring meetings to demand a more democratic kind of international decision-making. Similar protests took place in Prague, Czech Republic in September of that year. By dragging the Fund and the Bank into the light of public scrutiny, the Washington protests re-invigorated a public dialogue about the growing wealth inequalities within and among nations, and they put the institutions on notice that they can't continue business as usual.

BACKGROUND AND PURPOSES

The IMF resulted from lengthy discussions of separate American, British, Canadian, and French proposals drafted during World War II. The British "Keynes Plan" envisaged an international clearing union that would create an international means of payment called "bancor." Each country's central bank would accept payments in bancor without limit from other central banks. Debtor countries could obtain bancor by using automatic overdraft facilities with the clearing union. The limits to these overdrafts would be generous and would grow automatically with each member country's total of imports and exports. Charges of 1 or 2 percent a year would be levied on both creditor and debtor positions in excess of specified limits. This slight discouragement to unbalanced positions did not rule out the possibility of large imbalances covered by automatic American credits to the rest of the world, perhaps amounting to many billions of dollars. Part of the credits might eventually turn out to be gifts because of the provision for canceling creditor-country claims not used in international trade within a specified time period. The rival American plan took its name from Harry Dexter White of the U.S. Treasury. White rejected the overdraft principle and the possibility of automatic American credits in vast and only loosely limited amounts. Instead, he proposed a currency pool to which members would make definite contributions only and from which countries might borrow to tide themselves over short-term balance of payments deficits. Both plans looked forward to a world substantially free of controls imposed for balance of payments purposes. Both sought exchange-rate stability without restoring an international gold standard and without destroying national independence in monetary and fiscal policies. According to the usual interpretation, the British plan put more emphasis on national independence and the American plan on exchange-rate stability reminiscent of the gold standard. The compromise finally reached resembled the American proposal more than the British.

The Articles of Agreement of the International Monetary Fund (and also the articles of its sister institution, the International Bank for Reconstruction and Development of the World Bank, were drafted and signed by representatives of forty-four nations at Bretton Woods, New Hampshire, in July 1944. By the end of 1945, enough countries had ratified the agreement to bring the fund into existence. The board of governors first met in March 1946, adopted bylaws, and decided to locate the fund's headquarters in Washington, D.C. One year later the fund was ready for actual exchange operations.

According to its Articles of Agreement, the purposes of the International Monetary Fund are to promote international monetary cooperation, facilitate the expansion of international trade for the sake of high levels of employment and real income, promote exchange-rate stability and avoid competitive depreciation, work for a multilateral system of current international payments and for elimination of exchange controls over current transactions, create confidence among member nations and give them the opportunity to correct balance of payments maladjustments while avoiding measures destructive of national and international prosperity, and make balance of payments disequilibriums shorter and less severe than they would otherwise be.

Recognizing that these goals could not all be achieved promptly, Article XIV of the agreement provided for a postwar "transitional period" during which the member countries might violate the general ban on exchange controls over current account transactions. No definite length for the transition period was stated, but countries maintaining exchange controls more than five years after the start of fund operations (that is, beyond 1952) were expected to consult the fund about them every year. Actually, consultations about general economic policies have become an annual routine with all members, not just with members in violation of the standard decontrol obligations. Such consultations, requiring voluminous documentation, have even become the main activity of the fund, the one using up the most man-hours.

The "purposes" just mentioned are vague. More specifically, the fund provides drawing rights (in effect, loans) to help its members meet temporary deficits without resort to exchange controls, exchange-rate adjustments, or internal deflation. Member countries are supposed to "live with" or "ride out" purely temporary deficits, drawing on the fund when necessary to supplement their own accumulated reserves of gold and foreign exchange. The fund is not meant to use up its resources, however, hopelessly palliating "fundamental disequilibrium." A country faced with a "fundamental" deficit in its international transactions may be expected to seek a remedy in devaluing its currency. An opposite situation of "fundamental" balance of payments surplus would presumably call for upward revaluation. Such adjustments were expected to be infrequent.

The balance of payments (BOP) account is a statistical record of the economic transactions during a given year between residents (individuals, businesses, and governments) of one country and residents of the rest of the world. The BOP account consists of the current account, the capital account, and foreign currency reserves. The current account primarily records a country's net exports of goods and services. The current account is the cash flow element of the BOP account. If a country exports more than it imports, the current account is in a surplus position and the country has a positive cash flow. If a country imports more than it exports, the current account is in a deficit position and the country has a negative cash flow--the country's residents are not earning enough foreign currency through their exports to pay for what they buy from other countries. Countries, like people, can spend more than they take in only if they draw down their savings or borrow funds. A current account deficit, therefore, must be financed either by drawing down a country's foreign currency reserves or by borrowing funds from abroad. The capital account records a country's foreign borrowing. When a bond is sold to residents of another country, the payment, a capital inflow, is entered as a credit in the capital account. If a country's total receipts (exports plus capital inflows) fall short of its total payments (imports plus capital outflows), it has a BOP deficit and must draw on its foreign currency reserves to meet its obligations for the remaining payments. Persistent current account deficits eventually exhaust a country's credit and foreign currency reserves, just as a persistent negative cash flow for consumers eventually exhausts their credit cards and savings account.

If a country, say Brazil, has a BOP deficit--for example, U.S. dollar receipts from abroad are less than U.S. dollar payments due abroad--Brazil can, for a time, draw on its dollar reserves. Alternatively, Brazil can borrow dollars from the IMF by exchanging Brazilian reals for U.S. dollars. The IMF uses an analytic framework, known as financial programming, to determine the amount of the loan and the macroeconomic adjustments that are needed to eventually establish BOP equilibrium. Typically, the amount of the loan is equal to a country's upcoming foreign debt obligations and the macroeconomic adjustments are intended to reduce imports and increase exports to enable the country to earn sufficient foreign exchange in the future to pay its bills, including the newly incurred IMF debt.

Conceptually, therefore, IMF loans come at the price of "conditionality," the policy adjustments that IMF officials believe will correct a recipient's country BOP deficit. The usual strategy for correcting a BOP deficit is to reduce domestic demand, and thus imports, through the imposition of credit ceilings, reductions in government spending, and tax increases. In addition, the IMF calls for the removal of export barriers. Currency devaluations are also used to promote net exports. For example, reducing the exchange rate for one Brazilian real from $4 to $2 reduces imports by making U.S. goods twice as expensive in local real prices and increases exports by making Brazilian goods half as expensive in U.S. dollars. Conceptually, IMF adjustment programs seek to rapidly correct BOP deficits.

Membership Qualifications: Any country may apply for membership to the IMF. The application will be considered first by the IMF's Executive Board. After its consideration, the Executive Board will submit a report to the Board of Governors of the IMF with recommendations in the form of a "Membership Resolution." These recommendations cover the amount of quota in the IMF, the form of payment of the subscription, and other customary terms and conditions of membership. After the Board of Governors has adopted the "Membership Resolution," the applicant state needs to take the legal steps required under its own law to enable it to sign the IMF's Articles of Agreement and to fulfill the obligations of IMF membership.

A member's quota in the IMF determines the amount of its subscription, its voting weight, its access to IMF financing, and its allocation of SDRs. A member state cannot unilaterally increase its quota-increases must be approved of by the Executive Board. For example, in 2001, China was prevented from increasing its quota as high as it wished, ensuring it remained at the level of the smallest G7 economy (Canada). Since then, its contribution has been allowed to be increased slightly further. As of 2006, participating nations were discussing changes to the voting formula, to increase equity.

Assistance and Reforms: The primary mission of the IMF is to provide financial assistance to countries that experience serious financial difficulties. Member states with balance of payments problems may request loans and/or organizational management of their national economies. In return, the countries are usually required to launch certain reforms, which have often been dubbed the "Washington Consensus". These reforms are generally required because countries with fixed exchange rate policies can engage in fiscal, monetary, and political practices which may lead to the crisis itself. For example, nations with severe budget deficits, rampant inflation, strict price controls, or significantly over-valued or under-valued currencies run the risk of facing balance of payment crises in their future. Thus, the structural adjustment programs are at least ostensibly intended to ensure that the IMF is actually helping to prevent financial crises rather than merely funding financial recklessness.

However, this approach is not without its critics, as described below. Many proponents of the IMF contend that some criticisms are the result of the fact that many people are not familiar with the operations and objectives of the IMF, and blame a lack of transparency within the IMF for this, as well as the dense nature of international finance in general. Suggestions for improving these understandings have included greater community outreach efforts, tighter accounting standards, possible regulatory oversight, and changes in the organizational structure of the IMF to include fewer economists, whom many fear are attempting to use developing countries as nothing more than lab rats. Some fear, however, that some of these reforms to the IMF itself introduce political considerations rather than economic considerations, many of which may have resulted in the financial crises in the first place. According to Ulrich Beck, the International Monetary Fund is an international risk community combating the threat of a global financial crisis.

The role of the two Bretton Woods institutions has been controversial to some since the late Cold War period. Critics claim that IMF policy makers deliberately supported capitalistic military dictatorships friendly to American and European corporations. Critics also claim that the IMF is generally apathetic or hostile to their views of democracy, human rights, and labor rights. The controversy has helped spark the anti-globalization movement. Others claim the IMF has little power to democratize sovereign states, although that is not its stated objective, which is to advise and promote financial stability. Arguments in favor of the IMF say that economic stability is a precursor to democracy.

Two criticisms from economists have been that financial aid is always bound to so-called "Conditionalities", including Structural Adjustment Programs. Conditionalities, it is claimed, retard social stability and hence inhibit the stated goals of the IMF, while Structural Adjustment Programs lead to an increase in poverty in recipient countries.

Typically the IMF and its supporters advocate a Keynesian approach. As such, adherents of supply-side economics generally find themselves in open disagreement with the IMF. The IMF frequently advocates currency devaluation, criticized by proponents of supply-side economics as inflationary. Secondly they link higher taxes under "austerity programmes" with economic contraction.

Currency devaluation is recommended by the IMF to the governments of poor nations with struggling economies. Supply-side economists claim these Keynesian IMF policies are destructive to economic prosperity. That said, the IMF sometimes advocates "austerity programmes," increasing taxes even when the economy is weak, in order to generate government revenue and balance budget deficits, which is the opposite of Keynesian policy. These policies were criticised by Joseph E. Stiglitz, former chief economist and Senior Vice President at the World Bank, in his book Globalization and Its Discontents. He argued that by converting to a more Monetarist approach, the fund no longer had a valid purpose, as it was designed to provide funds for countries to carry out Keynesian reflations.

Complaints are also directed toward International Monetary Fund gold reserve being undervalued. At its inception in 1945, the IMF pegged gold at 35 dollars per Troy ounce of gold. In 1973 the Nixon administration lifted the fixed asset value of gold in favour of a world market price. Hence the fixed exchange rates of currencies tied to gold were switched to a floating rate, also based on market price and exchange. This largely came about because Petrodollars outside the United States were more than could be backed by the gold at Fort Knox under the fixed exchange rate system. The fixed rate system only served to limit the amount of assistance the organization could use to help debt-ridden countries. Current IMF rules prohibit members from linking their currencies to gold.

Most altermondialists, like ATTAC, believe that IMF interventions aggravate the poverty and debt of Third World and developing countries. According to the analysis by Yves Engler, the IMF is considered to be responsible for worsening or actually creating famine in Malawi (2002), Ethiopia (2003) and Niger (2005). The IMF, in turn, has documented evidence to the contrary.

Opposition to the IMF is often fragmented. For instance, advocates of supply-side economics would generally regard the policies advocated by ATTAC to be little different in form to the ideas peddled by the IMF. In other words, they would see ATTAC tax-and-spend policies and the IMF's austerity policies as being fundamentally similar.

Argentina, which had been considered by the IMF to be a model country in its compliance to policy proposals by the Bretton Woods institutions, experienced a catastrophic economic crisis in 2001, generally believed to have been caused by IMF-induced budget restrictions-which undercut the government's ability to sustain national infrastructure even in crucial areas such as health, education, and security-and privatization of strategically vital national resources. The crisis added to widespread hatred of this institution in Argentina and other South American countries, with many blaming the IMF for the region's economic problems. The current-as of early 2006-trend towards moderate left-wing governments in the region and a growing concern with the development of a regional economic policy largely independent of big business pressures has been ascribed to this crisis.

Another example of where IMF Structural Adjustment Programmes aggravated the problem was in Kenya. Before IMF got involved in the country, the Kenya central bank oversaw all currency movement in and out of the country. IMF mandated that Kenya central bank had to allow easier currency movement. However, the adjustment resulted in very little foreign investment, but allowed Kamlesh Manusuklal Damji Pattni, with the help of corrupt government officials, to siphon out billions of Kenya shillings in what came to be known as the Goldenberg scandal, leaving the country in a state worse than that which it was in before the IMF reforms were implemented.

That the IMF is perceived to intervene only in countries that experience years of dire economic conditions has certainly hurt its reputation. The financial collapses it intervenes in are products of uneven capitalist development sometimes exacerbated by government mismanagement, but mismanagement is often cited by rich nations as the source of the financial crises. These collapses tend to lead to years of economic difficulty that can be addressed in various ways, but IMF Structural Adjustment Policies consistently serve to open up or "liberalize" economies to foreign capital rather than provide for economic recovery through statist policies such as government financed projects to achieve full employment. Thus, IMF policies further the notion that economic development in underdeveloped countries is dependent on attracting foreign investment rather than through a state-managed approach centered on full employment and progressive taxation. It is also true that politicians have used the IMF as an easy target for blame when they themselves have erred, using nationalism to gain easy political points.

Overall the IMF success record is perceived as limited. While it was created to help stabilize the global economy, since 1980 critics claim over 100 countries have experienced a banking collapse that they claim have reduced GDP by four percent or more, far more than at any time in Post-Depression history. The considerable delay in IMF response to a crisis, and the fact that it tends to only respond to rather than prevent them, has led many economists to argue for reform, they claim. In 2006, an IMF reform agenda called the Medium Term Strategy was widely endorsed by the institution's member countries. The agenda includes changes in IMF governance to enhance the role of developing countries in the institution's decision-making process and steps to deepen the effectiveness of its core mandate, which is known as economic surveillance or helping member countries adopt macroeconomic policies that will sustain global growth and reduce poverty.

Whatever the feelings people in the Western world have for the IMF, research by the Pew Research Center shows that more than 60 percent of Asians and 70 percent of Africans feel that the IMF and the World Bank have a positive effect on their country. This may largely be due to the fact that the media and textbooks in developing countries' schools describe the IMF as having a positive role in their countries, despite claims that there has been an increase in poverty, increase in the debt-burden, and a reduction of economic growth that IMF opponents argue its policies have resulted in.

In 2005, the IMF was the first multilateral financial institution to implement a sweeping debt-relief program for the world's poorest countries known as the Multilateral Debt Relief Initiative. By year-end 2006, 23 countries mostly in sub-Saharan Africa and Central America had received total relief of debts owed the IMF.

PAST MANAGING DIRECTORS

An unwritten rule establishes that the IMF's managing director must be European and that the president of the World Bank must be from the United States. Executive Directors, who confirm the managing director are voted in by Finance Ministers from countries they represent. The First Deputy Managing Director of the IMF, the second-in-command, has traditionally been (and is today) an American.

The IMF is for the most part controlled by the major Western Powers, with voting rights on the Executive board based on a quota derived from a monetary stake in the institution. Rarely does the board vote and pass issues contradicting the will of the US or Europeans.

There have been some exceptions in the past. Dr. Mohamed Finaish from Libya, the Executive Director representing the majority of the Arab World and Pakistan, was a tireless defender of the developing nations' rights at the IMF. He stood steadfast in his beliefs and principles for fourteen years until his defeat in the 1992 elections to an Egyptian IMF Staff Member.

FEATURES OF THE ENHANCED DSBB

The International Monetary Fund's Dissemination Standards Bulletin Board (DSBB) provides access to the Special Data Dissemination Standard (SDDS), the General Data Dissemination System (GDDS), and the Data Quality Reference (DQRS) sites.

- The SDDS was established in 1996 to guide countries that have, or that might seek, access to international capital markets in the dissemination of economic and financial data to the public. This site provides information about economic and financial data disseminated by member countries that subscribe to the SDDS.
- The GDDS was established in 1997 to guide countries in the provision to the public of comprehensive, timely, accessible, and reliable economic, financial, and socio-demographic data. This site provides information on data produced and disseminated by member countries that participate in the GDDS.
- The Data Quality Reference Site (DQRS), which was created to foster a common understanding of data quality, provides access to contributions in the field and includes a selection of articles and other sources related to data quality issues.

THE BRETTON WOODS CONFERENCE

One participant described it as 'a quiet, green and soothing garden of the gods, circled by mountain ramparts'. A press reporter grew lyrical as he surveyed the scenery.

Viewed from this wicker chair on the curving porch of the Mt. Washington Hotel the Presidential range of New Hampshire etches zigzag indentations into the azure sky. A dark line against a twisting path of earthy green-that of the merging tracks of the world-famous cog railroad-climbs to the summit of New England's highest peak, Mt. Washington. On its crest, Tip-Top House and the radio tower stand out like a village in a mirage. In the foreground the darker greens of pine and hemlock vie with the lighter shades of oaks and birch. Set in the midst of these the brilliant green of one of the golf fairways forms a grassy floor. A sand trap glistens in the morning sun. Directly below, the wild Ammonoosuc plunges unseen but noisily on its way to join the sea.

The majestic beauty of the surroundings was in striking contrast to the temporary bedlam created by the arrival of about 700 people from more than forty countries. In addition to the official delegates, there were advisers, assistants, stenographers, newsmen, observers, technicians, and so on. Many of them spoke no English at all. The trains that brought them to Bretton Woods were dubbed 'the Tower of Babel on wheels'.

The Mount Washington Hotel, one of the most luxurious summer hotels in the world, had been closed for two years. Of Spanish Renaissance architecture, the hotel was surrounded by the White Mountain National Forest, which covers nearly 1 million acres. The management had only about a month to prepare for the onrush. Painters and cleaners were still busy applying the finishing touches. Rooms were mixed up, offices for the delegates had to be hastily improvised, and there was a general feeling of ineffective goodwill. A group of Army Military Police joined in the work, and even outworked some of the hired labour in the final cleaning of the premises.

Bretton Woods, the postal address of the hotel, was only a stop on the railway. It had no store, not even a main street. The hotel was self sufficient with its own power-plant, dress shops, beauty parlour, bowling alleys, barber shop, and stock ticker-tape. There were two cinemas, a swimming pool, tennis courts, and stables. A church was located in the hotel grounds.

The extraordinary bustle and confusion regarding the allocation of rooms, complicated by the lack of staff, hot water, beds, and so on, caused at least one casualty on the first day of the conference: the news went around that the new manager of the hotel had either drunk himself out of his job, or else had given up in despair and left. While the foreign delegations acquainted themselves with their new surroundings, Morgenthau and White set to work. Shortly after their arrival,

Morgenthau called a meeting of the American delegates to prepare them for the commission and committee meetings. While some of the delegates, such as Dean Acheson and Marriner Eccles, had been exposed to the plans before the conference, most them knew practically nothing, except what they may have read in the press or heard in Congressional committees. There was Fred Vinson, 'the judge'; Leo Crowley, Administrator of the Foreign Economic Administration; Miss Mabel Newcomer, professor at Vassar College; Representatives Brent Spence and Jesse Wolcott; Senators Robert Wagner and Charles Tobey; and Edward Brown, president of a large Chicago bank, 'a large, industrious, outspoken man who represented the tractable element of the banking community'. He had been at Atlantic City.

Morgenthau asked White to explain the salient points regarding the Fund and the Bank, and to give 'a broad outline of what the American experts feel as in the interest of our country as a result of the work in Atlantic City'.

The purpose of the meetings in Atlantic City, White said, had been purely exploratory. It had been useful to ascertain the differences of opinion, the major issues troubling the various delegates, so as to provide a basis for discussion and determine the position to take on the various points. He would confine himself to the major issues and differences: With the Fund, the first major issue is the question of quotas.... In the first place, all countries want larger quotas, but the countries that will give us the most trouble... are as follows: China insists that she shall have fourth place....France is insisting on fifth place and India is insisting on fifth place... and has sent a pretty high-powered delegation here....The smaller countries all want larger quotas. The most troublesome will be Australia who is participating to all extent far beyond the proper role of a country of her size and importance.... The South American countries would like a larger quota. Now, it is the South American countries who in this are going to be important to us for reasons that we will discuss later.

The American position had been that the aggregate quotas would not be more than $8000 million to $8300 million, that the American quota would not be larger than $2750 million, and that the British Empire as a whole would have a little less. 'Russia will get third place and she will have about ten per cent of the quotas. There is no problem-I mean, there is general agreement there as long as she had third place.'

The next point of importance was the amount of gold to be subscribed. The only problem here was that Russia insisted on a reduction of 50 per cent, and argued that all other countries that had suffered war damage should have a reduction, relative to the amount of destruction suffered. All the invaded countries supported this Russian claim, and Britain, though it had not been invaded, wanted the same treatment.

Then came the question of voting power. The American had taken the position that voting power and quota should approximately be the same. Smaller countries had objected, and wanted to start every country off with 100 votes. But White did not 'want to budge'.

One of the main points in dispute between the American the British delegations was the degree of flexibility of exchanges and the conditions under which a country could alter its exchange rate. The British, remembering the depression that followed their return to gold, were saying 'that they are never going to be in a position like that again, in which they are tied to the gold standard and have to suffer a depression merely to suit somebody's notions on monetary theories'. Those, like Keynes, who had warned against a return to gold, were now completely in the ascendancy, and the whole British people, with the exception of some banking groups, objected to anything that resembled the gold standard. Although the Fund provided for some flexibility, the British wanted more; 'Our position here is quite the opposite.' We wanted to prevent a return to the 1930s, with floating exchanges, unilateral decisions exchange depreciation. He realised that, if the British delegation made too many compromises, 'Parliament will throw it out.'

Edward Brown wanted to know why 'Russia doesn't need the Fund. It has a complete system of State trading-state industry. It doesn't make any difference to them whether the ruble is five cents or five dollars. They want to get some other things; they would like to keep a market for their newly mined gold.' But White, for reasons which he would point out later, thought 'the Fund needs Russia'.

Brown also thought that many of the small countries put in claims which they did not expect to get. Morgenthau agreed: the Mexicans would raise the silver question, but only for home consumption, and would not press it too hard. 'So I mean, these fellows are good horse traders, but I think among our delegates we have a couple of pretty good horse traders, outside myself-I trade cows.' As for Keynes, he had his hands full with the British Empire. 'He has an incipient revolution on his hands and... we will let the British Empire fight it out without making us a cat's paw.'

The next important point of difference, White said, was the pressure on debtor and creditor countries. The other countries had suggested that pressure should be put on creditor countries, and by that they meant mainly the United States. They expected that the United States would continue to export more than it imported, and to drain the world's gold. So they wanted these creditor countries to adopt a policy which would put less pressure on the exchange of the debtor countries, and 'enable them to sell more goods here. We have been perfectly adamant on that point. We have taken the position of absolutely no, on that. And that has created a good deal of discussion and will continue to create some.' The debtor countries, on the other hand, would have to pay deterrent charges, and the more they borrowed from the Fund the higher the charges would be, so that they would be under pressure to put their balance of payments in order. To the objection of one delegate that deterrent charges might accelerate the indebtedness of a country, instead of reducing it, White answered that these charges were low, but that it was necessary to create an inducement for the country to restore equilibrium.

He also explained that there was little risk for the United States in participating in the Fund. The amount of gold would remain stable, and, if a country devalued, it would have to put up more of its currency to make up for the difference.

The British and a number of other nations, White said, had insisted that their access to the Fund's resources were a matter of right, but the American delegation had persistently taken thc attitude that the Board of Directors of the Fund had the power to refuse the Fund's facilities, even though the quota might be available. That was the way the provision now read, 'but it reads in a way that is not too easy to see if you read it quickly'.

In drafting the provision the lawyers had taken great care, Luxford added; 'the language gives us clearly that right, but we have tried to avoid emphasizing it more than you have to'. Although there were technical experts at Atlantic City who disputed Luxford's interpretation. White was certain that he was right.

White also objected to the allegations of those who said that the Fund would go 'bust', and that the United States would loose the money it put in. '... we have surrounded this thing with protective devices at every point. That doesn't mean it is without risk.' If another war broke out, and 'a country says, "Yes, you have balances here, but try and get them", nothing can protect you against that kind of relationship'. But, otherwise, 'Our lawyers have done a job', White concluded.

If the worse came to the worst, members could always withdraw: 'we did that for our own sake... most countries feel that it is satisfactory to them, because it enables them quite appropriately to tell their Congress they are sovereign'.

White explained some of the other matters which had not been resolved, and answered the questions of the delegates so as to prepare them to defend the American position in the commissions and committees, or wherever they were being buttonholed by foreign representatives.

Morgenthau recommended, 'So again, if we play this as a team, if we have any differences, let's have them here in the room and over the bar... we have gotten off to a good start. We have some very good New Hampshire sunshine and weather, and let's play this as a team, looking over a broad horizon for future generations."

THE CONFERENCE AT WORK

After listening to the message President Roosevelt had sent to the conference, the chairman of the Chinese, Czechoslovakian, Mexican, Brazilian, Canadian and Russian delegations spoke in the name of their countries. After his nomination as president of the conference, Secretary Morgenthau stated that 'what we do here will shape to a significant degree the nature of the world in which we are to live'. The delegates were not asked to make definitive agreements binding on any of them; they would refer the proposals to their respective governments for acceptance or rejection.

We can accomplish this task only if we approach it not as bargainers but as partners-not as rivals but as men who recognize that their common welfare depends, in peace as in war, upon mutual trust and joint endeavor. We are to concern ourselves here with essential steps in the creation of a dynamic world economy.... This is the indispensable cornerstone of freedom and security. All else must be built upon this. For freedom of opportunity is the foundation for all other freedoms...On battlefronts the world over, the young men of all our united countries have been dying together-dying for a common purpose. It is not beyond our powers to enable the young men of all our countries to live together-to put their energies, their skills, their aspirations into mutual enrichment and peaceful progress.

As had been planned by White, Commission I (International Monetary Fund), of which he was to be chairman, was to be subdivided into four committees. Commission II (Bank for Reconstruction and Development) was to be headed by Keynes. Commission III was to concern itself with 'Other Means of International Financial Co-operation'.

The four committees of commission I were as follows:

- Committee 1-Purposes, Policies and Quotas of the Fund;
- Committee 2-Operations of the Fund;
- Committee 3-Organisation and Management;
- Committee 4-Form and Status of the Fund.

All the chairmen and reporters of these committees were non-American, They were all referred to as representatives of their respective countries, with the exception of the French, who represented the French Comité. The French resented this, but in the course of the conference some of the differences between General de Gaulle and President Roosevelt were settled in Washington, and the French gradually came to be referred to as French delegates.

As in Atlantic City, each committee was assigned a number of subjects which it had to discuss and, if possible, agree upon. The secretaries of the committees, who were the people White had trained, plus some new ones, trained by White's pupils, wrote up the minutes of the committee meetings and reported to the commission.

It soon became evident that some of the chairmen and reporters of the committees did not speak English, or spoke it very poorly. 'The Russian delegate... turned the meeting over to his Canadian colleague as soon as he had made his inaugural speech (in Russian). This sensible procedure has not unfortunately been imitated by other chairmen, with the result that several of the committees moved with maddening slowness.'

Dr E. A. Goldenweiser, director of research and statistics of the Board of Governors of the Federal Reserve System, and a member of the American delegation, brought back these observations:

It was very hard work. The delegates of each country usually met by themselves in the morning. There were always two or three meetings of committees and commissions and sub-committees, and later there would be the big task of having all that combined, written and distributed by the next morning. There was a large force of stenographers and multigraphers who worked day and night. They had shifts and... did an "amazingly good job in taking material that sometimes wasn't finished until two or three in the morning. One, of the nice features of the meeting was a little group of Boy Scouts who were acting as pages, and helped a good deal in keeping things moving and distributing things smoothly.

It was a combination of settling various conflicting interests, and at the same time hammering out specific provisions. I am not too familiar myself with all of the provisions. They are inevitably complex because of the subject, and they are written in a legal language, which I have always found it difficult to understand.

There were a great many varieties of people and a great many varieties of unintelligible English spoken. Most everything was said in what was supposed to be English. The Russians didn't speak English; neither did their interpreters. The French spoke English but always had trouble in being satisfied that their exact meaning was properly translated by their interpreters....

The Russians were an interesting group. I could not help feeling that they were struggling between the firing squad on the one hand and the English language on the other. They seemed to be very much afraid of the reactions in their own country, and didn't dare to make a step without consultation by 'phone or cable with their Government. (Dr Goldenweiser was born in Russia, and spent his boyhood there.) He gave this appreciation of Keynes: the outstanding personality at Bretton Woods was Lord Keynes. He shone in two respects-in the fact that he is, of course, one of the brightest lights of mankind in both thinking and expression and in his ability to influence people, and he shone also by being the world's worst chairman. He presided over meetings of the Bank in a way that was entirely intolerable because he had his own documents all fixed up so that he could go through in a hurry....He spoke while he was sitting down in a meeting and it was difficult to hear him. He spoke indistinctly when presiding and was impatient of any difference of opinion. His function at Bretton Woods was primarily performed in a suite of rooms on the second floor to which everybody went for inspiration and guidance and compromise.

It might be noted here that Lord and Lady Keynes had their suite just above the rooms occupied by Secretary and Mrs. Morgenthau. The penetrating rhythm of the exercises performed by the prima ballerina, unaware that her routine practising could be heard through the ceiling beneath, occasionally prevented Morgenthau, worried and tense about the outcome of the conference, from going to sleep.

During three weeks the overcrowded hotel would be filled with the extraordinary hustle and bustle of a polyglot conference. More than 700 people had to be accommodated, Since not enough room was available at the hotel itself some had to be lodged at nearby hostelries.

COMMISSION AND COMMITTEE MEETINGS

On 3 July, the second day of the conference, the plenary session was devoted to the selection of permanent Officers, the creation of committees and the election of those who were to direct the activities of the conference. The chairman of the New Zealand delegation presented the nominees for membership of the steering committee and the three main commissions. All we're unanimously approved.

Commission I was given the task of dealing with the Fund. White told Morgenthau that he would preside over that commission: 'The importance why we need somebody to chairman this, who knows the complete matter, is that he should prevent coming to a vote on matters which he doesn't wish to come to a vote on, and in general arranging the discussion in such a way that we are never caught with an agreement among the Commission on something that we don't want, because then it is too late.'

'I don't know anybody more competent', said Morgenthau.

The secretaries of the committees, who were to write up the minutes of the meetings, were designated by White. They were all Americans. At the beginning of the conference, a memorandum had been distributed to the delegates, which said that the 'Secretaries, like all other officers of the Conference, are on this occasion international officials and for all practical purposes temporarily lose not only their national identity but their allegiance to the organizations, governmental or otherwise, with which they are affiliated'. This had the ring of true internationalism. They were, in reality, the people who had been trained by White in Atlantic City (or had been trained by people who had been trained there). Senator Tobey, in his own state of New Hampshire, made a moving speech: It is our common aspiration, I believe, that, assembled here among these eternal hills, we shall, under a deep conviction of the needs of humanity, discard trivia and refuse to be turned away from our great purpose to give to the people of the world new hope and courage through the constructive results which we pray may come from this historic conference.... Every great effort in human history has had its saboteurs, men who utter critic peep and cynic bark. There are some of these around the perimeter of this Conference.... As we confer together here today, amidst the eternal hills, inspired by the sublime beauty around us, and as the shadows of passing clouds above leave their impress for a moment on the slopes of yonder mountains, may the contemplation of the tragic sufferings and sacrifices of every nation bind us together in brotherly love.... Two thousand years ago Christ was hanged on a cross, a spear thrust in his side....There are nations represented here today who, too, have had their sides pierced and a crown of thorns pressed upon them by the sufferings of war.... Gentlemen, we must not, we cannot, we dare not fail. The hopes and aspirations of the common people of each of our countries rest in us.

With the first committee meetings due to take place on 4 July, the American delegation discussed the strategy to follow. The first and most important question that would be brought up, and in which practically every country was extremely interested, was the table of quotas. No satisfactory formula had been found, and no complete list had been published, although many nations had been told what their quota was to be. The British had been working on it in an effort to increase the quotas of the Commonwealth countries, No delegation could go back home, after a table had been published, and meet the charge that they had been bad negotiators. So it was necessary to come to some agreement with the British before announcing the list of quotas. Australia, said White, was 'very rambunctious and almost belligerent in the attitude that she should have a much larger quota.... There will be a cat-and-dog fight, anyhow, because every country will want to change. Our safeguard is, however, that if the maximum is fixed, any increase that any country gets has to come out of some other country.... It will be a struggle between countries.' One good idea was to hold back a kitty: 'They will make strong arguments...and if you can give them a little something, they feel that they have negotiated... and I think they feel better.' Dr Goldenweiser did not think it was a dignified situation for America to be bargaining 'with all these people about little items of twenty-five or fifty million dollars'. Why not give them a figure and say 'This is where we stand', and if there is any change the whole American delegation will have to decide.

'It would make them mad at us, though', said Luxford. 'Why should we be the scapegoat for thirty-nine countries?'

'That is right', said White.

The foreign delegates would be told that the total was $8000 million, but the real total would be $8400 million dollars. 'They have got to fight around a couple of days and get nowhere.' If you told them in advance that the total would be increased, they would 'prolong the discussion interminably because they wouldn't believe that is your final figure'.

The next point concerned the rules under which the committee meetings were to be held. White said he had prepared many alternatives, which usually did not change the substance, but were formulated in more appropriate language. It was not necessary for the United States delegates to take much part in the discussions, 'but the boys that will be with you will be able to indicate whether they think something ought to be said, but I think you will find that most of the others will want to talk'.

Would the rules of the committee be some 'catch as catch can'?, Vinson asked. No, they would be very informal, he was told.

'Just make one general rule', Dr Goldenweiser suggested, 'that anybody can talk as long as he pleases provided he doesn't say anything. Separate the business of the Committee from the talk.' He thought his remark might be facetious, but it was rather close to what White wanted.

'You have got to go through the motions', someone suggested; 'the Chairman should go through the motions, at least of asking whether there are any' alternatives because, after all, these are the alternatives of Atlantic City and there were thirty countries not represented'.

The committees met twice every day. The meetings were staggered, to enable all national delegations to be represented adequately. The committees on the Fund devoted most of their time ironing out technical differences rather than establishing broad lines of agreement. The basis of all discussions was the joint statement and the alternatives submitted by the various countries, Keynes, after he saw the results of the Atlantic City conference, as they had been drafted by White and his group, thought he would have to submit a separate draft, but recognised soon that this would have mixed things up considerably, and gave up the idea.

This was the first international meeting of its kind and importance in which the US Treasury had taken a leading part. It soon became evident that some method had to be devised in order to achieve what had to be achieved, within the time limit available.

'You can argue and argue', said Luxford, 'and we haven't good arguments for some of the things we have to push through.'

There is no question that you can't vote on every provision', White thought, 'but pursue the same tactics on others. Speaking of legalities for a moment, supposing the chairman, after hearing the discussion, four or five for and one against, and he says that the chair rules that the sense of the meeting is as follows, can at some time subsequently the British say there was no vote and that wasn't the sense of the meeting, and re-open the thing?'

Acheson did not have the rules for international conferences with him, but he thought that delegates could ask for a roll-call vote. Luxford did not think that would be satisfactory: 'But the trouble is, you are going to find so many of these countries so very articulate who are in opposition, whereas the Latin Americans will just sit there until they vote.'

'I think what you could do', Acheson suggested, 'is to have a yea and nay vote if you can't tell by the noise, and ask them to raise their hands.' But White did not like that. He preferred to ascertain the sense of the meeting by the general attitude of the delegates. 'It is much safer... if it is legal.'

'That is perfectly all right', said Luxford, the lawyer, 'if they don't object.'

The procedure White had in mind also made it possible for, him, as chairman of the commission, to delegate to a 'special committee', which would hold no public debates, any question on which it seemed 'difficult to reach agreement. This allowed the matter to be settled behind closed doors, within the group of technical advisers."

For about two weeks the committees and the commissions met, and reviewed the provisions put before them, making suggestions, recommending changes, and putting forward new proposals. The level at which these discussions were held was, in general, very high. In addition to economists of international reputation, there were many government and central bank officials of outstanding competence in monetary affairs. There were Professor Robertson, Professor (later Lord) Robbins, Mr. Redvers Opie, Mr. Robert Brand, and several officials from Whitehall and the Bank of England. There were Mr. Louis Rasminsky from Canada, Professor Mossi from France, Mr Varvaressos, governor of the Bank of Greece, Dr. Beyen from Holland, Mr C. Gutt from Belgium, and many others who were counted among the best brains in the world on international monetary relations. They participated in the various specialist committees looking at the provisions on such matters as the following: conditions of membership, subscriptions, time and place of payment of quotas, revision of quotas, the obligatory gold contribution, the transactions of members with the Fund and with nonmember countries, the scarce-currency clause, members' obligations, the pressure to be exerted on debtor countries, the conditions under which a change in parity would be authorised (although the term 'fundamental disequilibrium' was never defined), the charges to be paid to the Fund, control of capital movements, management of the Fund, publication of reports, where the Fund's gold should be held, withdrawal from the Fund, the transitional period, and even the liquidation of the Fund. The secretary of each committee wrote the minutes of the meeting and passed them on to the commission, pointing out where agreement had been reached, and where there was disagreement. White took up the problem from there.

These discussions were of the greatest importance. Mr. Istel probably expressed the general feeling of the delegates when he said, 'We have worked so hard in examining the detailed texts that it is difficult at the present juncture to get an overall picture. " ' Every day, the 'Journal' of the conference would keep the delegates advised of the main decisions and events of the previous day. It was hard work, and very useful.

Obviously, each delegation had its own special interests arid problems. The Mexican delegation kept insisting that silver be considered, next to gold, as a monetary metal: Mr. Suarez stated that 'a large part of humanity will continue to believe in silver', and said that the problem was 'small in economic dimensions, but large in human implications'. The South African delegate stressed the importance of gold, but he could relax about the subject. The Indian delegation wanted the conference to take up the matter of the sterling balances India had accumulated in London, and that were frozen there; the American delegation refused to consider this matter, on the grounds that it concerned only the British and Indian governments. But, whether the delegates were aware of it or not, the important decisions were made behind closed doors between the American delegation and the foreign delegation involved. While Harry White and his small group of 'technical advisers' kept absolute control over the text of the articles to be included in the agreement, the powerhouse of the conference was in Morgenthau's office, where some of the most difficult and troublesome issues had to be settled. It is to the most important of these that we now turn. The technicalities of the subjects debated in commission and committee meetings are of interest only to specialists.

PROVISIONS OF QUOTAS

As expected, the allocation of quotas, which involved practically every delegation, was a very difficult and dangerous subject. From the beginning, White had indicated that the aggregate quota should not exceed $8000 million, with a possible margin. Russia's quota was to be not less than 10 per cent, and China's was to rank fourth. The total voting power of the British Commonwealth as determined by the quotas should not exceed that of the United States.

The ranking of the major nations having been thus determined, this still left the field open for a scramble for quotas by the delegations of the smaller and less powerful countries. Britain supported the demands of India, Australia and others for an increase of their quotas. During the early days of the conference, however, the Russians threw a spanner into the works by informing the Americans that they could not accept a quota less than the British. Such a major adjustment was obviously impossible if the aggregate was to be kept to $8000 million. This piece of information was leaked to the press, adding to the annoyance of the American delegation, Keynes had a confidential discussion with White, Acheson and Vinson on the subject, it was difficult to see any solution without decreasing the United States quota or increasing the aggregate. The Americans, in addition, felt themselves under the necessity of allowing increases to Brazil, Mexico and Cuba. Keynes balanced their demands 'by pressing vehemently for a further increase for India and 'Saying that we hoped something could be done for Australia also'. Such a position could obviously not be supported publicly, and an agreement had to be reached behind the scenes; otherwise, the floodgates would be thrown wide open, Keynes advocated an increase of the total quotas.

Delegations from the smaller and less powerful countries, spurred by national and personal considerations-the matter of prestige in the ranking of one's country and its economic importance relative its rivals, and the delegates' desire to earn grateful acknowledgement of their own performance and achievements at the conference-manoeuvred with the American delegation to obtain satisfaction. On the allocation of quotas, as on practically everything else, the American delegation was the ultimate arbiter.

Although Committee I was supposed to discuss and decide about the quotas, it was obvious that such a controversial matter, which for almost every delegation was the one of principal concern, could not be handled there. On 4 July the committee 'agreed to postpone temporarily the discussion of quotas until a paper on this subject had been distributed'. The American delegation then went on to consult separately each of the other delegations.

The question of the quotas was crucial and central. When, at one meeting, some of the delegates refused to consider one matter because they said they could not consider it intelligently unless they had their quotas, White immediately solved the problem. As he explained to the American delegation, he appointed a quota committee. 'This is a formal Quota Committee, which presumably will report the quotas to the Commission, but we won't call them to meet. United States is chairman, We won't call them to meet until we have the quota settled, but at least we met the requirements of the moment."'

2

Breton Woods System

THE BANK FOR RECONSTRUCTION AND DEVELOPMENT

From the beginning White had fully identified himself with the Fund. It was his idea and was to be his contribution to a better world. Keynes, while not losing interest in the Fund, had recently come to believe that the Bank was more urgent and important, and the European governments in residence in London tended to agree. While White was the driving force for the Fund, Keynes moved swiftly in Commission II to complete an agreement on the Bank.

Before his departure from London, and on the boat sailing to New York, he had prepared a proposal which had been received with enthusiasm by the Europeans. He had discussed it with White at Atlantic City, and White had approved of it. But Keynes had to move fast, and some of the other delegates attending the Commission II meetings had complained about the fact that he was running what was practically a one-man show.

On 8 July Keynes had cabled London that it had been reported to him that the British press was expressing pessimism about the outcome of the Bretton Woods Conference.

I believe this is a misreading of the position though a natural one. In fact great progress on most contentious and difficult issues is being made behind the scenes. In open Committee 44 nations are of course capable of wasting as much time as is at their disposal. But in the course of coming week

I believe we shall be in a position to crystallize quite suddenly on concrete and agreed conclusions.

We are only now beginning to work seriously on the Bank. But that appears surprisingly free from controversial issues. There are several improvements needed to make set-up really workable from a practical point of view; but nothing so far as I am aware controversial between Delegations.

On 13 July, however, Morgenthau opened the meeting of the American steering committee by stating, 'Theunis was so mad he shook. Souza Costa was just furious. The head delegate from India was just as furious as he could be.'

Acheson, who was the chief American delegate to the commission on the Bank refused to continue the role in which he was cast. One of the problems was that Keynes, having started working on the Bank much later than White on the Fund, was in a great hurry. 'Keynes' performances... are completely understandable, and although tactless... all he could do.' White said that there was no comparison between the two projects, and, while Acheson did not want to 'waste time by arguing', Morgenthau asked him to explain what he was concerned about. 'Let's be very frank for a minute. If I may be frank, when Dean gets irritated, it is so rare; I realize the cause must be grave.'

'The first problem about the Bank', Acheson said, 'is that the commission meetings on the Bank, which are conducted by Keynes, are being rushed in a perfectly impossible and outrageous way. Now, that comes from the fact that Keynes is under great pressure, He knows this thing inside out so that when anybody says Section 15-C he knows what it is. Nobody else in the room-knows. So before you have an opportunity to turn to Section 15-C and see what he is talking about, he says, "I hear no objection to that", and it is passed. Well, everybody is trying to find Section 15-C. He then says, we are now talking about Section 26-D. Then they begin fiddling around with their papers, and before you find that, it is passed.'

Morgenthau, as president of the conference, was perfectly willing 'to go and call on him and in a very nice way tell him that at least half a dozen people have come to me perfectly livid and I think he is making a mistake, and I am going to ask him very respectfully if he wouldn't do the thing at half speed'.

Acheson, of course, understood Keynes's problem, and suggested that when you are asking him to slow up this thing you are still making it possible for him to finish by Wednesday when the train leaves'.

White thought that Acheson should not let things go on like that: 'Just because Keynes is an autocrat doesn't mean that you have to take it. You stand up and you say you don't like the way things are running.' He would attend the next meeting and get up on his feet. 'Nobody talks to him. They are either too scared to talk to him or too nice to talk to him, but I am sure that if he is called to task strongly, and you have the crowd behind you, he will modify his procedure.'

'Could you do it privately rather than publicly?', Morgenthau asked.

'Maybe', said White.

There was another and more serious problem, said Acheson, and that was the problem of the American delegation. When they went to a meeting of the commission, they did not know what their view was, so they could not present it forcefully and clearly. They simply had no Organisation to do it. There had been a committee meeting where the American delegate had agreed to something which was the direct opposite of what everybody had said was the policy of the United States. 'Up comes Angell and says, "He is a liar, we never agreed." So I got up and said this was all a mistake, we never agreed to this, whereupon somebody else came rushing up and handed me a report. Another committee had agreed to the opposite. I was going almost nuts.'

In Commission I, White had a tremendous Organisation, and all the experts were working on the Fund. But in Commission II, 'as far as I can see, all the decisions to make judgements on the merits and which I am wholly incompetent to make judgments on is thrown on me. The whole business of negotiating and talking with people is thrown on me. The whole burden of being Chairman of the Drafting Commission is thrown on me. The whole burden of presiding at these Commissions is thrown at me, and this afternoon when Commission Two met, there was not one single person in the room from five o'clock, when the Commission met, until a quarter of seven, when you came in who had ever been in a single meeting or knew what the dickens was going on. Now, I will go on and do anything that I am asked to do, but the responsibility which is in somebody's mind is one which I am not discharging and cannot discharge.' Acheson went on to say that in fact he knew nothing about the Bank; 'I am playing this by ear.'

What Acheson wanted he was going to get, said White. He had every intention of giving him all the expert help he would need, once he was through with the Fund. Most of the people Acheson was using were very helpful in specific tasks, but they had not been involved long enough, and it was impossible to build an Organisation in a few days.

There was another problem, however. Acheson thought that the procedure adopted by White had got the commission and committees on the Bank 'in the most chaotic mess in the world. The only way I believe you can iron it out is to get the Steering Committee together and find out what we are doing. The thing is buzzing around in a perfectly nonsensical manner. We appointed ad hoc committees, section committees, drafting committees and all kinds of committees, A draft comes in from somewhere and nobody reads it, so it gets referred to somebody else; the delegates are going crazy.'

White did not think it was that bad. 'To some extent it is, Harry', Acheson insisted. Most of the people who were there knew only one-tenth or one-hundredth of what he knew himself, Vinson seemed to agree with White that the procedure was really very simple. The Russians had come down at noon, and they were very much concerned about the exchange rates, but they did not want to bring it up in an open meeting; so the matter was settled between the American and the Russian delegations. When there was disagreement on some point, 'instead of referring it back to the committees or instead of discussing it at any length in the committees, we let a few people discuss it, and immediately referred it to the ad hoc committees, created especially for that purpose, to refer back to the Fund Commission, and not to the committees', White explained. 'The procedure is very simple, Dean.'

GOLD AND THE US DOLLAR

Putting the dollar next to gold at the centre of the postwar monetary system had been uppermost in Harry White's mind ever since he started thinking about the subject. Early in 1943, before any plan was published, he had told a group of economists, 'The dollar is the one great currency in whose strength there is universal confidence. It will probably become the cornerstone of the postwar structure of stable currencies. In the early drafts of his plan, however, he stated that any attempt to make an existing currency the international unit of account 'would be opposed on the grounds that it would seem to give the country possessing that, currency some slight advantage either in international publicity or in trade'.

As we have seen, in September 1943 Keynes told White that the United Kingdom did not contemplate going on to a gold or a dollar standard, but might be prepared to accept a unitas standard. Whenever the matter was brought up, he categorically rejected the idea that the dollar should be given a special status, and he continued to take the same line at Atlantic City, when the subject briefly cropped up there. There seems to be no evidence that the Americans discussed the subject with any other delegates. However, though the Statement of Principles, as it was submitted to the Bretton Woods Conference, clearly stated that 'The par value of a member's currency... shall be expressed in terms of gold', White knew that the international bankers were extremely anxious to see the dollar become the international currency of the future.

A few days before leaving for Atlantic City, he made, in the face of persistent opposition by a few large banks, a statement to the press. 'He said that he had just spent a day in discussion with bankers, and that this showed 'differences of points of view on some matters.' 'A great part of the bankers' fears',

Dr White said, 'arose from their lack of understanding of the plan, and not knowing all the other things we have in mind. The statement of principles is a mere skeleton, but there will be a lot of flesh on those bones before we are through."' To put the flesh on the bones took three simple operations, of which only White and his closest assistants at the Bretton Woods Conference were aware. It is doubtful that even Morgenthau was involved. While it made White a little nervous, until the process was completed, it was in fact the easiest hurdle to overcome during the conference, and the one that had the most far-reaching consequences for the future. Since only a small group of 'technicians' were informed, it did not become a point of general debate.

The first move was made on 6 July, at the 2.30 p.m. meeting of Committee 2. Many provisions and their alternatives were discussed that day. Professor Robertson was the British delegate. Also present were Professor Mosse from France, Mr. de Iongh from Holland, and several other monetary experts. The consideration of a Mexican proposal about silver was postponed. The Dutch delegate proposed that the wording 'offer to' appearing in one provision be replaced by 'buy the currency'. There was a discussion about scarce currencies.

The Greek delegate, Mr. Varvaressos, suggested that the reports made by the Fund should be communicated, since they were confidential, to a 'member government', and not to the country, as it was stated. This was referred to the language committee.

Then came Alternative A, p. 16. This alternative, submitted, by the American delegate, provided that 'The par value of the currency of each member shall be expressed in terms of gold, as a common denominator, or in terms of a gold-convertible currency unit of the weight and fineness in effect on July 1, 1944'. This alternative was later presented in the official record of the conference (p.1651) as an American and British proposal, which is not accurate. It was, in fact, one of the numerous alternatives worked out by White and his group. Keynes obviously would never have agreed to the proposal, and he was not aware of it.

The American delegate explained that the purpose of this alternative was 'insignificant', and that it dealt with several problems. It was 'so worded to show no obligation to sell gold was implied'. He assumed 'there will exist a gold-convertible currency by definition within the terms of this agreement'. There was no further discussion, and the alternative was approved. It became part of the mass of material the committees and commissions were piling up day after day, and it does not seem that any of the delegates had noticed its implications. On 12 July the British delegation cabled London, 'Norwegian resolution proposed that books of Fund and Bank should be kept in Figures for international monetary unit equivalent to 10 dollars in present gold value of United States currency. This revives the proposal that accounts should be kept in Unitas and we regard it as already dead.' Having been approved by the committee, the provision then went to the commission,

The second move was made a week later, during the 2.30 p.m. meeting of Commission I on 13 July. Harry White was chairman. Just before the meeting he had told Morgenthau, 'The commission meeting this afternoon is extremely important. This is where we either fish or cut bait on most of these things.

The agenda again was heavy. One of the points to be discussed was the date on which countries joining the Fund should make their initial contribution of gold and gold-convertible exchange. This was a minor point, and, since the 'delegations did not have time to consider the matter, the Committee agreed to refer this question directly to your Commission'.

The Indian delegate asked for a definition of gold-convertible currency, which had been discussed, and of which Keynes had said it did not exist. The question as put related to the gold-convertible contributions only, and not to the par value of currencies.

Robertson, against Keynes's instructions, but as the responsible British delegate, suggested that the words 'gold and gold-convertible currency' be replaced by 'net official holdings of gold and U.S. dollars', and remarked that this would involve several changes elsewhere. This was White's opportunity. Using his authority as chairman, he referred the matter to a special committee, which took it out of any further discussion.

That evening he was satisfied. He told Morgenthau that the commission on the Fund 'covered quite a little material. A good deal of it was passed, and some of it was referred back to a special committee which is to consider it tonight.

The special committee was the group of technicians headed by White. It prepared for inclusion in the Final Act a number of provisions that were never discussed, nor even, brought up. The argument (referred to earlier) between Acheson and White over procedure took place after White had expressed his satisfaction.

'You have a very complicated procedure', Acheson said. 'First of all, you get a report of the Drafting Committees, Committee One, and Committee so and so. Those things are all brought up. People think they are about ready to vote on something. Then they discover that it isn't true because it has to be referred to an ad hoc Committee or a Special Committee, and then it has to go to the Drafting Committee....'

As far as the Fund was concerned, all Acheson's confusion was in his own mind, said White. The commission on the Fund was 'running as smooth as silk, and I don't know where you get your idea. There is no confusion as far as the Fund is concerned. All the important problems have been settled. They have either gone then-'

I am sure they have been settled,' snapped Acheson, 'but I don't think the delegates know that.'

They didn't; but, except for Keynes, what difference would it have made? After the meeting, White joined his group of technicians, and worked with them until three o'clock in the morning, He reported to Morgenthau the next day that the draft on the Fund was in excellent shape.

The change from 'gold' to 'gold and US dollars' was lost in the ninety-six page document the chairmen of the delegations would sign a few days later. Whether or not any of them noticed it, or understood its implications, it seems that none of them expressed any reservations about it. Keynes would not find out until later, when he studied the Final Act. Henry Ford, who celebrated his eighty-first birthday shortly after the end of the Bretton Woods Conference, told press reporters that he had not followed what had happened at the conference, but that he had always favored a universal currency. 'That currency', he added, 'should be our own dollar.'

LIQUIDATION OF THE BANK FOR INTERNATIONAL SETTLEMENTS

BE IT RESOLVED that the United Nations Monetary and 'Financial Conference recommends the liquidation of the Bank for International Settlements at Basel. It is suggested that the liquidation shall begin at the earliest possible date, and that the Governments of the United Nations now at war with Germany, appoint a Commission of Investigation, in order to examine the management and transactions of the bank during the present war.

White had been informed about this proposal immediately, and was obviously in favour. He said that Norway, France and Belgium supported it, and I think they could line up a majority. But England has been very busily at work, trying to get them to withdraw, and they tell me that the State Department here is also supporting the English'.

But Acheson thought it would be undesirable to discuss the Bank for International Settlements (BIS) at the conference.

'McKittrick would be forced to resign', said White. 'I would support the motion of the Norwegian delegate, I think it would be a salutary thing for the world.' Morgenthau agreed: following the invasion of Czechoslovakia, the BIS had turned over to the Germans the Czechoslovak gold. Luxford felt that the dissolution itself would not be too important, but it would be a symbol, since the bank was 'by virtue of the Nazi occupation of the countries of Europe, now... in the hand of the Nazis'.

Edward Brown, the banker, was embarrassed. At the request of the Hoover Administration, his bank and three New York banks had participated in the foundation of the BIS, and shares had been distributed to the public. The Norwegian delegate, Keilhau, had just made an attack on the president of the bank,

McKittrick; the BIS ought to be dissolved, said Brown, but this was not the place to discuss it.

Acheson was of the Same Opinion: this concerned foreign relations, he said, and it was up to the Secretary of State to express his opinion, 'I would be delighted to talk with Cordell Hull about this', said Morgenthau. 'I am fairly confident what his answer would be.'

The Norwegian proposal was strenuously opposed particularly by the Dutch delegation, whose chairman, Beyen, had been president of the BIS when the Czech gold was turned over to Germany. On 19 July the Norwegian and Dutch delegation communicated to the press a new proposal that they were submitting, recommending 'the liquidation of the Bank for International Settlements at the earliest possible moment'. It would be considered in commission the following day.

When he learned about this new resolution, which was milder than the first, Keynes wrote to Morgenthau, 'We are entirely in accord with the general purpose... What we cannot manage is a recommendation from Commission III to Commission I to write some specific agreement into the International Monetary Fund. For technical reasons this... would inevitably prevent us from participating either in the Fund or in the Bank until after the expiry of an indefinite period.'

Keynes delivered the message personally, Morgenthau told his staff, Lord Keynes came in here at about seven-forty, and the man was livid over this BIS thing, and said that if this thing went through at nine o'clock he was going to get up and leave the Conference. He didn't use the language that he had been double-crossed, but he said that this was the first time this has happened, but the inference was that he had been double-crossed and this thing had been given out in advance of the meeting... to the press, which he thought most unfair.... He said that he thought the people responsible should be rapped over the knuckles. What he said is just amongst the people here in the room and I don't want it to go any further. So I told him please to quiet down, that I would see my people and we decided that we would let the thing go over until tomorrow morning... he really was very much disturbed, and I don't think he was putting on an act. He said the BIS, politically, is just as unpopular, if not more so, in England than in America.

This may have been so, but Keynes was aware of the fact that Britain was bound by the obligations to which it had subscribed in joining the BIS, and could not simply repudiate them. He had suggested that, at the date of the constitution of the Fund, 'the necessary steps will be taken to liquidate the Bank for International Settlements'. But White and his staff had seen to it that the proposal put forward was stronger. They wanted the Bank liquidated as quickly as possible, In addition, lining up the Fund with the BIS, 'in the way Keynes suggested, I think, would be most unfortunate', said White. 'It would make it appear that that is a direct competitor.'

Morgenthau was puzzled that Beyen should have associated himself with this proposal: 'I am not sure that fellow Beyen didn't pull a fast one on us too', he said. 'Getting us to do something which he knew that Keynes would object to.'

Luxford gave the explanation: 'No, he didn't get us to do it. He fought it tooth and nail. We forced him to give us the right technical language against his will.'

White was very much disturbed that it had not been possible to pass the first Norwegian resolution. 'They will try very much to get this to look just the opposite of what we want. They will try to give the BIS status and a clean bill of health by saying it should continue in operation until the Fund comes and then it ought to pass out because it is doing approximately the same work. In the first place, it makes it more difficult for us in the Fund, because they can say, "Why don't you give the BIS more powers?" In the second place, it would look as though they were a perfectly good institution, it is just that the Fund has a little broader powers. And in the third place, it would be a public recognition of the fact, by forty-four nations, that the BIS is a good institution and should continue until the Fund....

Well, I am confident', Morgenthau interrupted, 'that if we can get Keynes down here face to face and make him agree to something on the spot, that I can be successful....'

Shortly afterwards, Keynes walked in with several members of the British delegation. Morgenthau handed him the proposal about the liquidation 'at the earliest possible moment'. 'I don't quite know what the earliest possible moment is', said Mr. Bolton, who accompanied Keynes.

'Not very early!' was Keynes's reply. He then came back to his own proposal, which recommended the liquidation after the establishment of the Fund. 'The only difference', he said, 'is that that says it is contingent upon the establishment of the Fund. This says it shall be liquidated whether there is a Fund or not. I don't think we want to keep the damned thing alive, do we?'

'Amen, brother!', said Vinson.

From the conversation that followed, in which Keynes said it was 'very wrong' that the proposal had been revealed to the press though it had not been passed by the committee, it became clear that White and his staff had in fact engineered the whole manoeuvre, using the Dutch and Norwegian delegates as a front.

The recommendation for the liquidation of the Bank for International Settlements 'at the earliest possible moment' was agreed upon by the conference and included in the Final Act. Once more, Keynes established himself as a prophet. The liquidation would not come 'very early'.

LOCATION OF FUND AND BANK

During the meeting in Atlantic City, White had indicated that he wanted he head offices of the Fund and Bank to be located in the United States. Keynes had advised London, and the answer had been that this would not be acceptable. White had prepared for submission to the conference a proposal to the effect chat 'The principal office of the Fund shall be located in the member having the largest quota.' Keynes had submitted a proposal suggesting that the decision about the location be made at the first meeting of the board of governors.

London had not quite understood Keynes's motives; after all the emphasis that the Fund would be a technical and not a political organisation, it would be a pity if the first task of the board of governors were to be to settle a highly political and controversial matter such as the location of the Fund. The question would have to be settled behind the scenes.

Keynes wrote White a 'personal and private' letter, dated 9 July, advising that he had tabled a proposal about the location of the Bank's headquarters, and that this was similar to his Proposal about the location of the Fund's. This was a most difficult matter to settle, and he had just received a telegram from the Chancellor of the Exchequer stating that no agreement was to be made without his express authority.

'The only comment I would like to make on this', White told the American delegates, 'is if you don't get this settled in the Conference, it certainly is reduced, and that is why they want to postpone. Maybe they hope to get some arrangement whereby they will get some and we will get others. I think it is important enough for us to push the issue here in the Conference where I am sure we will get a favorable vote.'

Morgenthau asked the Congressional delegates how they felt about it. It would have a material effect, said Wolcott; 'there has always been a certain jealousy that the financial center of the world is London, England'. If the United States were going to participate, it should have the head offices. The other Congressmen agreed. Senator Wagner thought that if the United States did not have the head offices it would be almost impossible to obtain Congressional approval of the Fund.

'Then the answer is that we have got to fight it out here and now', Morgenthau concluded.

Several delegations were on Keynes's side. 'Canadians, Dutch and Belgians all tell us that if London wants to remain in business even our present proposal goes dangerously far', he cabled. There was no hope of securing agreement on any location outside the United States during the time at their disposal. He asked that the Chancellor give him clear instructions. The Americans were emphatic that the matter should be settled at the conference. 'But if we are to be defeated on this perhaps we should retire with dignity by withdrawing our amendment.'

The Chancellor asked Keynes to make it clear to the American delegation that the considerable opposition the government would have to face would be gravely augmented by any decision that the Fund be located in the United States. He asked Keynes to hold the proposal, irrespective of the result, for the time being. If it were not possible to obtain a decision in favour of London or Amsterdam or some other appropriate European centre, opinion would be able to express itself. If it were possible to have the Fund in London or in some European capital, 'then we should raise no objection to the location of the Bank being in the United States'.

On 13 July Morgenthau discussed with the American delegation a letter he had just received from Keynes. The decision about the location of the Fund was a highly political matter to be decided by governments, and not by a monetary conference. The question could not be considered without reference to the location of other international bodies with which the Fund would have to co-operate. He hoped that the participating governments could reach a decision on the matter before the first meeting of the board of governors. "But I must particularly emphasise in this letter that in the opinion of my government it would not be a proper course to settle a political matter, such as this, by equal voting of the financial or technical Delegates from the wide variety of nations here assembled.

White thought that the British wanted the headquarters of either the Fund or the Bank to be in Britain. 'They don't care, as long as they have one, because they feel otherwise there are important things to follow. I think we are strategically in an invulnerable position to get it now, if you wait, I don't know what you will get, because they can't back out on the basis that they don't like where the head office is. Their public won't stand for it and the world won't stand for it, So the thing to do is to put it through on a vote here. If they don't like it, it is too bad.'

The Congressional delegates again confirmed their position. Also, many South American and smaller countries would feel more comfortable if the gold of the Fund were stored in the United States.

'New York has become the financial center of the world. These British are just fighting uphill. There is no question about that', said White. He did not even think that Morgenthau should answer Keynes's letter: 'he isn't saying anything he didn't say before.... Moreover, we are putting in twice as much money as anybody else, three times as much. On the face of it, it is preposterous that the head office should be any place else. We can vote it any place we want, by members, by votes, and we will win. They know it, and that is why they don't want to come to a vote. I don't see why we should put ourselves in a position to be subject to political manipulation.

'And if Churchill called Roosevelt, requesting a postponement of the decision?, Luxford wondered.

The President would not answer such a question without first contacting the American delegation at the conference, said Morgenthau.

'The vote will take place tomorrow', White decided. 'If the President should call up, we will say we are very sorry, but the Delegates have all voted on it. That will give him a good answer to Churchill. We can't hold up everything.'

'That is no answer,' Morgenthau concluded, 'but anyway, we have taken care of the meeting for tonight.

During a previous meeting White had suggested: 'Rather than bring that on with the British, why not postpone it until the last meeting of the Fund-just dodge it.... They are almost licked. What do they do? Publicly say, "We object because of some other reason?" ' But Morgenthau did not want to postpone it, and Luxford thought that 'if we are willing to take this thing to a vote basis, we can clean up the whole works.

The following morning Morgenthau went up to Keynes's suite, and told him that the American delegation was emphatic that Congress would not accept the Fund unless it were located in the United States; that a proposal for postponement would not be understood; and that in any event the ultimate decision must be regarded as a foregone conclusion. This problem arose out of the peculiar relationship between the Administration and Congress. He had regarded it as essential to associate Congress closely with the drafting of the agreement. So far, he had had an extraordinary and almost miraculous success. All Congressmen present at the conference, including not only

Republicans but also old-time isolationists and hostile critics had been brought round to enthusiastic support for the Fund and the Bank. The Republican senators were even telling Senator Taft, who had issued a critical statement, that he was not speaking for the party. Morgenthau begged Keynes to ask London not to upset the present mood of his team and pleaded that Whitehall should appreciate the special nature of his problem, which arose wholly from the relationship of Congress to the Administration, irrespective of politics. In passing on this message to the British government Keynes commented, 'I believe that we are on a losing wicket here.' He hoped that the Chancellor would instruct him either to withdraw the amendment or to argue, but not to press the matter. 'Eady, Brand and Ronald reluctantly concur.

In the light of Keynes's advice, the Chancellor agreed not to press the proposal, but to withdraw it. He wanted, however, to make it clear that British public and Parliamentary opinion were very sensitive on the point, and that the government was not debarred from making it a condition of acceptance of the plan that the head office of the Fund be located in Europe.

Morgenthau once more submitted the issue to the American delegation: 'I know you have expressed your opinion once before and I would like some sort of direction from the Committee. It is a question of New York versus London.'

'I stand pat', said Senator Tobey.

'I haven't changed', added Senator Wagner.

Congressman Spence was 'unalterably opposed to it and I am not going to change. I think you ought to talk to him as plainly as diplomacy will allow. I don't know how plain that is.'

'Well,' I am not a diplomat', said Morgenthau; 'I can talk pretty plain: I think this is the time to wave the flag.... It is the unanimous opinion... that we should not accede to Lord Keynes's request that this matter of location be postponed."'

The next day White reported that Professor Robbins of the British delegation had strongly urged him that the question of the location of the Fund should not immediately be raised at a public meeting, but should be left a few days, until the British had had an opportunity to obtain a reply from London. Vinson added that Robbins had said, 'We know we will be beaten and we hope to avoid being humiliated.'

'We can wait', said White.

In order to keep the American embassy in London informed, Morgenthau and Acheson sent a telegram stating that 'The most controversial point which we have had with the British during the course of the' Bretton Woods Conference has been the location of the head office of the Fund. We have taken the position all along that the head office must be located in the country which has the largest quota. In a conversation yesterday with Mr. Morgenthau the President instructed our Delegation to insist on this point.' Keynes was ready to give up his objections and would make a purely formal statement for the record. The decision on the matter had been postponed until 17 July.

On 17 July Keynes wrote to Morgenthau that the Chancellor had authorised him to withdraw the British amendment, 'but in doing so to place on record that in the view of His Majesty's Government the question where the headquarters of the Bank should be situated ought not to be considered without reference to the location of other international bodies'. He also mentioned the public and parliamentary opposition to the Fund that the decision about its headquarters was likely to create in Britain, and gave a reminder that the whole plan would eventually have to be put before the British government for its approval. Keynes said that, in order to avoid incomplete or inaccurate press reports, he would issue a statement announcing the withdrawal of his alternative, but making it clear at the same time that the location of the headquarters of the Fund was a matter for governments themselves, and not just a rather technical conference to decide.

The following day, the United States proposal that the headquarters of the Fund be located in the country having the largest quota-in other words, the United States was adopted that evening, Morgenthau discussed Keynes's press release.

The reservation by the United Kingdom was no different from any other reservation, said Luxford, 'It simply means that they object to it, but in the final analysis there is no choice as to whether they accept the Fund or not accept it, and they can't be rewriting the document. We can be very gracious. We are getting what we went after. We ought to let them do as much as they can do.'

At an earlier meeting Acheson, who had always been concerned about keeping strictly to the correct international procedure, had asked Morgenthau whether he could see Keynes s letter, because 'It ought to have some powerful consideration.' No one shared his view. It had been discussed and the American delegation was unanimous, 'more completely unanimous than it has ever been'. White did not think it necessary to bring the matter up again, 'Who is to determine where the head office is in an international conference? I should think it would be the conference. The governments are represented by the delegates. After they decide it, like any other point, any government can accept it or reject it.'

Acheson did not want to argue about it, he just wanted to ask a question.

'The question has to be argued about in order to come to a decision', said White.

Acheson was not scared of an argument; he was 'just too tired to make an argument, but I do want somebody to understand the question'.

'I see. Well, you restate it', said White.

The question that Keynes had raised, said Acheson, was whether a major policy decision that would normally be made among governments could be left to the groups meeting at Bretton Woods or postponed for a vote by the board of governors of the Fund after it had come into operation.

Morgenthau had sensed the intention of Acheson's question: 'What he is saying is that this, is a matter between governments, or foreign offices.'

Keynes had brought up the same question in Atlantic City, said White, saying that he hoped it would not be put in the draft on which the conference would vote, because the most appropriate time to determine where the Fund would be located would be after it got started.

'Are you through?' asked Morgenthau. 'May I simply say this, Dean, that whether it is done between governments or whether it is done here, this thing is a matter of postponing the day of reckoning.... Now, to me it boils down to this-and I will be willing to face this thing-these groups-once and for all-that the financial center of the world is going to be New York and we don't want to postpone this thing until another day where we may not be in as advantageous a position and maybe have them to get in a horse-trading position and maybe end up by having it in London. Now the advantage is ours here, and I personally think we should take it.'

'If the advantage was theirs, they would take it', said White.

THE FUND IS BORN

After two weeks of negotiations, Secretary Morgenthau issued a statement to the press:

The International Monetary Fund has been born. The achievement has been an unusually fine demonstration to the world that forty-four nations can get together to iron out their differences and decide how they will work together in post-war monetary matters. Not all countries have received all they hoped to get, but the spirit of give and take is the best kind of omen for international cooperation and for what we may expect when we get around the peace table. The few matters still outstanding are not of supreme importance.

In the morning session on 17 July, Keynes, Morgenthau and other delegates discussed a possible extension of the conference. Keynes had raised the question. In matters of fundamental difficulty or disagreement, he said, most questions had been resolved. 'But the technicians and draftsmen can handle the detail properly only when you have settled what it is all about, and I am afraid they are dreadfully behind-hand. They are doing a grand piece of work. It is not easy to keep track of it because none of us are seeing it as a whole, but in bits and pieces.' If they were hasty, errors and inconsistencies might slip in, and this would be dangerous. The British delegates concerned with the details were 'quite breaking up under the strain... their efficiency is getting very seriously impaired.' And so was their health. Then there was another consideration:

There are certain final technical matters we haven't considered at all, what the lawyers call the final act, which embodies the results of this Conference. No attempt has yet been made to draft that, and it hasn't been considered by anybody. At present, no one has seen, as a continuous narrative, the work that has been done, and I think it is not quite fair to the Delegations that they should be expected to pass so quickly on things they have never had a chance, really, of reading as a consecutive narrative. There was unanimous agreement that the conference should be extended.

'We have certain mechanical difficulties which I won't bore you with', said Morgenthau. 'We may have to get the President to get out an order to seize the hotel as of Wednesday night, and put troops in here to run it... we may have to carry the manager of the hotel out with two soldiers! If that is necessary, Judge Vinson will give the orders... we ought to fix a date and then not postpone it again, because we will be in considerable litigation here with the hotel.'

'We want to do as good a job as we can,' said White, 'because when it is available the whole world is going to examine this document. There will be lawyers and technicians and writers. They are going to go through this with a fine-toothed comb and find out and interpret every phrase, and as Lord Keynes has said, some of them may give rise to substantial problems.' Several of his people were 'getting irritable and a little inefficient. I felt myself cracking up last night and I went to bed at 10 o'clock, had some sleep, and I feel fine now.' He thought it would be possible to get through by Saturday night. 'So I would strongly urge that you don't leave here until Sunday.'

'As a technician,' said Luxford, 'I don't believe that you can promise that this job will be done by that time.'

'Well you just have to', Morgenthau told him; 'you can't stay on here forever.... Why last night did it suddenly dawn on you that you couldn't do it?' Judge Vinson intervened: 'Lord Keynes' men last night-Sir Wilfrid Eady and Mr. Robertson were just fagged. I am just merely saying that for Mr. Luxford.'

White also wanted time for a plenary session, a rather formal night occasion-in which the world can be informed of the successful conclusion of the Fund, and an indication that the Bank is going forward'.

Keynes suggested that the rest of the day 'be a whole holiday....Everybody wants to stop and think. I haven't been able to get hold of my technicians for three days.

There was unanimous agreement.

Two days later, Keynes walked upstairs to his own suite after dining with Morgenthau, and suffered a mild heart attack. Lady Keynes mentioned the fact to a friend she had met at the conference, and who was the mother of the Reuters correspondent. The news leaked out.

Keynes advised the Chancellor of the Exchequer that the conference would be extended.

The procedure of this conference is enormously complicated, the subjects under discussion are difficult and intricate, we are constantly sitting under chairmen who barely understand English and opportunities for the minor powers to waste time are unlimited. In the end we shall I believe produce satisfactory and workable document but here again there are lessons to be learned for future occasions.

In another telegram he said, 'With the exception of the Russians, who have pursued an unbroken policy of contracting into all benefits but out of all duties and obligations and a hesitation probably temporary by the Netherlands, all of the major delegations have agreed to subscribe to the Bank an amount of not less than their quota with the Fund.'

THE PRESS IS TAKEN INTO CONFIDENCE

On 2 July, during the morning session, Morgenthau discussed with the American delegates how to handle the press. 'The best plan in the world is no good if you can't get Congress to accept it', said White. It was necessary to meet the opposition that still prevailed in some influential papers, and get public opinion on the side of the Fund.

On the first day of the conference, every accredited representative of the press had received the full text of the master document that was to be the basis of all the discussions, and they were told that they would be given all facilities to remain informed about the proceedings of the conference. This was an innovation in the conduct of international conferences, and the reporters liked it. But Morgenthau felt that this was not enough. Senator Tobey said that he had met 'some saboteurs at this hotel doing all they can to stick a knife into this thing'. Representative Wolcott had just been told 'that this is throwing money down a rat hole'. As Republicans, they had been opposing the Fund, and were now expected to continue their opposition, which they did not want to do.

'If we are going to be successful', Wolcott said, 'we have to have public sentiment with us because public sentiment will control whatever action is taken by the Congress, and I think we have got to begin and start building public sentiment right today and now.' Utilising the medium of the press to beat the opponents to the punch and to take the edge off their criticism seemed the most effective way of building up public sentiment. The Congressmen obviously did not know enough about the subject to answer the questions that were asked by press reporters; they suggested that White hold a press meeting every afternoon to explain the purposes of the Fund and to answer questions. 'Let them have it with both barrels', Tobey recommended.

The method was extremely effective. The Chicago Daily News reported, Every afternoon at 3 Harry White, the dynamic assistant secretary of the Treasury Department, holds a 'seminar' for the press, at which he relates what progress, if any, has been made by the various committees, and discourses freely on the dark science of international finance. White is a medium-sized man with a trim mustache, rimless eyeglasses and thinning hair.

He formerly taught college economics, and as he gets into his stride with the 40 or more reporters who attend these sessions he seems to be back in the classroom. A reporter stumbles through a complicated inquiry, and White shakes his finger at him and says vigorously, 'That's a very intelligent question.' The reporter, who is a little in doubt about it in the first place undergoes a lifting of the spirit and begins to take notes furiously as White goes into rapid-fire account perhaps of the evils of unilateral action in the manipulation of foreign exchange.

On 6 July, Keynes appeared at one of these press conferences-the only occasion on which he did so, As usual, White was present. So far as the press was concerned, the event was obviously one of the highlights of the whole conference, For an hour and a half, Keynes and White answered questions fired at them by the correspondents. Keynes warned that, if the Fund were rejected, Britain might have to resort to bilateral barter agreements in order to protect its economy. He ridiculed the 'key currency' proposals, which would 'let the rest of the world go hang'. The Fund would make gold 'a monarch subject to constitutional limitations'.

No one with any practical sense would make the gold reserves of the world worthless, but gold should not exercise 'tyrannical powers over the world'.

'It is thought here', said a reporter, that the purpose of the Fund is to eliminate foreign exchange restrictions, but in your speech-a great point was made that the Fund will allow each country to Control all capital.'

'The object of the Fund', Keynes responded 'is to remove exchange restrictions as soon as possible. It provides that Capital movements must be controlled, and indeed that is an essential condition.... I think you will find there is no possible doubt about that in the provisions of the Fund.'

At that point White intervened to state that countries which chose to impose restrictions on capital movements were allowed to do so, but 'the United States does not wish to have them and they do not exist'.

Keynes explained that, in the long run, there had to be for every country a balance, between imports and exports. If the

United States went on exporting more than it imported, there was no remedy. 'The Fund can't solve continuing problems of this sort. It can just give the opportunity for settling it in an orderly way.' If he wished to criticise the Fund, he could make 'quite a good job of it'. But all the alternatives he had seen were very much worse.

Using the material provided by White during his seminars, by the daily conference journal, and by rumours and leaks, and the statements by delegates or prominent visitors, the press reported daily about the proceedings of the conference. Some correspondents were able to obtain confidential information about the attitude of the Russians, the conflict between Keynes and the American delegation about where the Fund should be located, and many other matters. Comments were generally neutral or favourable. Despite all the available information, much of what went on, however, remained mysterious. Walter Lippmann commented, 'It has been impossible for the general public to obtain any idea of what the Bretton Woods conference is about. Though it is concerned with questions which will affect men's lives deeply, the language of monetary policy is understood by very few men in any country.

The Christian Science Monitor noted that 'Fundamentals behind the monetary conference were partly hidden by the controversies over quotas, gold subscriptions, and other technicalities.' The monetary plans were a, game between debtors and creditors, between the United States and Great Britain, or between Wall Street and Washington'. Although White had taken great pains to convince the press that the commercial banks would profit from the operations of the Fund, which would deal only with government agencies, the papers which had opposed the Fund were not convinced.

The New York Times commented, 'The proposed agreement sets up a huge machinery and ignores all basic principles which must be adopted if such machinery could hope to be successful. American money poured into supporting weak foreign countries will be worse than wasted.

Another critical comment was that, instead of compelling a debtor nation to put its affairs in order, the Fund merely provided a breathing spell. While there was no objection to a breathing spell, the money provided would be wasted unless the breathing spell were used by the debtor country to strengthen its economic structures, so that it would not only get back to a sound monetary basis, but stay there.

As usual, the German press closely followed the monetary discussions. And so did the German government. Speaking to a group of economists and business leaders, Walther Funk said on 7 July 1944, while the Bretton Woods Conference was in process, that this was the wrong way to handle the problem. Instead of providing a complicated machinery to restore equilibrium in the balances of payments, it was much more effective to make sure that they did not get out of equilibrium. International commerce could not be maintained in orderly condition by monetary plans, but currencies had to be maintained in stable relations through commercial planning. If the Americans advocated a return to currencies backed by gold, this was only to make the dollar the international currency of the system. As for the Russians, they must be following the struggle between the two major capitalist countries with diabolical pleasure. In practice, the Russians were interested in the conference only because it assured them a market for their gold production, for which, because of the poverty of the Russian population, they had no internal use.

THE FRENCH CHAOS

In the early days of the Conference, the French delegation was referred to as the 'Comite', and it bothered the French delegates. President Roosevelt was furious at de Gaulle, and fed up with the general's manoeuvres to become the sole and undisputed leader of the French Committee of National Liberation. While the Bretton Woods conference was going on, the President, in Washington, modified his position, and became more favourable towards de Gaulle. By the end of the conference it had become customary to refer to the 'French' delegates, and they had become a little happier; but their problems were not over. Mr. Mendès France had flown from Algiers to the United States, and had briefly met Morgenthau on the stairs of the hotel. Morgenthau had understood that he was 'terribly upset' about the attitude of the American delegation: 'he can only draw one conclusion-that we are unfriendly to his Government', Mendès France had not threatened a French withdrawal, but the case was serious, and Morgenthau had another crisis on his hands. He promised to see the Frenchman in the evening. White reported that at a committee meeting Mendès France had warned that, because of the French quota, his government might not participate, and White thought it 'inexcusable for a country like France to make that statement'. Vinson, however, thought 'he had to make a strong statement, because, as I saw it, there is hostility in this group, and if he didn't put a strong speech in, it might be others around that might replace him. I didn't take his statement seriously.... I think he is a pretty fair poker player.'

One of the problems of the French delegation, causing them great anxiety, was the fact that Holland, Belgium and Luxembourg had recently signed the Benelux agreement. The combined quotas of these three countries was slightly larger than that of France, and the French feared that Benelux might get even closer together, and be given the fifth rank in the table of quotas, qualifying them automatically for a seat on the executive Committee of the Fund.

Morgenthau had agreed to see the French delegates on the evening of 15 July, at nine o'clock. He was there, but the French were late for the appointment, and everyone was becoming restless. Morgenthau suggested that White, Vinson and the other delegates wait for another five minutes and then go on with their own work, but soon afterwards Mendès France and Istel at last arrived. Morgenthau asked them to speak their mind. Mendès France explained that France had hoped to be number four, but that for political reasons China had been given number four, and France number five. This was understood and accepted. He had hoped, however, to be more successful on other matters, but, 'since we are here, on all questions we were interested in, we were refused'. In April he had been assured that, since France was considered a devastated country, it would have to pay only 75 per cent of its gold contribution. 'Then this thing was wiped out and we didn't receive it.' Morgenthau replied that France had not been singled out, and that this would apply to all countries. He was worried because Mendès France had told him that he would go back to Algiers saying that the Americans were against France.

Istel indicated that he was aware of the deal that had been made with the Russians, for whose sole benefit a special clause on newly-mined gold had been granted. At Morgenthau's request, France had earlier backed the proposal behind this, not knowing that in fact it would work to the disadvantage of France.

'But I don't want to discuss again all this question', said Mendès France. 'What I wanted to tell you is that, that I wanted to give you a few examples, and it is bad, but I can give you a lot of them. I wanted to give you a few examples to show you that every important decision was taken since we are here, and all this decision is without you willing it and without you and of course an enemy of my country, but these questions are always settled against our interest, and I give you the first example, which was this question about devastated countries. A second example is the example about quota. I am sure, and I don't say it to be polite, because I am sure you think it, I am sure you like my country and you want to be good with it, and I saw this morning when I spoke with you, that of course you were willing to find a solution and I am grateful to you, having made what you could, but in fact what happened, that in this situation, we didn't get what we hoped for and why-because when we started this question two or three days ago with Mr. White, we thought we would have a talk between us and he would have an agreement and this morning you told me it is too late.'

Morgenthau interrupted him: when this was discussed, the committee meeting was still going on, and the French delegation could have argued its case.

'No,' said Mendès France, 'because what happened, I went to this Committee this morning and we were suddenly given a list and we saw on this list we had four hundred and Fifty and I spoke and said we don't accept it. Then Lord Keynes said it is too late, "You can not change these things, it is a total which is eight and seven fifty and if somebody gets more, then it is necessary to take it to another man, because the total must not be changed." Then what was to do at this moment-I understood it was very difficult. Then I came to you and I saw you were willing to find something, but the direct difficulty, you told me, is that you have given a promise to the Chinese they must always be a hundred more than us and if you give us, for example, fifty, you have to give fifty to the Chinese, and the result is instead of having increased the fifty, you have increases of a hundred. But this promise you make to the Chinese, and if you made this promise, I have nothing to say against it, but this promise you made has a result that you give to the Chinese of course more than they have to receive, because you know, as well as we all know, that wasn't correct calculation with the correct quota, with the formula. We all know if China will not get so much than she has, then we have not to be a victim of this situation and when you told us, not you, but Mr. White, one month ago, that we will have five hundred, we thought it will be so, and now we only have four hundred and fifty.'

White had had to leave the meeting, and while Mendès France admitted that this had not been a firm commitment, he still wanted five hundred. White had promised to talk to the Secretary, but nothing further had been heard. The Frenchman had wanted to talk to Acheson, but that had not been useful, 'And then this morning when we received this sheet it was too late.... That is another example.'

'But', Morgenthau wondered, 'I asked you whether twenty-five million dollars would do any good. You said no.'

'You see, I am not a bargaining man.'

'I am not either, but I asked you if it would help any and you said it would be of no use.'

Vinson intervened: 'Now it seems to me in all friendliness that you are making a mountain out of a molehill.'

'And how will it look', said Mendès France, 'when I come back to my people and explain to them, "I went some months ago to Bretton Woods, and explained our position. I told them we want to ask this, this, and this, and in all these questions I have to tell you I come with zero." That is the fact. Then comes another example. Yes, it is very bad, as you know it is. Now, we have spoken with the Fund. Now we speak with the Bank. You have a council of Executive Directors in the Bank, the same kind as the Fund. That is to say, a council in which five permanent countries will be represented. And as our quota is the fifth, we thought that, like in the Fund, we ' will have the fifth seat. Now what happened today? We heard for the first time that only three permanent seats would be given.'

None of the American delegates had heard about this. It might have been suggested, but no position had been taken, and nothing had been decided,

'But please,' said Mendes France, 'but sometimes I come too early and sometimes I come too late. Then I prefer to come now too early as too late, because it is very expensive in these last days when I come too late.'

Morgenthau asked the American delegates whether France would have a seat if there were five members on the Executive Committee, Luxford thought that if there were five appointed members and France subscribed the fifth quota, she would have a seat.'

'But I don't want to speak about technical questions', said Mendès France. 'I want you to understand this. I must tell you frankly I have not an easy position in Algiers. I understand why you are laughing now.... Then when I go back to Algiers and have to explain all these things, my colleague will say, "You have lost on the quota, you have lost on the devastated countries, you have lost on these, and these, and these-then what do you bring back to us? What is the good news you bring back? What do I have to understand?" Then what I said this afternoon to the Commission-and I said it because it is true-it is not that I am leaving the Conference, but what I said-and it is worse-that if there are those I am describing now, my Government will not accept it, and I don't want to be in such a position.'

'If you don't mind my saying so,' Morgenthau remarked, 'I think your statement is a little bit too strong.'

'It is strong like the truth', the answer came back.

Morgenthau asked whether the request for a seat on the Executive Committee was the last one.

'It is the last one I wanted to give you, but if you want to have some others, I can give you-'

'It is enough', said Morgenthau. 'Let me ask this. I think that, Mr. Mendes France, about the Government and the little threat there which I don't like-'

'It isn't a threat, You must not think so. I give you my word it isn't a threat. It is an exact position. I have explained this morning about Belgium and Holland and Luxembourg.'

But Morgenthau had learned all about the customs union; he had learned his lesson. What worried the French was that the Benelux quotas would amount to 510, as against 450 for France.

'This was really the new fact which changed the position', Istel explained.

Vinson asked what was the position of Belgium, the Netherlands and Luxembourg 'in respect of France having a seat among the mighty'.

'It is very simple', Istel started to say, but Mendès France ordered him, 'Don't speak.'

'I will speak to you afterwards. You know the position of Luxembourg' was all lstel could add.

Morgenthau wanted the Frenchmen to understand how difficult it was, when you have 'forty-four nations to juggle and put together into a picture puzzle'. The thing that had bothered him, and which had now been corrected, was that the French delegates might have had the impression that anything he had done would be directed at France. 'I don't know who is handling this thing, but let's throw our weight to five Directors', Morgenthau suggested,

This satisfied the French delegates. 'Mr. Secretary,' said Mendès France, 'I must tell you, you spoke with me about this, and I thank you very much for having put five countries, and I told you, of course I would back it and I told you I am grateful.

But, please, you must understand that taking this position was not so easy with us, because on issues with Belgium and Holland it was not quite easy, but as I had promised you, I did it and I thank you for the idea you had for us.'

Luxford thought they had already asked for this at Atlantic City.

'Yes, and we thank you for it', said Istel.

'And I thank you for it', Mendès France echoed.

'Once is enough', said Morgenthau.

'But you had the feeling I had some bad idea', Mendeès France wondered.

No, Morgenthau was simply concerned that there had been this impression that the American delegation had been unfriendly to France, and 'I told you I would not go to bed until I tried to correct that impression. Now you say you have not got that impression and I can go to bed.' Thereupon the French delegates left, and Mrs. Morgenthau, who had followed the conversation, asked, 'Does he feel happier?'

'Yes,' said Morgenthau, 'he said tonight that he did not feel that the American Delegation and the Conference were opposed to France. Now I understood him to say this. That is the only thing that bothered him and the man is a very smart, intelligent fellow and I think, a very sincere fellow. And I certainly didn't know it, because you can't know all these things, but it never occurred to me that when we were fighting the Russians on the twenty-five percent that France was one of the most devastated countries and that they were affected. It never occurred to me.'

'Well,' said Morgenthau, 'let's call it a night.'

RUSSIANS: THE TOUGH CUSTOMERS

The position of the Russians had been anomalous from the beginning. Why, with their system of state trading and absolute government control over imports and exports, they should become part of an international organisation that would not allow restrictions on current transactions, but would be ready to assist governments whose citizens, by their multitude of uncoordinated decisions, had led the country temporarily to live beyond its means, was hard to see.

White had insisted all along that 'the Fund needs Russia', and Morgenthau shared this view, though, to get the reluctant Russians to Bretton Woods, they had all but had to drag them there. In the end Russia had sent to the conference a strong delegation, headed by Mr. M. S. Stepanov, Deputy People's Commissar of Foreign Trade.

Within the American delegation there was disagreement on how far to go along with the Russians, particularly because they were demanding that provisions applicable only to them be written into the Final Act.

They wanted, for instance, to be able to change the value of the rouble, if the change in parity did not affect international transactions, without having to refer the matter to the Fund. White had agreed, although he could not figure out what purpose it could be and neither could the Russians. We have asked them time and time again to cite us a single illustration of what they would wish to accomplish in parities that would not affect international transactions. They couldn't give an illustration, but you might conceive a hypothetical circumstance in which they would want to call their gold a different unit or something for domestic bookkeeping and still keep their exchange rates the same.

The provision, White thought, might save us a lot of trouble, because if this phrase isn't there, Congress might take the position, do we understand we can't alter the gold content of the dollar, which has always been our right, unless it is appropriate to correct a fundamental disequilibrium. If we could be able to answer 'no, you could do anything you want as long as it doesn't affect international transactions', we are talking at the kind of nonsensical level, but that is the level at which those discussions take place.

'What reason would we have, Harry, to change the gold value of the dollar if it didn't affect international transactions?', Marriner Eccles wanted to know.

'No reason' said White. 'It is nonsense.'

Brown, the banker, thought that putting in this provision would be an invitation to every other country to monkey with it and get them in trouble with the Fund.' The surest way to have the whole thing rejected by the American people, was to put it in. 'I think you have to meet the Russians head-on on this.'

Eccles thought that 'the Russians have... determined to have more than it is possible to give them, without breaking up the Conference'. The outlook was not very bright, and their interest in the success of the conference was entirely different from that of capitalistic countries. 'Their interest is openly to get this credit.'

'What is China's interest and Poland's interest and Greek interest?', White asked. He thought it was necessary to make concessions to Russia.

To Brown, the Russian attitude proved that for them this was not a stabilization fund, 'and as I see it, it is a grab-bag'.

This made White angry. He went into a long speech: 'No. I don't think that is an appropriate supposition.... A Stabilization Fund is a fund to provide exchange to take care of the cyclical swings in the demand for foreign exchange. Those cyclical swings may be caused by harvest failures, depreciation abroad, certain breakdowns of one kind or another when you are unable to export your goods at a price which will enable you to keep the imports you want. USSR has advantages which no other country has. She has large gold production, she has tremendous productive capacity, and last and most important, she herself can determine how much she is going to sell. No capitalistic country can do that, because they have to sell at a profit. Now then, when USSR says, very frankly, "We are going to use this Fund to buy things because this is a time of need and this is what a stabilization fund is for and we will pay you back after five, six or seven years", I say that is a stabilization operation and no different than what happens in any other country.... The reason why I go into detail here is because there is a tendency completely to distort the analysis and to point a finger at USSR, because they are saying frankly what the other countries are going to do anyway. What do you think Poland and the Netherlands or France or Belgium or China are going to do?

If they didn't do it, in my judgment, their financial ministers would be stupid. That is what they should do, and that is what the Fund is for, and the only consideration that we have to bear in mind is, can they repurchase that within the period we are thinking of, within the four, five, six, seven year period. If a country cannot repurchase it, then she has no business in getting some money from here, but should get it in thirty or forty year loans, and it is even questionable whether she should get it there.... From the point of view of the ability to repurchase foreign exchange which she buys from the Fund, I put USSR on top of the list and instead of giving her one billion dollars you could give her two billion and the Fund would operate still better and your exports would do a lot more business. That is quite a speech, but I think it is necessary in the light of the misunderstanding which is prevalent not only here but outside on what the nature of the Stabilization Fund is.'

'That is an honest difference in point of view', said Eccles. 'I don't agree with you. Your speech hasn't changed my point of view a particle.'

Neither did Brown like the agreement that had been made on the technical level 'that Russia should get eight hundred million. That was not published but you gave them an agreement to give them twenty-five per cent off in gold payments which isn't important, which wasn't published, just as the eight hundred million wasn't published but which is very important when you take the world as a whole as to the amount of gold you are going to get... you are going to hurt yourself. The newly-mined gold... two hundred million more than the eight hundred million that was agreed... twenty-five percent.... Now I think... the Conference is stalled absolutely stalled by these Russian demands. I think the time has come when unless it is resolved that the Conference will fail just because it can't complete its task within the two weeks, that it is necessary for us at this time to show our teeth, something which I dislike to do.'

'Not unless they are good teeth', said White.

Tell the Russians that the Fund is more to their benefit than to ours, Congressman Wolcott suggested. 'I don't like to say, "Take it or leave it", but that should be our attitude anyway.'

'I think the delegation should make up its mind and instruct the negotiators', Judge Vinson said.

But to Eccles, 'the question of negotiations is over. I think you have reached the point where you say this is taken up, this is the position and that is final. Let's adopt their tactics.'

White had been warned. He thought there was a chance in attempting to bargain. 'It is kind of a ticklish situation in which I really think we have the final cards, but they may not break out that way. You see, they may not turn it down that way. They will say, "We will consult with Moscow", maybe. And we sit and sweat and wait.'

'That will give us some time to go up to the mountain and play some golf', Wolcott concluded.

The Russians were tough negotiators. On 3 July the Soviet delegate had privately indicated to Morgenthau that he hoped the Russian quota would be only slightly less than the British quota, which meant $1200 million instead of the $800 million which had been discussed before. Morgenthau thought there must be some misunderstanding, but 'In spite of this regrettable misunderstanding... the delegation of the United States will associate itself in any efforts by the Soviet delegation to obtain an increase at this Conference in the quota for the Soviet Union.'

According to White: 'they are basing their desire to have a billion two on the grounds that from an economic point of view, from their economic potentialities, from the fact that they are a rapidly expanding economy and expect to play a major role in international monetary and economic affairs'. On the other hand, the Russians wanted a very substantial reduction in their gold contribution, 'because they say that during the next years they cannot get dollars or other currencies because they are not in a position to export anything until they restore their factories'.

On 11 July Morgenthau asked the Russians to come down and see him, because this was 'the first time I have had this experience in dealing with your government'. There had been an honest misunderstanding about the $800 million, but White had suggested two alternatives: either a $1200 million quota, or a $900 million quota with the right to reduce by 25 per cent the amount of gold contributed.

But the Russians wanted $1200 million and a 25 per cent reduction. Morgenthau was 'quite shocked that two great nations should begin what we call "to horse trade".... That isn't the spirit which my Government has approached this problem with; it isn't the spirit expressed by Mr. Molotov to me; it isn't the spirit of your Minister of Finance, where he said we would do this thing side by side, which means like partners.'

Stepanov did not understand English. The interpreter translated Morgenthau's words, and gave Stepanov's reply: 'Mr. Stepanov's idea is such that our Government really consented not to object against the positions which were made by your technical experts, in spite of the position of ours, because it was regarded to the mutual benefit and we didn't interfere, but wanted to collaborate with the Government of the United States.' Stepanov was of the opinion that 'there would be no difficulty in settling these problems if we try to understand each other properly. The Russian questions which we are not entitled to decide in case they have been already decided and agreed upon in Moscow-among these questions is the question concerning the loans of twenty-five per cent.' By 'loans' the interpreter meant something different, but Morgenthau understood what he wanted to say.

The quota suggested by White was very tentative, very approximate, the interpreter continued. But in Moscow 'those people who are in a position to see more clearly the data available for them concerning our financial position, they say that the amount which was just mentioned is approximate to that amount which we are entitled to get. And the American Delegation would see very clearly that we were right in this respect after we will give you the data concerning our financial position, including the national income.' Stepanov could not decide anything without the consent of Moscow.

Morgenthau was puzzled by this method of negotiation: 'I am not a diplomat, I am not a lawyer, I am just a farmer' he said. The interpreter answered. 'Mr. Stepanov says he is no diplomat himself-no lawyer, no financier, just a businessman.'

And he went on to say that Russia would be glad to support the position of your country and your personal proposition... we simply would like to occupy the place which we regard we are entitled to, according to the calculations which we have'.

Morgenthau said that he would be glad to recognise the-importance of Russia in the world, 'but we have no real data about Russian resources and therefore that is why I said we had to do this largely based on your military' successes. We have not-been furnished any data, you see?' After the Fund came into operation, Stepanov said, Russia would be glad to present all the data required, 'and you would see very clearly that this sum is very approximate 'to the exact sum you have arrived at on the basis of the American formula'.

Two days later, since nothing had been heard from the Russian delegation, Morgenthau saw Stepanov again. Unfortunately, no word had been received from Moscow. Mr. Stepanov 'is not sleeping too well at night waiting for the answer', the interpreter said. He had sent another cable but received no answer. 'What I would like to say to Mr. Stepanov, with all courtesy, is that the whole Conference is being held up, Morgenthau remarked. Ambassador Harriman had cabled from Moscow that the Russian delegation had received instructions but he had not been able to find out what the instructions were. There was going to be a meeting in the afternoon, and the American delegation would have to take position publicly on the Russian attitude. Morgenthau made the suggestion that the American delegation would support the $1200 million quota, and would also agree that the newly-mined gold would not have to be counted as part of the national reserves. This, he thought, was more important than a 25 per cent reduction in the gold contribution. Since the position of Russia was unique, in that it was the only country that had suffered devastation from the war and was at the same time a gold-producing country, by taking this position the American delegation would keep out of trouble with the other countries that had been devastated. If Russia received a special treatment because of the war damage, 'then all the other countries who have also been devastated will want the same treatment'.

The meeting where the quotas were to be announced was being held shortly, and it was necessary to make a decision.

'Now, we feel very sorry that we have to do this thing publicly, and that we can't wait', said Morgenthau; and we don't want to be discourteous. But we must go forward, and therefore at this two o'clock meeting when this question on the quotas comes up, that will be the position of the American Delegation. And I sincerely hope that when Mr. Stepanov gets word from Moscow that he will be able to concur.'

'Mr. Stepanov wants to thank you, sir, sincerely', said the interpreter, 'for your very good attitude towards our position.'

Having obtained about all they wanted, the Russians came to see Morgenthau the following day. They wanted to bring up again the point that a country would be allowed to change the par value of its currency if this did not affect the international transactions of the other members of the Fund. White had already gone a long way to meet the Russian demand, and had changed the paragraph which now said that the Fund would 'concur' in a proposed change, if it was 'satisfied that the proposed change does not affect international transactions of the member proposing the change'. The Russians wanted this to read that the country could, in that case, change the value without the consent of the Fund, Stepanov suggested that just the USSR should be given that right.

But White objected, 'If we did, it might be clear to the technicians, but it would create a storm of protest and suspicion on the part of the people who do not understand-in Congress and with the public.'

This was becoming too complicated for Morgenthau and he asked White to carry on the discussion. White said that, as a-result of the redrafting they had agreed upon, the two provisions were almost identical. There was no difference of substance.

'Mr. White finds that both languages are identical, then Mr. Stepanov proposes to take our wording', said the interpreter.

'Not identical; almost identical. The substance is the same', White answered.

'It is the "almost" we want to liquidate, do you see?'

White explained again that, since the Fund must agree, there was no difference in substance. But the Russians wanted their wording, which said that they would only have to inform the Fund of the proposed change: 'We have studied the American-proposal very carefully.... Still, we think that our proposition is the one that is feasible and that it 'will be accepted.'

There followed an intense discussion, each sticking to his own position, 'We will go in the other room and you just relax', Morgenthau told the Russians.

After a while the American group came back; White told the Russians that 'we have a suggestion that will meet you and probably please you'.

Luxford, the lawyer, started reading: ' "A change in the par value of a member's currency affecting the international transactions of members may be...."-you don't have to propose it, it doesn't affect it.'

'That is identical with yours', said White.

'And what about the changes that do not affect those transactions?', Stepanov wanted to know.

'Don't raise them', said White. 'That is identical. The reason why we have a little preference for that is because it doesn't highlight the change, do you see? But you don't raise the question.... Probably that is equally good, or better from your point of view; but it is better from ours, because it doesn't stand out.' As far as Stepanov could see, there was no more disagreement on substance. He agreed to it. But since the question was of great importance, Moscow would have to agree also. Therefore, he insisted on the wording he had proposed at the start of the conversation, since there was no difference of substance.

Morgenthau was exasperated; 'Mr. Stepanov has said two different things. First he said he would like time to consider the language of Mr. Luxford; then in the next breath he has changed his mind and has gone back to his own language.'

The 'interpreter explained that Mr. Stepanov had not changed his mind, but that he only wanted to point out that since there was no difference in substance, it would be easier for everyone to take his wording, since in that case he would not have to refer to his government.

'You mean you have to cable?'

'Cable. Mr. Stepanov says to avoid loss of time, he is offering his proposal.'

'I am laughing because he knows when he says "Cable" to me, I go like this!' said Morgenthau, gesturing.

'Same reaction on our side. It is a point of primary importance concerning our domestic affairs. There is no disagreement about the substance.'

'What is the use?' asked White,

'Well, look, on this particular issue,' said Morgenthau, 'I think it will be easier for the Conference to accept the language Mr. Luxford suggested, but we also like to be reasonable and therefore we will accept your language.'

'Thank you very much.'

'You tell Mr. Stepanov I am afraid it is the last time he is going to say thank you at this Conference!' responded Morgenthau, laughing.

There were more points to be discussed. The Russians wanted to know where the Fund's gold would be stored. Then there was the matter of the information that the Fund requested: Russia had never published many detailed statistics regarding newly-mined gold, national income, the index of prices, and so on, but it was ready to accept a programme such as the one proposed by the American delegation,

The Russians also thought that the rates of interest to be charged by the Fund were too high, and they were ready to discuss again the 25 per cent reduction in the gold contribution for devastated countries, bearing in mind that, since Russia had suffered the heaviest devastation, she would have the full reduction. They also had a few more points to make about the Bank. 'May I say this to Mr. Stepanov?' Morgenthau asked. 'He has brought up enough questions to take us ten hours to discuss, and Mr. White has a Commission at ten o'clock. What meeting is there now?'

'Why do they bring up all these things?' Morgenthau asked. There was no answer.

THE LAST DAYS

Secretary Morgenthau asked the chairmen of several delegations who were members of the steering committee to see him on 19 July at 9 p.m.

'I think we will start', he said, 'and maybe Lord Keynes can catch up.' He introduced Mr Frank Coe, the technical secretary-general of the conference, and asked him to explain the purpose of the meeting. Coe explained that it was necessary to constitute a coordinating committee to complete the documents of the conference. Because the commissions had been so careful in their work, the coordinating committee would have practically nothing to do. Therefore he suggested that it would not be necessary to call it together, 'unless some confusion should develop which would require such a body'. There was general agreement that authority for this job should be delegated to Secretary Morgenthau. 'The next piece of business is the resolution on the Final Act', said Morgenthau.

Frank Coe read a statement to the effect that the conference secretariat, of which he was leader, would be authorised to prepare the Final Act, containing the definitive texts of the conclusions approved by the conference, and that no changes would be made at the closing plenary session. The coordinating committee could review the text, and submit it to the final plenary session. 'The signature, therefore, of the Final Act would be essentially or entirely, a statement by the signer that he had attended the Conference and had witnessed these things being done', Coe added.

Mendès France wanted to know when the plenary session would take place. It had tentaively been arranged for 10 p.m. on Saturday, after the farewell dinner, he was told.

'At what time do we get the last papers?', Mendès France inquired.

'That will depend, of course upon the time that the Commissions complete their work and the Executive Session is held. It might be explained that each of those articles and resolutions will be considered twice by the plenary session; one, in Executive Session where there can be free discussion, and the last a mere formal approval.'

This too was agreed, 'If there is no other business, we could make this a record meeting', Morgenthau said happily.

The records seem not to contain any evidence, and probably never did, of whether Keynes was asked to attend the meeting.

The meeting over, White and his group could go ahead and write up the Final Act; the coordinating committee would not be called together, and there would be little time for anyone else to read much of the text.

White and his group worked day and night at combining the provisions that had been adopted by the various committees and commissions, plus those that had been secretly agreed upon in bilateral negotiations, and including those that had been prepared by the special committee and not been referred back to any commission meeting.

The completed Final Act contained ninety-six pages and was written mostly in lawyers' language, practically unintelligible to the layman; the chairmen or other chosen representatives of the delegations were to sign it by noon on the day following the closing plenary session (held at 9.45 p.m. on 22 July). Before that could happen, however, the conference went through some of its most dramatic moments.

On 21 July, Keynes took the time to write a long letter to Sir John Anderson, the Chancellor of the Exchequer, who was preparing for a visit to the United States:

> You should appreciate that you will be coming into an atmosphere of the greatest possible friendliness and good will. The Americans are inclined to be intolerably tiresome in method and in detail and with the execution of plans and in the mode of pressure they bring to bear.... One can and should approach them as a band of friends and brothers. They have their own difficult psychology and a dreadful tendency to suspicion and all the rest of it. But underneath, what I have just said is the real truth....

The fact that we have been able to work in such intimacy and for so long a period with the Americans, and more especially with the American Treasury, more as colleagues on the same side of the table, helping them to common ends and to make a good job of a piece of work, than trying to get something for ourselves has, as I think all of us agree, produced a relationship of intimacy and confidence which has never previously existed. We have tried most scrupulously to be reasonable and not to be greedy. We and we alone of the other Delegations have spent 90 per cent of our time trying to help them and not to make trouble for them. This is deeply understood and appreciated....

As I have already reported, one of the surprises has been the intimate and friendly relations with Morgenthau personally. As you know, I myself have known him for a considerable time. But until Bretton Woods I had never spent a minute with him that was not sticky. Now all that is completely changed. I have seen a good deal of him, and increasingly as time went on. Most of the interviews have been tete-a-tete. For the first time I have been able to discuss serious matters of business with him in quite long interviews without his getting into those moods which used to be so obstructive to proper relations. He could not have been more consistently kind and friendly, and even expansive....

The pressure of work here has been quite unbelievable... carried on in committees and commissions numbering anything up to 200 persons in rooms with bad acoustics, shouting through microphones, many of those present, often including the Chairman, with an imperfect knowledge of English, each wanting to get something on the record which would look well in the Press down at home, and one of the most important Delegations namely the Russians, only understanding what was afoot with the utmost difficulty and expense of time.... We have all of us worked every minute of our waking hours practically without intermission for what is now four weeks.... I have resolutely refused to go to any committees after dinner (except once only against orders which promptly led to a heart attack, so that I suffered from guilt not less than from bodily discomfort!); whereas the others have been sitting in committees night after night up to 3.30 a.m., starting again in the committee at 9.30 a.m. next morning. How people have stood it all is a miracle....

Our personal relations with the Russians have been very cordial and we have seen quite a lot of them socially. We like them exceedingly and, I think, they like us. Given time we should, I believe, gain their confidence and would then be able to help them a good deal. They want to thaw and collaborate. But the linguistic difficulties and very poor interpretation are a dreadful obstacle, Above all, they are put in a most awkward, and sometimes humiliating, position by the lack both of suitable instructions and of suitable direction from Moscow.

Well we have survived. In my opinion the final products are clear and even aesthetic in presentation. I hope you will like the substance and we feel that we have protected your position not too badly.

One of the knottiest problems the conference had to deal with was the Russians' attitude on the quotas. It had been stipulated that the quotas of each country would be the same in the Fund, where they meant access to the facilities, as in the Bank, where they had to be contributed and would be used by the neediest. All major countries had agreed to this, except the Russians, who insisted on a $1200 million quota in the Fund, but wanted to contribute only $900 million to the Bank. After protracted negotiations the American delegation had accepted this, and the press had become aware of it.

In order to break the deadlock, Judge Vinson asked the chairmen of a number of delegations to meet during the morning of 21 July. Several delegations indicated their willingness to increase their Bank quota, in order not to change the aggregate, while subscribing the part the Russians refused to take. Keynes appealed to the Soviet delegate, who was present but had not yet spoken: 'He has heard in the course of the last few minutes that Poland and China are prepared to make increased contributions to meet something that Russia cannot afford.'

The risks involved were limited, but, owing to language difficulties, this probably had not been understood by the Soviet delegation. The delegate from India had just remarked that, if the Russian contribution remained at $900 million, the Indian contribution 'will be half the Soviet contribution, which he would find difficult to justify. I do urge, most sincerely, that it is scarcely consistent with the honor and dignity of a great country to remain so uncompromising at this stage.'

The Soviet delegate was 'deeply moved by the willingness of other delegations to reach the goal which was mentioned'. He had, however, no authorisation to propose any other figure, In international organisations each country has to determine its contribution by its circumstances, and he could not see the necessity for taking into account other countries' circumstances too. Russia had suffered more from the war than India, He did not want to influence in any way any other delegation; it was up to each country to make its own decision.

That afternoon the same delegates met again, and Vinson had to announce that the Russian delegation had received no further communication from Moscow. China, Poland, the United States, Canada, and even the Latin American countries had all shown themselves prepared to increase their own contributions. Thus the total remained unchanged. Keynes suggested that the final table of contributions be presented at six o'clock that evening. There was unanimous agreement.

At seven o'clock that evening, the two principal Russian delegates came to see Morgenthau.

'Mr. Stepanov would like to tell you that he has the answer from Mr. Molotov', said the interpreter, 'and the answer is that he is happy to agree to your proposition.'

'Yes', was all Morgenthau could say.

'Mr. Molotov says that we will agree to increase our quota', the interpreter repeated.

'To how much?'

'To $1,200,000,000.'

'Mr. Molotov agrees to that?'

'He said that he agrees with Mr. Morgenthau.'

'Well, you tell Mr. Molotov that I want to thank him from the bottom of my heart. Now, I don't know what we will do, but I will have to send for Mr. Vinson and the others right away, and we will have to get busy.'

'Yes, Mr. Stepanov says that it is all right.'

Just so I understand', said Morgenthau, 'would you mind saying it once more?'

Mr. Stepanov repeated the message and the interpreter formulated it once more: 'Mr Molotov gives us the right to agree to a quota of $1,200,000,000 in the Bank. He said that he agrees with Mr. Morgenthau, and I should like to mention this too. Mr. Molotov says that he agrees to the size of the quota because Mr. Morgenthau asked the Soviet Delegation to do it.'

'I want you to say this to Mr. Molotov. This confirms the long time respect and confidence that I have in the Union of Soviet and Socialist Republics.'

'Mr. Stepanov says that he will telegraph what you told him just as it was said by yourself.'

'Well, this makes me very, very happy. The Conference was almost a success and now it is a complete success.

Before the Russian decision became known, Keynes had sent the following comment to London:

At the final discussion of subscriptions... Russia stood pat on 900 and lost much honour and dignity in the process.... The Americans have been outstandingly anxious to meet Russia on every point. The Russian stonewalling tactics have been successful in getting nearly all concessions for which they have asked. Nevertheless they have overplayed their hand and seriously diminished their prestige before every delegation here present.

Another problem that came up at the end of the conference resulted from the fact that the representatives of China, France, the USSR, Greece, Ethiopia, Yugoslavia, India, Australia, Egypt and New Zealand, while they agreed to sign the Final Act, wanted to express reservations of one sort or another, most of them about their quotas.

At the executive plenary session on 20 July, Keynes took up the subject and wondered whether there is not a possibility of some misunderstanding in the minds of the Delegates who wish to make reservations on particular points. So far as the U.K. Delegation is concerned we, in common with all other Delegations, reserve the opinion of our Government on the document as a whole and on every part of it... we are at the present stage in no way committed to anything. We do not even recommend our Governments to adopt the result.

By expressing reservations on part of the document, the countries concerned seemed to suggest that the rest was in some sense accepted, and this might create some misapprehension of the position of those countries that expressed no reservations. He suggested that the reservations be retained in the minutes of the commission, but not be made part of the Final Act.

Judge Vinson appealed to the delegations that had made reservations not 'to make the task of friends more difficult'. He assured the Chinese delegates that the United States was not unmindful of the 'historic friendship that has existed throughout the years between China and our country; tell me that the United States does not recognize the glorious courageous effort that China has made'. As for France, 'we learned it at our mother's knees that France came to us years ago when we were in need. 1917 when millions of our sons joined common cause with France and others of her kind a historic statement was made by an American when he stood before the tomb of Lafayette, saluted and said, "Lafayette we are here." ' He trusted and prayed that all delegations that had expressed reservations on the question of quotas would reconsider their position.

Following these appeals, the reservations were withdrawn. They remained recorded in the minutes of the commission, but were not included in the Final Act.

During the morning of 22 July, the American delegation met for the last time. Morgenthau was happy. The previous night, at 11 o'clock, he had got the idea that it might be nice if the President sent a message of congratulations to the Conference on the conclusion'. He did not know where the

President was, but around midnight he had sent him a proposed draft for a telegram, and the President's approval had arrived in the morning.

He thanked everybody for the splendid work the American delegation had done. 'It has been a team. It has been the most successful group I have ever worked with, the most pleasant, and I think it has demonstrated to me that on this sort of thing it is the way we should work with Congress.'

One after the other the delegates complemented Morgenthau on his splendid leadership', on 'your remarkable patience and your genius in directing the Conference'. The members of Congress, both the Democrats and the Republicans, promised to do the best they could to 'carry this thing forward to success'.

Ned Brown the banker promised to 'do what I can to sell it to the bankers of the country', although he 'didn't give any guarantee'. The Republican senators' Morgenthau felt, could take care of the opposition in Congress: 'I will leave Taft to you', he told Senator Tobey. 'He is your personal meat. I think you could take him apart and put him together again so that you would not recognize what he looks like.'

Senator Tobey, in turn, paid tribute to 'something that has impressed me tremendously, and it is the genius of these two men, Luxford and Bernstein. I have watched them in action and it is wonderful the work they have done here and I want to compliment them and I appreciate all they have done.' Now that the conference was coming to an end, there was general agreement that 'every one here has to work as hard as they have been working to sell it. Our job isn't done until it is sold.' Morgenthau suggested that the delegation meet in Washington from time to time, and 'go along step by step', as a permanent body, to organise the campaign that would have to be conducted in Congress and with public opinion.

'Speaking of continuing our conversations in Washington,' Morgenthau concluded, 'I think the New Hampshire air has contributed much to the clear thinking of everybody,... Believe me, if the United States Government had a summer capital, I think it would increase the work by a hundred per cent.'

A formal dinner marked the closing plenary session. When almost everyone was already seated, Keynes's chair was still empty, He came in a little late, 'Tired, pale as a sheet, he was walking round the long table to his empty seat. Spontaneously everyone in the room stood up in complete silence while he made his way to his chair. It was an unspoken moving tribute to the master, the true prophet of this gathering,'

The message from President Roosevelt asking Morgenthau to convey his heartiest congratulations to the delegates on the successful completion of their difficult task was read: 'They have prepared two further foundation stones for the structure of lasting peace and security.'

Keynes had been asked to address the conference for the last time, and to submit the motion to accept the Final Act. He rose and said, I feel it a signal honour that I am asked to move the acceptance of the Final Act.

We, the Delegates of this Conference, Mr. President, have been trying to accomplish something very difficult to accomplish.... We have had to perform at one and the same time the tasks appropriate to the economist, to the financier, to the politician, to the journalist, to the propagandist, to the lawyer, to the statesman-even, I think, to the prophet and to the soothsayer.

Nor has the magic of the microphone been able, silently and swiftly perambulant at the hands of our attendant sprites, the faithful Scouts, Puck coming to the aid of Bottom, to undo all the mischief first wrought in the Tower of Babel. He paid tribute to Secretary Morgenthau's 'wise and kindly guidance', and to 'the indomitable will and energy, always governed by good temper and humour, of Harry White'. But it had been teamwork, such as he had seldom experienced.

And for my own part, I should like to pay a particular tribute to our lawyers. All the more so because I confess that, generally speaking, I do not like lawyers. I have been known to complain that, to judge from results in this lawyer-ridden land, the Mayflower, when she sailed from Plymouth, must have been entirely filled with lawyers.... Too often lawyers busy themselves to make common sense illegal. Too often lawyers are men who turn poetry into prose and prose into jargon, Not so our lawyers here in Bretton Woods. On the contrary they have turned our jargon into prose and our prose into poetry.... I have only one complaint against them.... I wish that they had not covered so large a part of our birth certificate with such very detailed provisions for our burial service, hymns and lessons and all.

I am greatly encouraged, I confess, by the critical, sceptical, and even carping spirit in which our proceedings have been watched and welcomed in the outside world, How much better that our projects should begin in disillusion than that they should end in it!

The end of his address, in which he stated his hope that the brotherhood of man would 'become more than a mere phrase', is quoted at the beginning of this book.

One of the most dramatic moments of the conference occurred when Secretary Morgenthau announced that the Russian government had agreed to increase its quota in the Bank from $900 million to $1200 million.

The delegates applauded when they heard that the telegram from Moscow announcing this decision had just arrived. The Russian delegate expressed his gratitude to Secretary Morgenthau and stated,

The stabilization of the currencies of the various countries, the expansion of world trade, the balancing of international payments, long-term capital investments intended for the reconstruction and development of the democratic nations and especially for the restoration of economy of those countries who suffered severely from enemy occupation and hostilities-all these aspirations will have exceptional importance for the postwar organization of the World and for the maintenance and strengthening of peace and security.

Mr J. L. Ilsley, chairman of the Canadian delegation, hailed the results of the Conference as 'a great and even historic achievement'. He paid tribute to the technical competence of Harry White and his associates, to Morgenthau, and particularly to Keynes, who had so eloquently and fittingly presented the motion.

We find a happy fitness also in that delegate being Lord Keynes. Throughout the Conference, as indeed throughout his life, he has showered his ideas upon us and has occasionally nourished some of ours. His sudden insights, his revealing phrases, and, if I may say so, his passionate striving for what is reasonable and emancipating in human affairs, have contributed greatly to the progress and wisdom of our deliberations.

Mendès France, recalling the failures of the numerous economic and monetary conferences held between the two wars, stated that the delegates to the conference of Bretton Woods may be proud of having inaugurated a new era in the history of these conferences....Because, as it is impossible in the modern world to circumscribe wars, it will be impossible to avoid the spread of unemployment, economic stagnation, excessive economic fluctuations from one country to another with all their train of miseries and sufferings.

As president of the conference it fell upon Secretary Morgenthau to deliver the farewell address. He stressed the fact that nations at the conference had 'had to yield to one another not in respect to principles or essentials, but in respect to methods and procedural details.

The fact that we have done so... is a sign blazoned upon the horizon... that the peoples of the earth are learning to join hands and work in unity.'

The American delegation, like all other delegations, 'has at all times been conscious of its primary obligation-the protection of American interests, And the other representatives here have been no less loyal or devoted to the welfare of their own people.' But the only genuine safeguard for the national interests lay in international co-operation.

To seek the achievement of our aims separately through the planless senseless rivalry that divided us in the past, or through the outright economic aggression which turned neighbors into enemies, would be to invite ruin again upon us all. Worse, it would be once more to start our steps irretraceably down the steep, disastrous road to war, That sort of extreme nationalism belongs to an era that is dead, Today the only enlightened form of national self-interest lies in international accord. He took it as an axiom that governments would not tolerate prolonged and widespread unemployment any more. A revival of international trade was indispensable if full employment was to be achieved in a peaceful world, and with standards of living which will permit the realization of men's reasonable hopes'.

What are the fundamental conditions under which commerce among the nations can once more flourish?

First, there must be a reasonably stable standard of international exchange....

Second, long-term financial aid must be made available at reasonable rates to those countries whose industry and agriculture have been destroyed.... Objections to this Bank have been raised by some bankers and a few economists. The institutions proposed by the Bretton Woods Conference would indeed limit the control which certain private bankers have in the past exercised over international finance. It would by no means restrict the investment sphere in which bankers could engage. On the contrary, it would greatly expand this sphere by enlarging the volume of international investment and would act as an enormously effective stabilizer and guarantor of loans which they might make....

The effect would be to provide capital for those who need it at lower interest rates than in the past and to drive only the usurious money lenders out of the temple of international finance, For my own part, I cannot look upon this outcome with any sense of dismay. Capital, like any other commodity, should be free from monopoly control, and available upon reasonable terms to those who will put it to use for the general welfare....

This monetary agreement is but one step, of course, in the broad program of international action necessary for the shaping of a free future. But it is an indispensable step and a vital test of our intentions. We are at a crossroads, and we must go one way or the other. The Conference at Bretton Woods has erected a signpost-a signpost pointing down a highway broad enough for all men to walk in step and side by side. If they will set out together, there is nothing on earth that need stop them.

A band played the 'Star-Spangled Banner'.

All eyes were on Keynes, and, as he rose and moved to leave the room, the delegates stood up again and sang 'For He's a jolly Good Fellow' and applauded.

Some chairmen of the delegations moved to room B to sign the Final Act. Others signed it the next morning.

The delegates then boarded two special trains, bound for New York and Washington.

3

Borrowing from International Monetary Fund

GENERAL ARRANGEMENTS TO BORROW (GAB)

The GAB enable the IMF to borrow specified amounts of currencies from 11 industrial countries (or their central banks), under certain circumstances, at market-related rates of interest. The potential amount of credit available to the IMF under the GAB totals SDR 17 billion (about $23 billion), with an additional SDR 1.5 billion available under an associated arrangement with Saudi Arabia.

The GAB have been renewed nine times, most recently in November 2002 when the IMF Executive Board approved its renewal for a further period of five years from December 2003. In response to the growing pressures on the IMF's resources caused by the emergence of the debt crisis in Latin America in 1982, a broad review was undertaken in 1983. It resulted in a substantial increase in the credit lines made available under the GAB from about SDR 6 billion to SDR 17 billion, plus an additional SDR 1.5 billion under an associated arrangement with Saudi Arabia.

Other major amendments to earlier GAB provisions permit the IMF to use the GAB to finance lending to nonparticipants in the GAB, if the IMF faces a situation where it has inadequate resources of its own. The earlier GAB carried a rate of interest below market rates; this rate was raised at the time of the GAB enlargement to 100 percent of the SDR interest rate.

GAB Participants and Credit Amounts (After December 26, 1983)

Participant	Amount (in millions of SDRs)
United States	4,250.0
Deutsche Bundesbank	2,380.0
Japan	2,125.0
France	1,700.0
United Kingdom	1,700.0
Italy	1,105.0
Swiss National Bank	1,020.0
Canada	892.5
Netherlands	850.0
Belgium	595.0
Sveriges Riksbank	382.5
Total	17,000.0
Credit arrangement with Saudi Arabia in association with the GAB	1,500.0

NEW ARRANGEMENTS TO BORROW

Following the Mexican financial crisis in 1994, concern that substantially more resources might be needed to respond to future financial crises prompted participants in the 1995 G-7 Halifax Summit to call on the G-10 and other financially strong countries to develop financing arrangements that would double the amount available to the IMF under the GAB. The IMF's Executive Board adopted a decision establishing the NAB that became effective in November 1998. The NAB are a set of credit arrangements between the IMF and 26 members and institutions to provide supplementary resources to the IMF to forestall or cope with an impairment of the international monetary system or to deal with an exceptional threat to the stability of that system. Commitments from individual participants are based on relative economic strength, as measured by actual IMF quotas, as a predominant criterion. An IMF member or institution that is not currently a participant in the NAB may be accepted as a participant at the time of a renewal of the decision, if the IMF and participants representing 80 percent of the total credit arrangements agree to the request. New participants may also be accepted at other times, by way of an amendment to the NAB adopted by the IMF's Executive Board, and with the concurrence of participants representing 85 percent of total credit arrangements.

In November 2002, the NAB decision was renewed for a further period of five years from November 2003. Also, the Banco Central de Chile (as an official institution of Chile) became a new participant with a credit arrangement of SDR 340 million, effective February 2003.2

How do GAB and NAB relate to each other?

The NAB do not replace the existing GAB, which remain in force. However, the NAB would typically be the first and principal recourse in the event of a need to provide supplementary resources to the IMF. The maximum amount of resources available to the IMF under its borrowing arrangements is SDR 34 billion (about $45 billion), double the amount available under the GAB alone.

WHEN HAVE THEY BEEN ACTIVATED?

A proposal for calls on the GAB or the NAB by the IMF's Managing Director can become effective only if it is accepted by the GAB or NAB participants, and the proposal is then approved by the Executive Board. The NAB have been activated once-to finance a Stand-By Arrangement for Brazil in December 1998, when the IMF called on funding of SDR 9.1 billion, of which SDR 2.9 billion was used. The GAB have been activated ten times. The last time was in July 1998 for an amount of SDR 6.3 billion in connection with the financing of an Extended Arrangement for Russia. Of that amount, only SDR 1.4 billion was used. The activations for both Russia and Brazil were canceled in March 1999, when the Fund repaid the outstanding amount following the entry into effect of the Eleventh General Review of Quotas and payment of the bulk of the quota increases.

NAB Participants and Credit Amounts

Participant	Amount (millions of SDRs)
Australia	801
Austria	408
Banco Central de Chile	340
Belgium	957
Canada	1,381
Denmark	367
Deutsche Bundesbank	3,519
Finland	340
France	2,549
Hong Kong Monetary Authority	340
Italy	1,753
Japan	3,519
Korea	340
Kuwait	341
Luxembourg	340
Malaysia	340
Netherlands	1,302
Norway	379
Saudi Arabia	1,761
Singapore	340
Spain	665
Sveriges Riksbank	850
Swiss National Bank	1,540
Thailand	340
United Kingdom	2,549
United States	6,640
Total	34,000

1. Total may not equal sum of components due to rounding.
2. The total amount of NAB credit arrangements remained at SDR 34 billion, with Chile's contribution offset by proportionate reductions in the contributions of existing participants with credit arrangements above the SDR 340 million minimum.

IMF SURVEILLANCE

In today's globalized economy, in which there is a greater risk that domestic policy mistakes will spill over onto other countries, it is essential to have a mechanism to monitor countries' economic policies. This includes policy developments expected over the next year or two, and their likely consequences.

The IMF has a mandate under its Articles of Agreement to exercise firm surveillance over the exchange rate policies of members in order to oversee the international monetary system and ensure its effective operation. To this end, the IMF assesses whether a country's economic developments and policies are consistent with the achievement of sustainable growth and domestic and external stability. In this way, the IMF seeks to provide a preventive mechanism that is capable of signaling dangers on the horizon and anticipating the need for policy action.

Stepping Up Surveillance

The IMF recognizes that the effectiveness of surveillance depends critically upon:

- *Provision of Information*: Timely, reliable, and comprehensive data are essential. The IMF encourages countries to introduce greater transparency and fuller disclosure-for instance by providing data on forward transactions by central banks and private short-term debt. Further efforts are needed to strengthen members' data provision to the IMF and the public. This can now be done through the Special Data Dissemination Standard (SDS) for members having, or seeking, access to international capital markets. The SDS is being modified to incorporate more stringent requirements regarding the publication of international reserves data.
- *Continuity of Surveillance*: To ensure more continuous surveillance, the IMF has intensified its efforts in several areas, including supplementing annual consultations with interim staff visits to member countries, and frequent informal Board meetings to review major developments in selected member countries.

- *Focus of Surveillance*: Surveillance at the country level should: monitor international capital flows more actively to identify potential trouble spots and pay more explicit attention to policy interdependence and the risks of contagion. In light of the Asian crisis, the IMF recognizes that the focus of surveillance must extend further and more deeply beyond short-term macroeconomic issues. This would mean a closer examination of the functioning of the financial sector, capital account issues, and external vulnerability, at a much more detailed level.
- *Clarity and Candor of IMF Advice*: The crucial role of credibility and the restoration of market confidence in the Asian crisis underlines the importance of policy transparency. The IMF is placing greater emphasis on transparency by the staff in communicating its views on economic developments in member countries.
- *Peer Pressure*: The effectiveness of IMF advice benefits from supportive peer pressure. Regular staff input into regional surveillance mechanisms could strengthen regional peer pressure for the implementation of good policies.

In the wake of the Mexican crisis, the IMF took several steps to strengthen the effectiveness of surveillance to better anticipate future crises. These initiatives are being built upon in light of the Asian crisis, with greater consideration being given to how surveillance practices can be strengthened to improve the IMF's ability to convince members to follow policies that are in their own best interest and avoid disruptions in the economies of other members. While surveillance can play an important role in crisis prevention, it must also be supported by responsible policies at the national level and by the private sector.

SURVEILLANCE IN PRACTICE

How does the IMF Fulfill its Surveillance Mandate?

Article IV Consultations. In accordance with Article IV of its Articles of Agreement, the IMF holds consultations, normally every year, with each of its members. These consultations focus on the member's fiscal, exchange rate, and monetary policies;

its balance of payments and external debt developments; and the impact of its policies on the country's external accounts. These consultations are not limited to macroeconomic policies, but touch on all policies that significantly affect the economic performance of a country, including those that effect the labor market, society, the environment, and governance. With the intensified global integration of financial markets, the IMF is also taking into account more explicitly capital account and financial and banking sector issues.

Multilateral and regional surveillance. The IMF's World Economic Outlook, prepared twice a year, and the annual International Capital Markets Report, provide opportunities to assess the global implications of members' policies and to review key developments and prospects in the international monetary system. Regular discussions are also held with regional economic institutions, including in the context of Economic and Monetary Union (EMU) in Europe.

PUBLICITY AND OPENNESS

To encourage debate and promote consensus-building for important policy choices, many IMF members have increased the transparency of their economic policy making in recent years. In this context, a growing number of countries have released the IMF staff's concluding statement following Article IV consultation discussions. The IMF's Executive Board supports greater transparency in the IMF's policies and activities. Recent initiatives include:

- Since 1994, the IMF has released background papers on recent economic developments in individual countries for most member countries, providing information and analysis assembled during annual country consultations.
- Since May 1997, the IMF has been releasing the conclusions of the Article IV consultations by the Executive Board in the form of PINs-Public Information Notices. In the past 18 months, an increasing number of countries concerned have agreed to their publication, with some 80 percent of all recent annual country consultations resulting in the release of a PIN.

OTHER TYPES OF SURVEILLANCE

While Article IV consultations remain the main form of collaboration between the IMF and a member country, some members have sought closer rapport in other ways, including:

- Precautionary arrangements, by which members agree to an IMF arrangement but do not intend to use resources committed by the IMF under such an arrangement; precautionary arrangements are useful in signaling the IMF's endorsement of a member's policies and boosting confidence in those policies;
- Informal staff monitoring, which includes the standard Article IV consultation process, but is often supplemented by interim visits, with a more intensive dialogue with the IMF staff against the background of quantitative benchmarks; informal monitoring does not, however, constitute formal IMF endorsement of the member's policies;
- Enhanced surveillance, established in 1985, provides members not using IMF resources with close IMF monitoring. The procedure does not constitute formal IMF endorsement of the member's policies.
- The IMF strongly encourages countries using IMF resources to publish their policy framework papers and letters of intent. For instance, the letters of intent of Indonesia, Thailand, and Korea have been published by the authorities and are being posted on the IMF's own website.
- The IMF has published several internal reviews of its operations in the past few years. Internal reviews have been complemented by external evaluations of Fund operations. In 1997, for example, an external evaluation was conducted on the IMF's concessional lending facility, the Enhanced Structural Adjustment Facility (ESAF). Another external evaluation is now under way on IMF Surveillance.

EVERY CURRENCY CRUMBLES

Currencies, being made of paper, are highly flammable, and governments are forever trying to put out the fires. Thus a half decade before the bonfire of the baht, the rupiah and the yen, there was the conflagration of the markka, the lira and the pound. The dollar, today's global standard of value, was smoldering ominously as recently as 1992.

Monetary crises are almost as old as money. What is different today is the size of these episodes. It isn't every monetary era that features recurrent seismic shifts in the exchange values of so-called major currencies. On Wednesday morning, after coordinated American and Japanese intervention, the weakling yen became 5 percent less weak in a matter of hours.

People with even a little bit of money ought to be asking what it's made of. J. S. G. Boggs, an American artist, has made an important contribution to monetary theory with his lifelike paintings of dollar bills. So authentic do these works appear--at least at first glance, before Mr. Boggs's own signature ornamentation becomes apparent--that the Secret Service has investigated him for counterfeiting. "All money is art," Mr. Boggs has responded.

Currency management is a political art. The intrinsic value of a unit of currency is the cost of the paper and printing. The stated value of a unit of currency derives from the confidence of the holder in the promises of the issuing government.

It cannot undergird confidence that the monetary fires are becoming six-and seven-alarmers. Writing in 1993 about the crisis of the European Rate Mechanism (in which George Soros bested the Bank of England by correctly anticipating a devaluation of the pound), a central bankers' organization commented: "Despite its geographical confinement to Europe, it is probably no exaggeration to say that the period from late 1991 to early 1993 witnessed the most severe and widespread foreign exchange market crisis since the breakdown of the Bretton Woods System 20 years ago." But the European crisis has been handily eclipsed by the Asian one.

Monetary systems have broken down every generation or so for the past century. The true-blue international gold standard didn't survive World War I. Its successor, a half-strength gold standard, didn't survive the Great Depression. The Bretton

Woods regime--in which the dollar was convertible into gold and the other, lesser currencies were convertible into the dollar--didn't survive the inflationary period of the late 1960's and early 1970's.

Today, the unnamed successor to Bretton Woods is showing its years. The present-day system is also dollar-based, but it differs from Bretton Woods in that the dollar is no longer anchored to anything. It is defined as 100 cents and only as 100 cents. Its value is derived not from a specified weight of gold, as it was up until Aug. 15, 1971, but from the confidence of the market.

For the moment, the market is highly confident. So is the world at large. In 1996, the Federal Reserve Board estimated that some 60 percent of all American currency in existence circulates overseas. The dollar has become the Coca-Cola of monetary brands.

However, as Madison Avenue knows as well as Wall Street, brand loyalties are fickle. In the early 1890's, the United States Treasury was obliged to seek a bailout from the Morgan bank. During the great inflation of the 1970's, Italian hotel clerks, offered payments in dollars, rolled their eyes. The yen, today reckoned dangerously weak at 140 or so to the dollar, was 360 as recently as 1971. The tendency of the purchasing power of every paper currency down through the ages is to regress. Is there any good reason that the dollar, universally esteemed today, should be different?

None: Certainly, the deterioration of the American balance-of-payments position doesn't bode well for the dollar's long-term exchange rate. Consuming more than it produces, the United States must finance the shortfall. And it is privileged to be able to pay its overseas bills with dollars, the currency that it alone can legally produce. Thailand would be a richer country today if the world would accept baht, and nothing but baht, in exchange for goods and services. It won't, of course. America and the dollar are uniquely blessed.

Or Were: France and Germany have led the movement to create a pan-European currency, one that would compete with the dollar as both a store of value and a medium of exchange. The euro, as the new monetary brand is called, constitutes the first serious competitive threat to the dollar since the glory days of the pound sterling.

In a world without a fixed standard of value, a currency is strong or weak only in relation to other currencies. The dollar's "strength," therefore, is a mirror image of--for example--the yen's "weakness." It is not necessarily a reflection of the excellence of the American economy.

And no degree of excellence can forestall a new monetary crisis indefinitely. Some monetary systems are better than others, and some last longer than others, but each and every one comes a cropper. The bezant, the standard gold coin of the Byzantine empire, was minted for 800 years at the same weight and fineness. The gold may still be in existence (in fact--no small recommendation for gold bullion--it probably is), but the empire has fallen.

After the 1994 crisis involving the Mexican peso, the world's financial establishment vowed to stave off a recurrence. Even as the experts delivered their speeches, however, Asian banks were overlending and Asian businesses were overborrowing; the credit-cum-currency eruption followed in short order. Naturally, officials and editorialists are now calling for even better fire prevention systems.

But "stability," the goal so sought after, is ever unattainable. The history of currencies is unambiguous. The law is, Ashes to ashes and dust to dust.

IMF'S KOHLER SEES MORE RISKS TO GLOBAL ECONOMY

Washington, Sept 19 (Reuters): The head of the International Monetary Fund said on Thursday that risks to the global economic outlook have increased in recent months but the recovery should still continue. In a speech before the IMF's annual meetings here next week, the lender's managing director, Horst Koehler, said the United States should avoid falling back into chronic overspending while Europe and Japan should do more to bolster their economic growth prospects.

"The global economy has shown remarkable resilience in the face of multiple shocks over the past two years," Koehler told the Council on Foreign Relations. "Nevertheless, we need to be concerned about the strength and durability of the ongoing economic recovery, and the stability of the international financial system."

"Risks to the global economic outlook today are clearly tilted more to the downside than they were a few months ago," he said, adding, "On balance, we do still expect that the recovery will continue."

Koehler said the heightened risks included the continued fallout from the collapse of the equity bubble, corporate scandals that have undermined investor confidence, crises in some emerging economies like Brazil and Argentina, regional political tensions and volatility in world oil prices.

BOOST CONFIDENCE

He said it was crucial for leading economies to take steps to boost confidence, including steps to improve accounting standards and stamp out corporate corruption.

"The United States should beware of falling back into chronic public sector deficits," Koehler said. "Europe and Japan have to be more serious about accelerating structural reforms, to unlock self-sustained growth."

He also said Japan "should act decisively to bring an end to deflation" and more work was needed to bring a successful conclusion to the latest round of world trade talks.

Koehler also used his speech to hone his vision on how the IMF should be reformed, making a number of new suggestions.

Topping those reforms were his first public statement that the IMF should act as a whistle-blower on countries that are going astray--something that the Bush administration has been seeking but the lender has resisted so far.

"We have a responsibility to speak out when countries live too long beyond their means, not least because the poor suffer most from disorderly adjustment, high inflation and volatility," Koehler said. Critics have said that if the IMF had blown the whistle on Argentina earlier, it would have been forced to restructure its debts earlier, and could have avoided the messy debt default it undertook early this year after the IMF cut off aid due to a myriad of broken promises.

And with corporate scandals like Enron and WorldCom dominating headlines over the past year, Koehler suggested the IMF could play a role. He said the lender, in cooperation with the World Bank and Financial Stability Forum, could work on harmonizing accounting standards, enhancing corporate disclosure and ways to better align management incentives better with shareholder objectives.

The IMF chief also said he supports changing the lender's quota system so its decision-making board would more accurately reflect the economic strength of emerging economies and give a better voice for African nations.

Asian nations have complained they are under represented on the IMF's board compared to their European counterparts, while most African nations are represented by just two of the lender's 24 board members.

With the size of the global economy growing, Koehler also raised the possibility that rich nations might begin considering giving the IMF more cash to do its work.

Koehler reiterated the IMF should do more work on crisis prevention and should support countries with good policies and "be prepared to say 'no'" to recalcitrant nations and, as a rule, make fewer massive bailouts.

On Brazil, which recently secured a $30 billion IMF bailout, Koehler said, "I am confident that Brazil will stay the course of sound policies in the period ahead, regain the full confidence of international financial markets, and resume a strong growth path." "The main problem in Latin America has not been too much reform, but too little. We have seen in Argentina that it is dangerous to stop halfway."

THE IMF: THROWING MORE FUEL ON THE WORLD ECONOMIC BONFIRE

Free-Market capitalism remains the most effective instrument for economic growth and for raising the standard of living of most people. But just as the reckless laissez faire capitalism of the 19th century spawned Marxism, so the indiscriminate globalism of the 1990s may generate a worldwide assault on the very concept of free financial markets. Globalism views the entire world as one market in which the most efficient and competitive prosper. It accepts-and even welcomes-that the free market will relentlessly sift the efficient from the inefficient, even at the cost of periodic economic and social dislocation.

Even well-established free-market democracies do not accept limitless suffering in the name of the market, and have taken measures to provide a social safety net and to curb market excesses by regulation. The international financial system does not as yet have these firebreaks. Nor is there much of a recognition that it needs them.

Ours is the first period experiencing a genuinely global economic system. Markets in different parts of the world interact continuously. Modern communications enable them to respond instantaneously. Sophisticated credit instruments provide unprecedented liquidity. Hedge funds, the trading departments of international banks and institutional investors possess the reach, power and resources to profit from market swings in either direction, and even to bring them about. It is market stability that they find uncongenial.

Broadly speaking, direct foreign investment benefits from the well-being of the societies in which it operates; it runs the risks and is entitled to the benefits of the host country. By contrast, modern speculative capital benefits from exploiting emerging trends before the general public does. It drives upswings into bubbles and down cycles into crises, and in a time-frame that cannot be significantly affected by the kind of macroeconomic remedies being urged on the political leaders.

For example, when Asian credit-worthiness began to fall, financial institutions and fund managers holding the debt were tempted to sell Asian currencies short, thereby accelerating devaluation and compounding the difficulty of repaying debt. Speculators were acting rationally, but the result was a deeper, more vicious and more intractable crisis.

To maintain their overall performance, speculators, as losses mounted in Asia, were driven to cash in their holdings in Latin America and thereby spread the crisis. Regulators in the United States, Europe and Japan have not succeeded in dampening the increased volatility of the market. And small and medium-sized countries are defenseless in the face of it.

The International Monetary Fund, the principal international institution for dealing with the crisis, too often compounds the political instability. Forced by the current crisis into assuming functions for which it was never designed, the IMF has utterly failed to grasp the political impact of its actions.

In the name of free-market orthodoxy, it usually attempts-in an almost academic manner-to remove all at once every weakness in the economic system of the afflicted country, regardless of whether these caused the crisis or not.

In the process, it too often weakens the political structure and with it the precondition of meaningful reform. Like a doctor who has only one pill for every conceivable illness, its nearly invariable remedies mandate austerity, high interest rates to prevent capital outflows and major devaluations to discourage imports and encourage exports.

The inevitable result is a dramatic drop in the standard of living, exploding unemployment and growing hardship weakening the political institutions necessary to carry out the IMF program.

The situation in Southeast Asia is a case in point. Crony capitalism, corruption and inadequate supervision of banks were serious shortcomings. But they did not cause the immediate crisis; they were a cost of doing business, not a barrier to it. Until little more than a year ago, Asia was the fastest growing region in the world, its progress underpinned by high savings rates, disciplined work ethic and responsible fiscal behavior.

What triggered the crisis were factors largely out of national or regional control. The various countries had exchange rates linked to the U.S. dollar. When the dollar appreciated significantly starting in 1995, and the yen fell sharply, Southeast Asian exports became less competitive and export earnings fell.

At the same time, the dollar pegs created unprecedented opportunities for speculation. It was possible to borrow dollars in New York and lend them locally for at least twice the cost of borrowing-at no apparent currency risk. The borrowers invested in real estate and excess plant capacity, creating a dangerous bubble. Local currency became overvalued and local currency holders converted into dollars, inviting speculative raids-all without significant warnings from international financial institutions.

When the crisis spread to Indonesia, the largest country of Southeast Asia, the threat to the global financial system could no longer be ignored. At U.S. urging, the IMF intervened in both situations with its standard remedies, leading to massive austerity. Thailand's democratic institutions have so far proved relatively resilient. But for how long can it sustain interest rates of more than 40 percent, a negative growth of 8 percent and a 42 percent devaluation of its currency?

In Indonesia-a rich country with vast resources and an economy which was praised by the World Bank in July 1997 for its efficient management-the IMF, advised by an administration afraid of being accused of having political ties to leading Indonesian financial institutions, decided to make its assistance conditional on remedying virtually every ill of which the society suffered. It demanded the closing of 15 banks, the ending of monopolies on food and heating oil, and the end of subsidies.

But when 15 banks are closed in the middle of a crisis, a run on other banks follows inevitably. The ending of subsidies raised food and fuel prices, causing riots aimed at the Chinese minority that controls much of the economy. As a result, as much as $60 billion of Chinese money fled Indonesia, or more than the IMF could possibly provide. A currency crisis had been turned into an economic disaster.

For a few months, a special Treasury representative worked with the government and the IMF to ease the pressures. But by April the IMF was back at the old stand. This time the explosion swept away the Suharto regime. A currency crisis, having been transmuted into an economic crisis, has become a crisis of political institutions. Any real economic reform stands suspended. The shortcomings of Suharto were real enough, but to try to deal with them concurrently with the currency crisis has produced a political vacuum in the most populous Islamic nation in the world.

All this might make sense if the IMF programs brought demonstrable relief. But in every country where the IMF has operated, successive programs have lowered the forecast of the growth rate which, in Indonesia, is now a negative 10 percent, in Thailand a negative 5 percent and in South Korea an optimistic positive 1 percent.

The inability of the IMF to operate where politics and economics intersect is shown by its experience in Russia. In Indonesia the IMF contributed to the destruction of the political framework by excessive emphasis on economics; in Russia it accelerated the collapse of the economy by overemphasizing politics. The IMF is, quite simply, not equipped for the task it has assumed.

The IMF must be transformed. It should be returned to its original purpose as a provider of expert advice and judgment, supplemented by short-term liquidity support. When the IMF focuses on multibillion-dollar loans, it plays a poker game it cannot possibly win; the house, in this case the market, simply has too much money. Congress should use the need for IMF replenishment to impose such changes.

4

Financing Methods and Rules

The IMF uses its financial resources to help members redress balance of payments problems and to help cushion the impact of adjustment. The IMF's financing is provided through both its general resources and its concessional financing facilities, which are administered separately. The extension of IMF credit is subject to Executive Board approval and, in most cases, to the member's commitment to take steps to address the causes of its payments imbalance. Members using the IMF's general resources "purchase" (or draw) other members' currencies or SDRs with an equivalent amount of their own currency. The IMF levies charges on these drawings and requires that members "repurchase" (or buy back) their own currency from the IMF with other members' currencies or SDRs within a specified time. Concessional financing under the Enhanced Structural Adjustment Facility (ESAF) is provided in the form of low-interest loans and grants under the HIPC (heavily indebted poor countries) debt initiative.

REGULAR FACILITIES

Reserve Tranche

A member has a reserve tranche position if the IMF's holdings of its currency in the General Resources Account, excluding those holdings that reflect the member's use of IMF resources, are less than its quota. A member may draw up to the full amount of its reserve tranche position at any time, subject only to the member's representation of a balance of payments need. A reserve tranche drawing does not constitute a use of IMF credit and is not subject to charges or to an expectation or obligation to repurchase.

Credit Tranches

IMF credit is subject to different conditionality and phasing, depending on whether it is made available in the first credit "tranche" (or segment) of 25 percent of a member's quota or in the upper credit tranches (any segment above 25 percent of quota). For drawings in the first credit tranche, members must demonstrate reasonable efforts to overcome their balance of payments difficulties.

Upper credit tranche drawings are made in installments, or phased, and are released when performance targets are met. Such drawings are normally associated with Stand-By or Extended Arrangements, which typically seek to resolve balance of payments difficulties and to support structural policy reforms where appropriate. Performance criteria and periodic reviews are used to assess policy implementation.

Stand-By Arrangements

Stand-By Arrangements give members the right to draw up to a specified amount of IMF resources during a prescribed period. Drawings are normally phased on a quarterly basis, with their release conditional upon meeting performance criteria and the completion of periodic reviews. Performance criteria generally cover bank credit, government or public sector borrowing, trade and payments restrictions, foreign borrowing, and international reserve levels. These criteria allow both the member and the IMF to assess progress and may signal the need for further corrective policies. Stand-By Arrangements typically cover a 12-18 month period (although they can extend up to three years). Repayments are to be made within 3¼ to 5 years of each drawing.

In 1997/98, the IMF approved commitments under nine new Stand-By Arrangements totaling SDR 27.3 billion. Stand-By Arrangements totaling SDR 26.7 billion were approved for Indonesia (SDR 7.3 billion), Korea (SDR 15.5 billion), the Philippines (SDR 1.0 billion), and Thailand (SDR 2.9 billion). The arrangement for Korea-the largest in the IMF's history-included SDR 10.0 billion available until December 1998 under the newly created Supplementary Reserve Facility (SRF). Stand-

By Arrangements totaling SDR 0.6 billion were also approved for Cape Verde, Estonia, Latvia, Ukraine, and Uruguay. As of April 30, 1998, 14 countries had Stand-By Arrangements with the IMF, with total commitments of SDR 28.3 billion and undrawn balances of SDR 12.4 billion. Commitments totaling SDR 1.2 billion have been approved since April 30, 1998. This includes an augmentation of SDR 1.0 billion for Indonesia.

Extended Fund Facility (EFF)

The EFF provides assistance for adjustment programs over longer periods and with generally larger amounts of financing than under Stand-By Arrangements. Extended Arrangements, which normally run for three years (and can be extended for a fourth), are designed to rectify balance of payments difficulties that stem largely from structural problems and require a longer period of adjustment.

A member requesting an Extended Arrangement outlines its objectives and policies for the period of the arrangement and presents a detailed statement each year of the policies and measures to be pursued over the next 12 months. The phasing and performance criteria are comparable to those of Stand-By Arrangements, although phasing on a semiannual basis is possible. Repayments are to be made within 4½ to 10 years of each drawing.

During 1997/98, four new Extended Arrangements totaling SDR 2.8 billion were approved for Argentina, Pakistan, Panama, and Yemen. In addition, the Extended Arrangement for the Philippines was augmented by SDR 0.3 billion. The Extended Arrangements for Pakistan and Yemen were approved in conjunction with ESAF arrangements. As of April 30, 1998, 13 countries had Extended Arrangements, with commitments totaling SDR 12.3 billion and undrawn balances of SDR 6.8 billion.

Overall, new commitments of IMF resources under Stand-By and Extended Arrangements amounted to SDR 30.4 billion in 1997/98. Of this total, nearly 90 percent was approved for Asian countries directly affected by the regional financial crisis. In July 1998, there was an augmentation of commitments amounting to SDR 6.3 billion for Russia, financed under the GAB.

SPECIAL FACILITIES OF IMF

The IMF's special facilities include the Compensatory and Contingency Financing Facility (CCFF), the Buffer Stock Financing Facility-which has not been used since 1984-and the Supplemental Reserve Facility (SRF).

Compensatory and Contingency Financing Facility

The export compensatory element of the CCFF provides timely financing to members experiencing a temporary shortfall in export earnings or an excess in cereal import costs, attributable to factors largely beyond the member's control. This element of the facility has been used particularly by commodity exporters. The contingency element helps members with IMF arrangements keep their adjustment programs on track when faced with unexpected adverse external shocks. The affected variables could include export earnings, import prices, and international interest rates; workers' remittances and tourism receipts may also be covered if they are a significant component in the member's current account. During the 1997/98 fiscal year, no member used the CCFF. In July 1998, the IMF approved financial support for Russia in the amount of SDR 2.16 billion under the CCFF to compensate for a shortfall in export earnings related mainly to lower crude oil prices.

Buffer Stock Financing Facility

Under this facility, the IMF helps finance members' contributions to approved international buffer stocks if the member demonstrates a balance of payments need. No drawings have been made under this facility for the past 14 years.

Supplemental Reserve Facility (SRF)

In December 1997, the Executive Board opened a new lending window-the SRF-for member countries experiencing exceptional balance of payments problems owing to a large short-term financing need resulting from a sudden and disruptive loss of market confidence reflected in pressure on the capital account and the member's reserves. Assistance under the SRF is available when there is a reasonable expectation that implementation of strong adjustment policies and adequate financing will result, in a short period, in early correction of the balance of payments difficulties.

Although resources under IMF facilities are available to all members, the SRF is likely to be used in cases where the magnitude of the outflows may create a risk of contagion that could potentially threaten the international monetary system. In approving a request for the use of IMF resources under the SRF, the IMF takes into account the financing provided by other creditors.

To minimize moral hazard, a member using resources under the SRF is encouraged to maintain the participation of creditors-both official and private-until the pressure on the balance of payments ceases.

Financing under the SRF, available in the form of additional resources under a Stand-By or Extended Arrangement, is committed for up to one year and generally available in two or more drawings. The first drawing is available at the time of approval of the financing, which normally coincides with the approval of the corresponding arrangement.

Countries drawing under the SRF are expected to repay within 1 to 1½ years of the date of each purchase. The Board may, however, extend this repayment period by up to one year, at which point repayment is obligatory. During the first year from the date of approval of financing to a country under the SRF, the use of IMF resources is subject to a surcharge of 300 basis points above the rate of charge on IMF loans.

This rate will be increased by 50 basis points at the end of that period and every six months thereafter until the surcharge reaches 500 basis points. The IMF first activated the SRF in December 1997, committing SDR 9.95 billion to Korea as part of its Stand-By Arrangement. In July 1998, SDR 4 billion was committed to Russia under the SRF as part of the augmentation of Russia's Extended Arrangement by SDR 6.3 billion.

CONCESSIONAL FACILITIES

Enhanced Structural Adjustment Facility (ESAF). This facility, which was established by the Executive Board in 1987 and extended and enlarged in February 1994, is the principal means by which the IMF provides financial support, in the form of highly concessional loans, to low-income member countries facing protracted balance of payments problems and loans and grants under the HIPC Initiative.

At the same time that the ESAF was extended and enlarged, no new resources were made available for its precursor-the Structural Adjustment Facility (SAF), which had been established in 1986. All remaining SAF resources were disbursed by end-1995. The objectives and primary features of the SAF were similar to those of the current ESAF, but programs supported under ESAF arrangements are more ambitious with regard to macroeconomic policy and structural reform measures.

ESAF resources are intended to support strong medium-term structural adjustment programs. Eligible members seeking ESAF resources must develop, with the assistance of the staffs of the IMF and the World Bank, a policy framework paper (PFP) for a three-year adjustment program. The PFP, which is updated annually, describes the authorities' economic objectives, macroeconomic and structural policies during the three-year period, and associated external financing needs and major sources of financing. The PFP, which is a document of the national authorities, is intended to ensure a consistent framework for economic policies and to attract financial and technical assistance in support of the adjustment program.

Adjustment measures under ESAF-supported programs are expected to strengthen substantially a country's balance of payments position and foster growth during the three-year period. Monitoring under ESAF arrangements is conducted through quarterly financial and structural benchmarks. In addition, semiannual performance criteria are set for key quantitative and structural targets. ESAF loans are disbursed semiannually, initially upon approval of an annual arrangement and subsequently based on the observance of performance criteria and after completion of a midterm review. ESAF loans are repaid in ten equal semiannual installments, beginning 5½ years and ending 10 years after the date of each disbursement. The interest rate on ESAF loans is 0.5 percent a year.

In 1997/98, the IMF approved eight new ESAF arrangements totaling SDR 1.7 billion for Cameroon, Côte d'Ivoire, Mongolia, Nicaragua, Pakistan, Senegal, Uganda, and Yemen, as well as an ESAF grant to Uganda under the HIPC Initiative. As of April 30, 1998, 33 ESAF arrangements were in effect.

Cumulative commitments under all SAF and ESAF arrangements approved since 1986 (excluding undisbursed amounts under expired and canceled arrangements) totaled SDR 9.9 billion as of April 30, 1998, compared with SDR 8.8 billion a year earlier. ESAF disbursements in 1997/98 totaled SDR 1.0 billion, compared with SDR 0.7 billion in 1996/97, bringing cumulative SAF and ESAF disbursements through April 30, 1998, to SDR 8.1 billion. Since April 30, 1998, seven new ESAF arrangements have been approved for a total of SDR 0.4 billion.

Financing the ESAF Trust

The resources to finance lending in support of ESAF arrangements are kept separate from the general resources of the IMF and are administered by the IMF as Trustee of the ESAF Trust. ESAF operations are conducted through three accounts with separate functions. The ESAF Trust borrows resources through the Loan Account for onlending to eligible members under ESAF arrangements, with the maturity of drawings coinciding with the maturity of loans to ESAF borrowers. Lenders have extended loans to the ESAF Trust on different interest rate terms, free of interest in one case and highly concessional in others. Also, most lenders making loans at market-related interest rates have made separate contributions to help reduce the interest rate charged to borrowers.

Subsidy contributions (including a contribution from the IMF's Special Disbursement Account in 1994) are channeled through the Subsidy Account and have taken the form of direct grants or deposits at concessional interest rates. These funds are invested by the Trust, with the subsidy contribution being equal to the interest rate differential. Resources are set aside in the Reserve Account to provide security to lenders' claims on the Trust against the risk of nonpayment by borrowers. These latter resources result mainly from repayments of SAF loans and the part of ESAF loans that was financed with SAF resources and ultimately originate in the profits from gold sales undertaken by the IMF in 1976-81.

Making the ESAF Self-Sustaining. Based on the broad agreement that the ESAF is, and will remain, the centerpiece of the IMF's support for the poorest countries, including in the context of the HIPC Initiative, the Executive Board in 1996 agreed on a framework for the continuation of ESAF operations. Under current projections, available ESAF resources are expected to be fully committed by mid-2000. A self-sustained ESAF, with a commitment capacity of about SDR 0.8 billion a year, would begin in the year 2005, or perhaps earlier, financed from the IMF-owned resources set aside in the Reserve Account, which will be freed as ESAF lenders are repaid.

This would leave an interim period of about four years during which financing of an estimated SDR 1.7 billion on an "as needed" basis would need to be mobilized to cover interest subsidies. In addition, financing needs for special ESAF operations under the HIPC Initiative are estimated to be SDR 1.1 billion on an "as needed" basis.

OTHER IMF POLICIES AND PROCEDURES

For specific circumstances that cannot be adequately addressed under its regular and special facilities, the IMF extends financing to member countries under a variety of special mechanisms. These include an emergency financing mechanism, support for currency stabilization funds, and emergency assistance to members facing balance of payments difficulties arising from sudden and unforeseeable natural disasters or in post-conflict situations. In addition, special accelerated procedures are available to facilitate rapid Board approval of IMF financial support in emergency cases.

Support for Currency Stabilization Funds

In September 1995, the Executive Board decided that in the framework of an upper credit tranche Stand-By or Extended Arrangement, the IMF could provide financial support for the establishment of a currency stabilization fund to bolster confidence, for a transitional period, in an exchange-rate-based stabilization strategy. For a currency stabilization fund to play its intended role, economic policies would have to be sufficiently tight to deliver an inflation path compatible with the targeted exchange rate anchor, so that little, if any, use of the currency stabilization fund for exchange market intervention would be expected. The most appropriate exchange rate arrangement to be supported by a currency stabilization fund would be an exchange rate peg with relatively narrow margins or a preannounced crawl.

IMF support would be conditional upon fiscal adjustment and credit creation consistent with targeted inflation, appropriate measures to deal with backward-looking automatic wage and other indexation schemes, a high degree of current account convertibility and an open trade regime and other measures to encourage a return of flight capital, contingency plans to deal with large capital account outflows or inflows, integrated management of foreign exchange reserves and intervention policy, and other structural and institutional elements designed to reduce inflation sharply. So far, no occasion has arisen for the IMF to provide financial support for currency stabilization funds.

Emergency Assistance

The IMF can also provide emergency financial assistance to a member facing balance of payments difficulties caused by a natural disaster and has provided such assistance on a number of occasions. The assistance is available through outright purchases, usually limited to 25 percent of quota, provided that the member is cooperating with the IMF to find a solution to its balance of payments problem. In most cases, this assistance has been followed by an arrangement with the IMF under one of its regular facilities.

In 1995, the policy on emergency assistance was expanded to cover countries in post-conflict situations. This assistance may be provided when the member's institutional or administrative capacity has been disrupted as a result of the conflict but there is still sufficient capacity for planning and policy implementation and a demonstrated commitment on the part of the authorities; there is an urgent balance of payments need; and IMF support could be catalytic and is part of a concerted international effort. Conditions for the assistance include a statement of economic policies, a quantified macroeconomic framework to the extent possible, and a statement of the authorities' intention to move as soon as possible to an upper credit tranche Stand-By or Extended Arrangement, or to an ESAF Arrangement. The conditionality is tailored to the individual country situation and to rebuilding the country's administrative and institutional capacity. In 1997/98, three countries (Albania, Rwanda, and Tajikistan) made purchases totaling SDR 30 million under the IMF's policy on emergency post-conflict assistance.

Emergency Financing Mechanism (EFM)

A set of procedures to facilitate rapid Executive Board approval of IMF financial support while ensuring the conditionality necessary to warrant such support, these emergency measures are to be used only in rare circumstances representing, or threatening to give rise to, a crisis in a member's external accounts that requires an immediate IMF response. The EFM was established by the Executive Board in September 1995, and it was first activated in support of the Philippines' request in July 1997 for an extension and augmentation of its three-year extended arrangement. It was used again in August, November, and December 1997, and in July 1998-together with the provision of exceptional financial support-for Thailand, Indonesia, Korea, and Russia, respectively.

ACCESS LIMITS ARE GUIDED BY QUOTAS

The rules governing access to the IMF's general resources apply uniformly to all members. Access is determined primarily by a member's balance of payments need, the strength of its adjustment policies, and its capacity to repay the IMF. Except for the Supplemental Reserve Facility (SRF), access is permitted up to limits defined in relation to the member's quota.

The Executive Board reviews the access limits in the credit tranches and under the Extended Fund Facility (EFF) annually in light of many elements, including the magnitude of members' payments problems and developments in the IMF's liquidity. Guided by the principle that strong adjustment programs deserve strong support and by the need to safeguard the monetary character and catalytic role of the IMF, the Executive Board decided that, for a three-year period beginning October 24, 1994, the annual limit for access to the IMF's general resources in the credit tranches and under extended arrangements would rise to 100 percent of quota from 68 percent of quota. The cumulative access limit was left unchanged at 300 percent of quota, net of scheduled repayments. At the November 1997 review, the Board decided to maintain the annual and cumulative access limits set in 1994 until the next review of access policies to be held not later than October 1998.

These limits may be exceeded in exceptional cases. The limits exclude drawings under the SRF, the Compensatory and Contingency Financing Facility (CCFF), and the Buffer Stock Financing Facility (BSFF), and loans under the Enhanced Structural Adjustment Facility (ESAF). Access under the SRF is not subject to limits in relation to quota.

The IMF determines access under the SRF based on the financing needs of the member; its capacity to pay, including in particular the strength of its program; its outstanding use of IMF credit; and its record in using IMF resources in the past and in cooperating with the IMF in surveillance, as well as the IMF's liquidity. The current overall access limit under the CCFF is set at 95 percent of a member's quota. For the BSFF, the access limit is 35 percent of quota.

Access under ESAF arrangements also differs according to members' balance of payments needs, the strength of their adjustment efforts, and their capacity to repay. An eligible member country may borrow a maximum of 190 percent of its quota under a three-year ESAF arrangement, although this limit may be increased, under exceptional circumstances, up to a maximum of 255 percent of quota.

EXTERNAL EVALUATION OF THE ESAF

In the spring of 1997, a panel of outside experts began work on an independent evaluation of SAF/ESAF-supported programs. This was the first time that an external evaluation of the IMF's work had been commissioned by the Executive Board. The evaluators used a case-study approach to examine social policies and the composition of government spending; developments in countries' external positions; and the determinants and influence of differing degrees of national ownership of ESAF-supported programs. They offered the following main recommendations:

Social Impact

- The IMF should seek ex ante assessments by the World Bank of the likely impact that ESAF-supported programs will have on the incomes of the poor and of the real projected value of social service provision. These impact assessments could be taken into account at the program design stage and should be updated during program implementation. The IMF should draw formally on the household poverty expertise of the World Bank.
- In program design, the IMF should explicitly analyze trade-offs between the short run and long run. The analysis would address sequencing issues, front-loading of structural reforms, and the efficiency costs of revenue measures.
- In the area of fiscal policy, IMF-World Bank collaboration should be increased to allow for more joint analysis and to address overlaps concerning the macroeconomic concerns of the IMF and the microeconomic concerns of the Bank.
- The ESAF should have a new role in the post-stabilization environment to help reforming governments build reputations and to enable the IMF to play a role

in potential ESAF countries that do not currently use the facility.

External Viability

- ESAF financing should be provided as budget support rather than to central banks.
- Equal or more weight should be given to indicators that relate total debt and debt service to GDP rather than to the traditional export-based indicators, as the latter are overly sensitive to an economy's openness.

Ownership and Governance

- Countries have primary responsibility for economic reform programs and they should develop and build a consensus behind a program capable of achieving sustainable growth. The IMF should make the negotiation process and conditionality regime more supportive of country ownership.
- The IMF should ensure greater flexibility in the negotiating frameworks, develop systematic mechanisms for ex-post support for country-initiated programs, strengthen resident representative missions in ESAF countries, engage in regular informal policy dialogue with the country's political leadership, and find ways to improve the IMF's image.
- Countries should create economic management teams comprising economic and social sector ministries and political leaders to oversee the reform process and hold national conferences where alternatives and trade-offs can be openly debated.

5

International Monetary Fund and its Operations

ROLE OF THE IMF

The IMF is a cooperative intergovernmental monetary and financial institution with near universal membership. Its policies and activities are guided by its charter, known as the Articles of Agreement (the Articles), and are conducted under a decision-making structure that has evolved over the years.

The IMF is unique among intergovernmental organizations in its combination of regulatory, consultative, and financial functions, which derive from the purposes for which it was established: to promote international monetary cooperation; to facilitate the balanced growth of international trade; to promote exchange rate stability; to assist in the establishment of a multilateral system of payments and in the elimination of foreign exchange restrictions that hamper the growth of world trade; to make its resources available to its members to correct balance of payments imbalances without resorting to trade and payments restrictions; and to provide a forum for consultation and collaboration on international monetary problems.

Thus, the IMF is concerned not only with the problems of individual countries but also with the working of the international monetary system as a whole. Its activities focus on promoting policies and strategies through which its members can work together to ensure a stable world financial system and sustainable economic growth.

The Articles effectively place the IMF at the center of the international monetary system. The IMF provides a forum for international monetary cooperation, and thus for an orderly evolution of the system, and it subjects a wide area of international monetary affairs to covenants of law, moral suasion, and understandings. The IMF must also stand ready to deal with crisis situations, not only those affecting individual members but also those representing threats to the international monetary system.

IMF policy and practice are constantly evolving in response to new challenges, most recently the further globalization of capital markets and the increased risk of financial crises and their spillover effects. The work of the IMF in the immediate future, as outlined by the Interim Committee at its meeting in April 1998 (the Spring 1998 Interim Committee), will be shaped importantly by exploring ways to prevent, manage, and resolve financial crises.

As an immediate response to the Asian financial crisis, in late 1997 the IMF established a new credit facility--the Supplemental Reserve Facility (SRF)--to address potentially large but short-term financing needs that emanate mainly from the capital account, reflecting a loss of market confidence. To make its financial assistance more expeditious, the IMF put into use during the Asian financial crisis the rapid procedures of the Emergency Financing Mechanism that had been set up in the aftermath of the Mexican crisis in 1995.

SURVEILLANCE

Central to the IMF's purposes and operations is the mandate, under the Articles of Agreement, to "exercise firm surveillance" over the policies of its members in complying with their obligations. Under the Articles, each member undertakes to collaborate with the IMF and other members to ensure orderly exchange arrangements and to promote a stable system of exchange rates. Members' specific obligations under Article IV include directing their economic and financial policies to foster economic growth with reasonable price stability, seeking to promote stability by fostering orderly economic and financial conditions, and avoiding manipulation of exchange rates to prevent balance of payments adjustment or to gain unfair competitive advantage over other members. Members are also obliged to follow exchange rate policies compatible with these undertakings.

The IMF exercises surveillance through both multilateral and bilateral means. Multilateral surveillance consists of Executive Board reviews of developments in the international monetary system based principally on the staff's World Economic Outlook reports and through periodic discussions of developments, prospects, and key policy issues in international capital markets. Bilateral surveillance takes the form of consultations with individual member countries, conducted annually for most members, under Article IV of the IMF's Articles of Agreement.

After the 1994-95 Mexican crisis, efforts to strengthen IMF surveillance included more intensive treatment of issues relating to members' financial sectors. In March 1996 the Executive Board examined the relationship between banking system soundness and macroeconomic and structural policies, as well as ways in which issues in bank soundness could be incorporated into IMF surveillance, IMF-supported programs, and technical assistance.

The increasing globalization of capital markets, together with the possibility of abrupt changes in capital flows and the risk of contagion, may result in large financial imbalances, as experienced by Mexico in early 1995 and several of the emerging Asian economies in 1997-98. The April 1998 Interim Committee envisaged that the future work of the IMF should include strengthening financial systems by continuing the work already in progress in various forums to develop supervisory frameworks consistent with internationally accepted practices and strengthened standards for bank and nonbank financial entities, and by advancing work in other areas such as accounting, auditing, disclosure, asset valuation, and corporate governance.

The Committee called on the IMF to work with other concerned institutions and organizations responsible for the development of standards and guidelines in these areas. The

Committee also called for intensifying IMF surveillance of financial sector issues and capital flows, giving particular attention to policy interdependence and the risks of contagion.

The timely provision of macroeconomic and financial data by member countries is of crucial importance for the smooth functioning of markets. Accordingly, the IMF has developed a set of standards to guide members in the provision of these data to the public A two-tier approach has been followed, comprising a special standard intended to guide members that have or may seek access to international capital markets, and a general standard to guide all IMF members. The Special Data Dissemination Standard (SDDS) opened for subscription in April 1996.

Although subscription is voluntary, it carries a commitment by the subscribing member to observe the standard and provide information about its data and data dissemination practices--metadata--for posting on the Internet on the IMF's Dissemination Standards Bulletin Board (DSBB), which opened to the public in September 1996. As of June 30, 1998, 46 members had subscribed to the SDDS and 40 of them have their metadata posted on the DSBB, some with electronic links that enable users to move between the DSBB and the actual data maintained by countries on their Internet sites.

In the period through end-1998 subscribers must bring their statistical practices fully into line with the SDDS, while members that subscribe after 1998 will be required to meet all the SDDS requirements at the time of subscription. The second of the two standards, the General Data Dissemination System (GDDS), established in December 1997, emphasizes the development and dissemination of comprehensive statistical frameworks and economic and financial indicators. The implementation of the GDDS will be phased over the next six to seven years and will be carried out in consultation with other regional and international organizations that have expertise in the areas covered by the system.

The April 1998 Interim Committee noted that the effectiveness of the IMF's surveillance depends critically on the timely availability of accurate information, and stated that if there were persistent deficiencies in disclosing relevant information for the IMF's surveillance, the conclusion of Article IV consultations should be delayed. In order to increase the availability and transparency of information regarding economic data and policies, the Committee called for the SDDS to be broadened and strengthened to cover additional financial data, including net reserves, short-term debt, and indicators of the stability of the financial sector. It also encouraged more members to agree to the release of Press (now Public) Information Notices on the conclusion of consultations with the IMF. The April 1998 Interim Committee also stated that the IMF's views on members' policies will need to be communicated effectively, possibly with a "tiered response" that would allow increasingly strong warnings to members that are considered to be seriously off course in their policies.

Reflecting the significance of good governance to achieve and sustain economic efficiency and growth, in July 1997 the Executive Board adopted guidelines covering the role of the IMF on issues of governance.

These guidelines seek to provide greater attention to IMF involvement in economic aspects of governance, in particular through (1) a more comprehensive treatment, in the context of both Article IV consultations and IMF-supported programs, of those governance issues within the IMF's mandate and expertise; (2) a more proactive approach in advocating policies and the development of institutions and administrative systems that eliminate the opportunity for bribery, corruption, and fraudulent activity in the management of public resources; (3) an evenhanded treatment of governance issues in all member countries; and (4) enhanced collaboration with other bilateral and multilateral institutions, in particular the World Bank, to make better use of complementary areas of expertise.

The IMF's contribution to good governance would be in fostering an improved management of public resources through reforms of public sector institutions, and supporting the development and maintenance of a transparent and stable economic and regulatory environment conducive to efficient private sector activities. The April 1998 Interim Committee adopted a code of good practices to serve as a guide for members to increase fiscal transparency, and thereby enhance the accountability and credibility of fiscal policy as a key feature of good governance.

GLOBAL LIQUIDITY

Because the IMF is responsible for the smooth functioning of the international monetary and payments system, it is particularly concerned with global liquidity--that is, with the level and composition of reserves available to member nations to meet their trade and payments requirements, and their access to capital markets.

The IMF is a repository of part of members' liquid international reserves in the form of reserve positions and loan claims on the institution. When there is a global need to supplement world reserves, the IMF can be a source of additional liquidity through the allocation to its members of the special drawing right (SDR), a reserve asset created by international decision. Moreover, the IMF has a promotional role in fulfilling the objective, as established in its Articles, of making the SDR the principal reserve asset of the international monetary system. However, there has not been agreement on the existence of a global need to increase liquidity and no general allocation of SDRs has been made since 1981.

In March 1996, the IMF arranged a seminar attended by outside experts and IMF staff where the general sentiment was that it was unlikely that the SDR would become the principal reserve asset of the international monetary system but that it had an important role in the IMF's financial operations and as a safety net for dealing with serious difficulties that could arise in the functioning of the international monetary system.

There was agreement at the seminar on the need to find ways to solve the "equity issue" arising from the fact that many members had never received an SDR allocation. This issue had already been discussed thoroughly by the Executive Board, and is now being addressed by a proposed amendment of the Articles approved by the Board of Governors to allow a special allocation of SDRs.

CAPITAL ACCOUNT CONVERTIBILITY

Recognizing the increasing importance of capital flows in the international monetary system, the IMF has been intensively examining the issue of capital account convertibility. The April 1997 Interim Committee emphasized that an open and liberal system of capital movements is beneficial to the world economy and considered the IMF uniquely placed to promote the orderly liberalization of capital movements and to play a central role in this effort. The Committee endorsed the concept of an amendment to the IMF's Articles of Agreement to make the promotion of capital account liberalization a specific purpose of the IMF and to give it appropriate jurisdiction over capital movements. Following Executive Board discussion of possible transitional arrangements and approval policies, and legal aspects of capital movements, the September 1997 Interim Committee invited the Executive Board to complete its work on the proposed amendment of the IMF's Articles of Agreement through the establishment of carefully defined and consistently applied obligations regarding the liberalization of capital movements. It was emphasized that safeguards and transitional arrangements are necessary for the success of this major endeavor, and flexible approval policies would have to be adopted.

The April 1998 Interim Committee reaffirmed the view that a new chapter should be added to the Bretton Woods Agreement by making the liberalization of capital movements one of the purposes of the IMF and extending, as needed, the IMF's jurisdiction for that purpose. The Committee called for an appropriate amendment of the Articles to be submitted for its consideration as soon as possible.

USE OF IMF RESOURCES AND OTHER ASSISTANCE TO MEMBER COUNTRIES

Surveillance through Article IV consultations is the main channel for collaboration between the IMF and its members. In addition, for members facing balance of payments difficulties, formal financial arrangements for the immediate use of IMF resources provide a framework for more intensive collaboration.

The IMF maintains a pool of resources from which to help finance temporary imbalances in the balance of payments of its members. These resources are of a revolving character and are primarily derived from currencies and SDRs made available by members as their quota subscriptions. The IMF may supplement these resources by borrowing. To use IMF resources, a member must represent to the institution that it has a need to do so because of its balance of payments or reserve position or developments in its reserves. The use of IMF resources is based on the uniform and nondiscriminatory treatment of members, with due regard paid to their domestic social and political objectives. The IMF's policies encourage members to have recourse to the IMF's financial facilities at an early stage of a member's balance of payments problems. Financial assistance provided by the IMF allows members to correct their payments imbalances without having to resort to trade and payments restrictions. The IMF acts as a catalyst to the extent that policy adjustments implemented by members undertaking IMF-supported programs help generate additional financial assistance from other sources, such as private and official creditors. The IMF functions as a financial intermediary insofar as it recycles funds from surplus to deficit countries.

The use of IMF resources typically takes place under an IMF arrangement, a decision of the IMF that gives the member assurance that the institution stands ready to provide foreign exchange or SDRs in accordance with the terms of the decision during a specified period of time. An IMF arrangement is approved by the Executive Board in support of an economic program under which the member undertakes a set of policy actions to reduce external and internal economic imbalances.

Apart from the resources derived from members' quota subscriptions, the IMF administers other resources that are made available to low-income member countries facing protracted balance of payments problems. Such assistance is provided in the form of highly concessional loans to support medium-term macroeconomic and structural adjustment programs. Assistance is also provided to eligible heavily indebted poor countries, where debt burdens are unsustainable, in the form of grants through a trust administered by the IMF to support the reduction of debt-service burdens to sustainable levels.

Precautionary arrangements and program monitoring are used to assist members interested in boosting confidence in their economic management. Under a Stand-By or an Extended Arrangement that the member treats as precautionary, the member agrees to meet the conditions applied for such use of the IMF's resources but expresses its intention not to draw on them. This expression of intent is not binding; consequently, as with an arrangement under which a member is expected to draw, approval of a precautionary arrangement signifies the IMF's endorsement of the member's policies according to the standards applicable to the particular form of arrangement. Program monitoring by the IMF staff can be provided outside the context of an arrangement; such monitoring is generally requested by members in need of policy advice and technical support during a specific period--for example, preceding the negotiation of an arrangement with the IMF if a record of performance needs to be established, during a World Bank lending program, or following an intense period of collaboration under a series of IMF arrangements.

The enhanced surveillance procedure also has been used to assist a member to boost domestic and external confidence in its continuing efforts to pursue appropriate adjustment policies and to help secure financial support. The procedure was adopted in 1985 to help members address their debt problems and improve relations with their creditors in the context of multi-year debt-rescheduling arrangements. Use of the procedure, which has been very limited, requires approval by the Executive Board for a specified period of usually 12 months. During this period, economic developments in the member country are monitored by the IMF, and an assessment of the country's economic program is provided by the staff to the Executive Board.

Enhanced surveillance does not represent an endorsement of a country's policies by the IMF, although the staff's assessment could be presented by the member to official and private creditors and donors for their consideration. Enhanced surveillance is undertaken only at the request of a member country and usually only in those cases in which the member has a strong record of adjustment under IMF-supported programs. In 1993, the possibility of applying the enhanced surveillance procedure was broadened from assisting in resolving issues related to debt restructurings to cover any situation where a member would find this form of monitoring by the IMF helpful.

The surveillance of the policies of IMF members who are participants in monetary unions presents special characteristics. Such members have transferred certain competencies in the economic and monetary fields to the monetary union and therefore at the individual level they are limited in their ability to conduct independent economic and monetary policies On January 1, 1999, the European Economic and Monetary Union (EMU) is scheduled to be established, and the special features of the IMF's surveillance of the policies of its members, as well as operational aspects arising from the adoption of the euro as a common currency for EMU members, are being considered.

A compendium of good practices for the banking sector, with the Core Principles of the Basle Committee included as an annex, is contained in IMF, Toward a Framework for Financial Stability, World Economic and Financial Surveys (Washington, 1997).

FINANCIAL STRUCTURE

The financial transactions and operations of the IMF are conducted through the General Department, the SDR Department, and the Administered Accounts. The transactions of the IMF in the General Resources Account are exchanges of monetary assets by the IMF for other monetary assets. The operations of the IMF are other uses or receipts of monetary assets by the IMF.

The IMF is a quota-based institution. When a country becomes a member of the IMF, an amount not exceeding 25 percent of its quota has to be paid in SDRs or usable currencies ("reserve assets") specified by the IMF and the balance in the member's own currency, normally in the form of nonnegotiable, non-interest-bearing notes (essentially promissory notes). The portion of a member's quota paid in reserve assets becomes its initial reserve tranche in the IMF (known as the "gold tranche" before the Second Amendment of the Articles, when this reserve asset was paid in gold. The reserve tranche position can be defined as the amount by which a member's quota exceeds the IMF's holdings of its own currency. A member may draw up to the full amount of its reserve tranche position at any time (subject only to its representation to the IMF that it has a balance of payments need) by transferring to the IMF an equivalent amount of its own currency.

The IMF's unit of account is the special drawing right (SDR), whose value is calculated daily on the basis of a "valuation basket" comprising five major currencies. The IMF's financial year runs from May 1 to April 30, with financial quarters starting in May, August, November, and February.

ACCOUNTS IN MEMBER COUNTRIES

Each member is required to designate a fiscal agency and a depository to conduct its financial dealings with the IMF. The fiscal agency may be the member's treasury (ministry of finance), central bank, official monetary agency, stabilization fund, or other similar entity. The IMF can deal only with, or through, the designated fiscal agency, which is accordingly authorized to carry out on behalf of the member country all operations and transactions authorized under the Articles. In addition, each member is required to designate its central bank as a depository for all IMF holdings of its currency. If it has no central bank, the member can designate another institution such as a monetary agency or even a commercial bank, that is acceptable to the IMF.

A depository is required to pay out of the IMF's holdings of the member's currency, on demand and without delay, sums to any payee named by the IMF in the member's own territory, and hold securities for safe custody on behalf of the IMF if the member issues nonnegotiable, non-interest-bearing notes, or similar instruments, in substitution for part of its currency holdings. In addition, each member guarantees all assets of the

IMF against loss resulting from failure or default on the part of the designated depository.

Each depository maintains (without any service charge or commission) two accounts, the IMF No. 1 Account and the IMF No. 2 Account, and some depositories also maintain a Securities Account at the option of the member. The balances in these accounts, which originate, in the first instance, from the payment to the IMF of the member's quota subscription, do not yield any interest for the IMF.

The No. 1 Account is used for IMF transactions and operations, including subscription payments, purchases, repurchases, repayment of borrowing, and sales of the member's currency. Provided that a minimum is maintained in the No. 1 Account, as explained below, all these transactions can also be carried out through the IMF Securities Account.

A member may establish an IMF Securities Account to hold nonnegotiable non-interest-bearing notes, or similar obligations, payable to the IMF on demand if the currency is needed for the IMF's operations and transactions. The depository holds these notes for safekeeping and acts as the agent of the IMF to obtain encashment of the notes in order to maintain at all times the minimum balance in the No. 1 Account. If any payment by the IMF reduces the balance in the No. 1 Account below a minimum of 1/4 of 1 percent of the member's quota, the balance is to be restored to that level by the next business day through the encashment of sufficient notes.

The No. 2 Account is used for the IMF's administrative expenditures and receipts (for example, receipts from sales of IMF publications) in the member's currency and within its territory. Small, out-of-pocket expenses, such as telecommunications charges, may be debited to this account on a quarterly basis.

General Department

Under the Articles, the IMF's General Department consists of the General Resources Account (GRA), the Special Disbursement Account (SDA), and the Investment Account (not activated as of June 30, 1998). The General Department also includes the Borrowed Resources Suspense Accounts, which were established by a decision of the Executive Board in May 1981 but which have been inactive since 1991 when remaining borrowed resources under the Enlarged Access Policy were disbursed to members.

Most transactions between member countries and the IMF take place through the GRA. This account handles, among other transactions and operations, the receipt of quota subscriptions, purchases and repurchases, receipt and refund of charges, payment of remuneration on members' creditor positions in the IMF, and repayment of principal to the IMF's lenders. The assets held in the GRA include currencies of member countries (held in the No. 1 Account, the No. 2 Account, and the Securities Account with each member), the IMF's own holdings of SDRs, and gold.

The Special Disbursement Account is the vehicle for (1) receiving and investing profits from the sale of the IMF's gold (that is, the net proceeds in excess of the book value of SDR 35 per fine ounce); and (2) making transfers for special purposes authorized in the Articles. The SDA was activated in 1981 initially to receive transfers from the Trust Fund, which had been funded from gold sales, upon its termination.

The IMF is authorized to establish an Investment Account in the General Department; to date, however, no decision has been taken to this effect. The assets in the Investment Account would be held separately from the General Resources Account and would not be subject to maintenance-of-value requirements. The Articles envisage that assets in the Investment Account could derive--if authorized by the requisite majority vote--from profits from the sale of the IMF's gold, from a transfer of currencies held in the GRA, or from the income or proceeds of investments in the account. With the exception of income from the account's investments, the total amount transferred to the Investment Account may not exceed the resources held in the IMF's General and Special Reserves. Investments may be made only in income-generating marketable obligations of international financial organizations or of the member whose currency is used for the investment. The income may be reinvested or used to meet the expenses of conducting the business of the IMF, including both operational and administrative expenses.

The Borrowed Resources Suspense Accounts were established to hold, transfer, convert, and invest (1) currencies borrowed by the IMF before they were transferred to the GRA for use in transactions or operations, and (2) currencies received by the IMF in repurchases financed with borrowed resources before repayments to lenders could be made. Members were not obligated to maintain the SDR value of their currencies held by the IMF in the Borrowed Resources Suspense Accounts, and as far as practicable the currencies were invested in SDR-denominated obligations. As mentioned above, since December 1991 no amount has been held in suspense in these accounts.

SDR DEPARTMENT

The IMF's SDR Department records all transactions and operations involving SDRs. The SDR is an interest-bearing asset allocated by the IMF to each member that is a participant in the SDR Department. As already noted, the IMF uses the SDR as its unit of account.

The IMF can hold SDRs in the GRA and can use them in transactions and operations. The GRA receives SDRs in partial payment of quota increases and in the settlement of charges and repurchases; it uses SDRs to finance purchases by members and to pay remuneration to members.

ADMINISTERED ACCOUNTS

The IMF may establish administered accounts for purposes, such as financial and technical assistance, that are consistent with the Articles. Accounts have been established to administer resources for support for the low-income and heavily indebted members (the Enhanced Structural Adjustment Facility and the Heavily Indebted Poor Countries Initiative).

There are several other Administered Accounts established for different purposes, including a Framework Administered Account to administer resources to finance technical assistance activities.

OPERATING COSTS

The expenses of conducting the business of the IMF's General Department along with the IMF's general overhead are paid from the net operational income of the General Resources Account. The expenses of conducting the business of the SDR Department are also paid from the GRA, which is reimbursed by the participants in the SDR Department at the end of each financial year. For this purpose, the IMF levies an assessment on the participants, at the same rate for all participants, in relation to their net cumulative allocations. Also at the end of each financial year, the ESAF Trust reimburses the GRA for the cost of administering the trust during the year. The General and SDR Departments and the Administered Accounts are operated, recorded, and accounted for separately, and no assets in one department or administered account may be used to discharge liabilities or to meet losses incurred in the administration of other accounts or departments.

IMF GETS SUPPORT FOR BANKRUPTCY PLAN

Washington (September 17, 2002 3:21 p.m. EDT): A landmark proposal that would make it easier for countries in economic crisis to restructure their foreign debt should receive a major endorsement at the upcoming annual meeting of the International Monetary Fund, a top IMF official said Tuesday.

IMF Deputy Managing Director Anne Krueger said she expected her proposal for creation of an international bankruptcy procedure for countries to be endorsed in broad terms by finance ministers representing the agency's members at the end of this month.

IMF officials expect its policy-setting panel will direct IMF staff to prepare the amendments to the IMF's charter that would be needed to put the bankruptcy process into operation. The wording on the change in the IMF's Articles of Agreement, under this schedule, would be debated at the spring meetings of the agency next April.

"I am confident we will get an endorsement... to move forward," Krueger told reporters at a briefing.

Krueger said the proposal had "come a long way in 10 months," referring to last November when she first put forward a new process to help countries facing severe financial difficulties and an unsustainable debt burden.

Krueger's plan would essentially give nations the same opportunity that companies have to file for bankruptcy, beginning a court-supervised process that allows them to continue operations while they develop a plan with creditors to restructure their debt.

The Bush administration was initially cool to the idea, arguing that the approach would take too long to put into place because it would require the 184 nations who are members of the IMF to agree to changing the institution's charter.

Treasury Secretary Paul O'Neill and his top aide on international economic issues, Treasury Undersecretary John Taylor, originally came out in support of a less far-sweeping approach that would encourage countries to insert new language into bond agreements that would allow a super majority of bond holders to agree to restructure debt in the event a country encounters financial difficulties. U.S. officials argued that such an approach could be implemented quickly while it could take years for the IMF to win approval of an amendment to its charter.

However, since Kreuger advanced the plan last November, Argentina was forced to declare the largest government debt default in history, stopping payments on a large portion of its $141 billion in foreign debt last December.

And this summer the IMF was forced to rush to the assistance of Brazil with a record $30 billion loan, hoping to calm investor fears that Latin America's largest economy was about to default on its foreign debt.

Krueger said there was an emerging consensus that a two-track approach was needed which would include both the new bond clauses plus a more sweeping approach that would put in place the equivalent of an international bankruptcy process.

She cautioned that there remained substantial work to be done on the precise wording of the new approach, which officials hope to be able to present at the spring meetings of the IMF and World Bank next April.

"Some of the last pieces are very important," she said. "That discussion is still going on."

Krueger's remarks came as she presented the IMF's annual report, which covered a 12-month period that ended last April. The report showed that the recession that hit the United States and then spread to other countries had increased demands on the IMF, which provides loans to countries to help them deal with economic troubles. For the 12 months ending in April, the IMF approved almost $50 billion in credit lines for member countries, almost triple the $17 billion in loans it had approved in the previous 12-month period.

The IMF and the World Bank will condense their normal weeklong annual meetings to just two days on the weekend of Sept. 28-29. The decision to sharply curtail this year's discussions was taken in an effort to hold down the cost of providing security for the meetings, which will draw large numbers of anti-globalization protesters.

Status of Arrangements As of April 30, 1999
(In thousands of SDRs)

General Resources Account: Stand-By Arrangements

Member	Date of Arrangement	Expiration	Total Amount Agreed	Undrawn Balance
Bosnia and Herzegovina	May 29 1998	May 28 1999	60,600	36,360
Brazil	Dec 02 1998	Dec 01 2001	13,024,800	5,969,700
Cape Verde	Feb 20 1998	May 31 1999	2,100	2,100
El Salvador	Sep 23 1998	Feb 22 2000	37,680	37,680
Korea	Dec 04 1997	Dec 03 2000.	15,500,000	1,268,750
Philippines	Apr 01 1998	Mar 31 2000	1,020,790	633,400
Thailand	Aug 20 1997	Jun 19 2000	2,900,000	500,000
Uruguay	Mar 29 1999	Mar 28 2000	70,000	70,000
Zimbabwe	Jun 01 1998	Jun 30 1999	130,650	91,450
Total			32,746,620	8,609,440

General Resources Account: Extended Arrangements

Member	Date of Arrangement	Expiration	Total Amount Agreed	Undrawn Balance
Argentina	Feb 04 1998	Feb 03 2001	2,080,000	2,080,000
Azerbaijan	Dec 20 1996	Dec 19 1999	58,500	15,800
Bulgaria	Sep 25 1998	Sep 24 2001	627,620	470,720
Croatia, Republic of	Mar 12 1997	Mar 11 2000	353,160	324,380
Indonesia	Aug 25 1998	Nov 05 2000	5,383,100	2,259,400
Jordan	Apr 15 1999	Apr 14 2002	127,880	117,220
Kazakhstan, Republic of	Jul 17 1996	Jul 16 1999	309,400	154,700
Moldova, Republic of	May 20 1996	May 19 2000	135,000	72,500
Pakistan	Oct 20 1997	Oct 19 2000	454,920	379,090
Panama	Dec 10 1997	Dec 09 2000	120,000	80,000
Ukraine	Sep 04 1998	Sep 03 2001	1,645,550	1,288,900
Yemen, Republic of	Oct 29 1997	Oct 28 2000	105,900	76,900
Total			11,401,030	7,319,610

Enhanced Structural Adjustment Facility Trust

Member	Date of Arrangement	Expiration	Total Amount Agreed	Undrawn Balance
Albania	May 13 1998	May 12 2001	35,300	23,530
Armenia, Republic of	Feb 14 1996	Dec 20 1999	109,350	20,925
Azerbaijan	Dec 20 1996	Jan 24 2000	93,600	17,550
Benin	Aug 28 1996	Jan 07 2000	27,180	14,496
Bolivia	Sep 18 1998	Sep 17 2001	100,960	84,134
Burkina Faso	Jun 14 1996	Sep 13 1999	39,780	6,630
Cameroon	Aug 20 1997	Aug 19 2000	162,120	54,040
Central African Republic	Jul 20 1998	Jul 19 2001	49,440	41,200

Congo, Republic of	Jun 28 1996	Jun 27 1999	69,480	55,584
Cote d'Ivoire	Mar 17 1998	Mar 16 2001	285,840	161,976
Ethiopia	Oct 11 1996	Oct 22 1999	88,470	58,980
Gambia, The	Jun 29 1998	Jun 28 2001	20,610	17,175
Georgia	Feb 28 1996	Jul 26 1999	166,500	27,750
Ghana	Jun 30 1995	Jun 29 1999	164,400	27,400
Guinea	Jan 13 1997	Jan 12 2000	70,800	23,600
Guyana	Jul 15 1998	Jul 14 2001	53,760	44,800
Haiti	Oct 18 1996	Oct 17 1999	91,050	75,875
Honduras	Mar 26 1999	Mar 25 2002	156,750	96,900
Kyrgyz Republic	Jun 26 1998	Jun 25 2001	73,380	43,000
Macedonia, former Yugoslav Republic of	Apr 11 1997	Apr 10 2000	54,560	27,279
Madagascar	Nov 27 1996	Nov 26 1999	81,360	54,240
Malawi	Oct 18 1995	Dec 16 1999	50,960	7,635
Mali	Apr 10 1996	Aug 05 1999	62,010	0
Mongolia	Jul 30 1997	Jul 29 2000	33,390	27,825
Mozambique	Jun 21 1996	Aug 24 1999	75,600	12,600
Nicaragua	Mar 18 1998	Mar 17 2001	148,955	67,270
Niger	Jun 12 1996	Aug 27 1999	57,960	9,660
Pakistan	Oct 20 1997	Oct 19 2000	682,380	417,010
Rwanda	Jun 24 1998	Jun 23 2001	71,400	47,600
Senegal	Apr 20 1998	Apr 19 2001	107,010	71,340
Tajikistan, Republic of	Jun 24 1998	Jun 23 2001	100,300	60,000
Tanzania	Nov 08 1996	Feb 07 2000	181,590	29,380
Uganda	Nov 10 1997	Nov 09 2000	100,425	43,518
Yemen, Republic of	Oct 29 1997	Oct 28 2000	264,750	140,750
Zambia	Mar 25 1999	Mar 24 2002	254,450	244,450
Total			4,185,870	2,156,101

Source: Treasurer's Department, Accounts and Financial Reports Division

Fund Credit Outstanding

As at April 30, 1999

The information provided is for your convenience and is not intended to replace other official IMF reports and statements. (in SDRs)

Member	General Resources Account (GRA) Purchases	Structural Adjustment Facility Enhanced Structural Adjustment Facility Trust Fund (SAF/ESAF/TF) Loans	Total
Albania	8,825,000	41,983,000	50,808,000
Algeria	1,345,595,000	0	1,345,595,000
Argentina	3,638,672,259	0	3,638,672,259
Armenia, Republic of	43,453,125	88,425,000	131,878,125
Azerbaijan	214,845,000	76,050,000	290,895,000
Bangladesh	98,125,000	184,118,750	282,243,750
Belarus, Republic of	160,174,999	0	160,174,999
Benin	0	67,547,500	67,547,500
Bolivia	0	179,462,500	179,462,500
Bosnia and Herzegovina	50,752,500	0	50,752,500
Brazil	7,055,100,000	0	7,055,100,000
Bulgaria	805,818,337	0	805,818,337
Burkina Faso	0	78,110,000	78,110,000
Burundi	0	13,114,000	13,114,000
Cambodia	4,687,501	42,000,000	46,687,501
Cameroon	26,075,000	108,080,000	134,155,000
Central African Republic	0	10,063,901	10,063,901
Chad	0	52,314,000	52,314,000
Comoros	0	1,800,000	1,800,000
Congo, Democratic Republic of	157,805,175	142,909,596	300,714,771
Congo, Republic of	8,802,500	13,896,000	22,698,500

Cote d'Ivoire	0	457,344,000	457,344,000
Croatia, Republic of	157,400,000	0	157,400,000
Djibouti	7,272,000	0	7,272,000
Dominican Republic	39,700,000	0	39,700,000
Ecuador	37,087,500	0	37,087,500
Equatorial Guinea	0	7,360,000	7,360,000
Estonia, Republic of	20,343,750	0	20,343,750
Ethiopia	0	72,556,000	72,556,000
Gabon	72,801,750	0	72,801,750
Gambia, The	0	7,315,000	7,315,000
Georgia	71,456,250	138,750,000	210,206,250
Ghana	0	230,060,000	230,060,000
Guinea	0	88,309,000	88,309,000
Guinea-Bissau	0	10,725,000	10,725,000
Guyana	0	104,003,720	104,003,720
Haiti	23,525,000	15,175,000	38,700,000
Honduras	47,500,000	91,038,000	138,538,000
India	211,750,000	0	211,750,000
Indonesia	6,792,820,000	0	6,792,820,000
Jamaica	72,375,000	0	72,375,000
Jordan	374,919,999	0	374,919,999
Kazakhstan, Republic of	426,664,375	0	426,664,375
Kenya	0	136,005,012	136,005,012
Korea	9,748,750,000	0	9,748,750,000
Kyrgyz Republic	24,187,500	118,530,000	142,717,500
Lao People's Democratic Republic	0	42,807,500	42,807,500
Latvia, Republic of	41,175,000	0	41,175,000
Lesotho	0	15,553,000	15,553,000
Liberia	201,456,706	23,653,957	225,110,663
Lithuania, Republic of	173,793,750	0	173,793,750
Macedonia, former Yugoslav Republic of	42,233,334	27,281,000	69,514,334

Madagascar	0	39,936,657	39,936,657
Malawi	4,771,875	60,995,000	65,766,875
Mali	0	140,229,000	140,229,000
Mauritania	0	76,650,000	76,650,000
Mexico	5,336,781,903	0	5,336,781,903
Moldova, Republic of	137,200,000	0	137,200,000
Mongolia	0	34,317,500	34,317,500
Mozambique	0	139,912,516	139,912,516
Nepal	0	16,039,000	16,039,000
Nicaragua	0	101,705,000	101,705,000
Niger	0	51,164,500	51,164,500
Pakistan	819,805,417	535,904,000	1,355,709,417
Panama	123,212,500	0	123,212,500
Papua New Guinea	25,192,500	0	25,192,500
Peru	588,957,406	0	588,957,406
Philippines	1,208,970,208	0	1,208,970,208
Romania	366,533,544	0	366,533,544
Russian Federation	12,923,285,875	0	12,923,285,875
Rwanda	21,568,750	27,304,000	48,872,750
St. Kitts and Nevis	1,625,000	0	1,625,000
Sao Tome and Principe	0	80,000	80,000
Senegal	0	198,798,000	198,798,000
Sierra Leone	11,580,000	123,868,000	135,448,000
Slovak Republic	115,451,250	0	115,451,250
Somalia	96,700,987	15,303,010	112,003,997
Sri Lanka	0	232,879,000	232,879,000
Sudan	480,049,501	59,227,764	539,277,265
Tajikistan, Republic of	30,000,000	40,300,000	70,300,000
Tanzania	0	215,340,000	215,340,000
Thailand	2,400,000,000	0	2,400,000,000
Togo	0	67,356,000	67,356,000
Tunisia	86,424,168	0	86,424,168
Turkey	188,812,500	0	188,812,500

Uganda	0	268,800,500	268,800,500
Ukraine	1,969,372,292	0	1,969,372,292
Uruguay	114,200,000	0	114,200,000
Uzbekistan, Republic of	164,425,000	0	164,425,000
Venezuela	842,070,934	0	842,070,934
Vietnam	29,213,332	241,600,000	270,813,332
Yemen, Republic of	161,375,000	124,000,000	285,375,000
Yugoslavia, Federal Republic of (Serbia/ Montenegro)	56,056,031	0	56,056,031
Zambia	0	853,431,540	853,431,540
Zimbabwe	141,125,003	132,450,000	273,575,003
Total	60,650,704,286	6,483,931,423	67,134,635,709

Source: Treasurer's Department, Accounts and Financial Reports Division

6

International Monetary Fund and its Sources of Finance

The IMF is a cooperative institution-in some ways like a credit union-which derives the bulk of its financial resources from its members' contributions (called quotas). Generally speaking, these resources are available for temporary lending to any member that experiences difficulties in paying its import bills and/or servicing its foreign debt, and that agrees to undertake reforms to correct the macroeconomic imbalances that underlie the problem.

Members' quota subscriptions constitute the largest source of funds at the IMF's disposal. Members pay 25 percent of their quota subscriptions in "acceptable" (hard) currencies or in SDRs (a special reserve asset created by the IMF), and the rest in their own domestic currency. A review of quotas is conducted every five years to determine whether they need to be adjusted in light of the growth of the world economy and changes in individual countries' economic positions. The quota increase under the latest General Review became effective in January 1999 and the payments for the bulk of the quota increase were received by the end of February 1999, bringing total quotas to about $300 billion.

In addition to quotas, the IMF can draw on lines of credit that have been established since 1962 with 11 industrialized countries. These credit arrangements, which are called the General Arrangements to Borrow (GAB), currently amount to about $23 billion. An additional $2 billion is available through an associated agreement with Saudi Arabia. In July 1998, the GAB were activated for $8.4 billion, of which only $1.9 billion was drawn.

Following the quota increase, the GAB activation was canceled and the borrowed amount was repaid in early March 1999. In January 1997, the IMF's Executive Board decided to supplement the GAB with a new set of credit lines with 25 member countries, called the New Arrangements to Borrow (NAB). This effectively doubled-to $46 billion-the total amount of credit potentially available to the IMF. The IMF activated the NAB for $12.7 billion in December 1998 to finance its lending to Brazil, of which $4.1 billion was disbursed. As with the GAB, the NAB borrowing was repaid by the Fund in March 1999 following the payments for the quota increase noted above.

The IMF can also borrow-and has in the past borrowed-from member governments or their monetary authorities for specific programs of benefit to its members.

Separately, acting as Trustee, the IMF also manages funds provided partly through sales of gold in the late 1970s and partly in various forms by its members for the purpose of helping the poorest developing countries. These resources are lent out at a concessional interest rate of 0.5 percent through the Enhanced Structural Adjustment Facility (ESAF).

HOW DOES THE IMF LEND?

IMF lending transactions (except for those under the ESAF) are not loans per se. Rather, IMF transactions are exchanges of one type of monetary asset for another, i.e., a member with a weak balance of payments position and in need of hard currencies will exchange some of its own currency for the currencies of members with strong balances of payments. In IMF parlance, the country seeking assistance is said to make a "purchase" of the stronger currencies it needs with an equivalent amount of its own currency.

In time the "borrower" has to buy back ("repurchase") its own currency with hard currencies. This purchase-repurchase scheme explains why, from an accounting perspective, the IMF's total resources never vary; only the composition of its currency holdings changes.

IMF LENDING: A SAMPLE TRANSACTION

Assume a country seeks the financial assistance of the IMF and that the IMF decides to use U.S. dollars to provide the assistance. The IMF's use of U.S. dollars results in an exchange of the borrowing ("purchasing") member's own currency for U.S. dollars; to repay the IMF, the purchaser (borrower) will be obliged to buy back ("repurchase") its own currency from the IMF. A "purchase" of U.S. dollars is recorded as a debit to the IMF's U.S. dollar account at the New York Federal Reserve Bank, and as a credit to the account of the borrowing member. As a result, the IMF's holdings of U.S. dollars are lower than the U.S.'s quota subscription and the United States assumes a creditor position with the IMF; the borrower correspondingly is in a debtor position.

CURRENCIES USED IN IMF TRANSACTIONS

The IMF's Executive Board decides periodically which currencies can be used when a member makes a purchase or a repurchase, based on an assessment of the strength of various currencies. The quarterly currency budget identifies those members with strong balance of payments and reserve positions, and sets the maximum amounts of each currency that can be used to meet expected financing by the IMF for the coming quarter. In November 1998, the IMF changed the method of allocating currencies in the quarterly budget so that the share of each member is now determined in proportion to its share in the quotas of the strong currency members. (Previously, shares had been allocated mainly, but not exclusively, in proportion to members' foreign exchange reserves.)

WHERE DO IMF FUNDS GO?

The IMF provides general balance of payments assistance. It does not provide financing for specific projects, which is a typical activity of development banks. The conditions for IMF assistance are subject to regular reviews by the IMF's Board. Assistance is typically made available in installments linked to the observance of specific conditions or "performance criteria" that must be satisfied before the next installment is released.

When a country purchases foreign exchange from the IMF with its own currency, it deposits its own currency in an account that the IMF maintains at the member's central bank. The foreign exchange provided by the IMF is deposited in an account maintained by the borrowing member in the country whose currency is being used, and becomes part of the international reserves of the recipient country, freely available for use by that country in the same manner as all other international reserves. Therefore, there is no meaningful way in which the use of IMF resources can be tracked, as might, for example, lending by a development bank for a specific project.

INTEREST RATES OF IMF

If a member makes a purchase from the IMF, it pays various charges to cover the IMF's operational expenses and to compensate the members whose currencies it is borrowing. The interest rate charged is linked to a weighted average of market interest rates on short-term instruments in the capital markets of France, Germany, Japan, the United Kingdom, and the United States. This rate varies from week to week. Presently:

- The borrower pays about ¼ of 1 percent in a (refundable) commitment fee, ½ of 1 percent of the amount borrowed in service charges, and interest charges at a variable rate, currently around 3.75 percent, for the use of the IMF's regular (non-concessional) lending facilities. A surcharge of 3 percent, progressing to 5 percent, is levied on amounts borrowed under a special, short-term facility (the Supplemental Reserve Facility).
- An IMF creditor country earns interest whenever other members borrow its currency from the IMF. This "rate of remuneration" varies with the rate of charge; it is currently around 3.50 percent.

A BAD SIDE OF BAILOUTS: SOME GO UNPENALIZED

Much of the $55 billion that has been pledged by the international community to South Korea--like the $40 billion for Indonesia and the $17 billion for Thailand before it--will ultimately go to lenders who dished out huge sums for risky projects that failed to pay off. The rescue plan centers on shaky Korean banks. The nation's industrialists, who borrowed billions of dollars from them for new factories and such, have not made enough profit to repay their debts. The banks, of course, got their money in part from Korean depositors. Other money came from foreigners--big European, American, and Japanese banks, for example--that lent enthusiastically to the Korean banks, in hopes of sharing in the profits.

The bailout money, from the International Monetary Fund, the World Bank, and individual countries, will be channeled through the Korean government and its central bank in great measure to the private banking system. In some cases, foreign creditors may be paid off directly. Mostly, the money will go to salvage some institutions and to close others while paying off creditors. The bailout will, in effect, repay the depositors and the foreign lenders. At the end of last year [1996], South Korean banks owed nearly $60 billion to foreign banks, according to the Bank for International Settlement.

"We keep blaming this crisis on corruption and bad banking practices," said Jeffrey Sachs, a Harvard economist. "But this all happened in the private marketplace. It was so often a case of big foreign lenders pushing their money on the Koreans and the Korean banks enthusiastically taking it in."

Of course, some of the bailout money is earmarked for specific projects, such as public works. That is particularly true of the World Bank's $10 billion contribution. But money that the Korean government is now spending on such projects will simply be freed up for the financial rescue.

All of the Asian aid packages, already totaling more than $100 billion, are prompting many economists and investment bankers to argue anew that bailouts, even when they accomplish their immediate goals, set a bad precedent. By making the lenders whole, they encourage more careless lending and fresh crises.

"If we practice bailing out countries whenever they get into trouble," said Richard Cooper, a Harvard economist, "then lenders everywhere will come to count on that and they will continue to make loans they should not make." That view, widely held, is producing numerous proposals for change. Mr. Cooper suggests that new regulations should be adopted by all countries that would cause the owners of banks--the shareholders--to lose their investments in such situations. That would make lenders more cautious, reducing bank failures and the need for bailouts. Robert Hormats, a vice president of Goldman, Sachs, argues that developing countries should adopt capital controls, dictating how loans can be dispersed, particularly those from abroad. That, too, could force lenders to be more cautious.

Henry Kaufman, an economist and money manager, says a new layer of international supervision and lending standards is needed. "There is simply no effort today to manage global liquidity," he said.

A national bailout is the only tool readily available today to reverse financial crises that a government cannot handle on its own. These crises are almost always rooted in the unrealistic view of lenders and borrowers that they will profit. When those profit hopes were dashed in Asia in recent months, devaluations, bankruptcies, and bank failures followed.

The IMF will feed the $55 billion to South Korea in stages. The money will go to the Ministry of Finance or the central bank, where it will augment Korean government funds. The additional funds may help restore confidence in the country and stabilize the slide in its currency.

Or it may be used to directly solve the banking crisis.

A Korean bank, for example, may have made a five-year, $100 million loan to an auto company, which has defaulted. The bank may have received its funds from $100 million in six-month loans from American and Japanese banks.

As long as the Korean economy seemed sound, even booming, the foreign banks were willing to roll over these short-term loans. Indeed, they were eager to do so because they were lending to Korean banks at much higher rates than they would charge domestic customers. But in the current crisis the American and Japanese banks, fearful of losing money, want quick repayment. And new lending from abroad dries up.

With the IMF bailout, the foreign banks may choose to roll over their loans, expecting that, in time, they will be repaid in full. That happened in Mexico. The $48 billion that was made available to the country, $20 billion of it from the United States, reassured most foreign investors, and they left their money in place. But the big Mexican debtor was the government, while in Asia's crisis, the private sector owes the money.

If the foreign banks--American and Japanese in this example--insist on quick repayment, the Korean government can do this as well, with its new found money. Or the process can be less direct. The Ministry of Finance can buy the bad loans from the Seoul bank. The Seoul bank, in turn, buys foreign currency with the proceeds and repays the American and Japanese banks.

A similar reimbursement process functions for Korean depositors whose money has gone to bad loans. The Korean government can replenish the deposits, in whole or in part, by buying up the bad loans, using general funds to do so. In this case, the IMF bailout adds to the government's available funds.

But for Joseph E. Stiglitz, chief economist at the World Bank, the bailout solution is unlikely to deter the unrealistic lending practices that inject money from all parts of the world into a Korea or a Thailand. "To the extent that private investors who made bad decisions are bailed out," he said in a speech, "their incentives will be distorted, exacerbating the problems governments face in trying to stabilize capital flows."

WHY SHOULD THE IMF LEND AT SUBSIDIZED INTEREST RATES?

This selection was excerpted from "The Political Economy of the IMF: A Public Choice Analysis," published in Perpetuating Poverty: The World Bank, the IMF, and the Developing World, edited by Doug Bandow and Ian Vasquez (1994). Roland Vaubel is a professor of economics at the University of Mannheim in Germany.

Member governments can borrow from the IMF at favorable interest rates instead of resorting to the international capital market. According to its Articles of Agreement (V.8.d and XX.2), the fund has to charge uniform interest rates to all borrowers, effectively paying the largest subsidies to the least creditworthy. The IMF also tends to give the greatest benefits to long-term debtors because, contrary to the Articles of Agreement (V.8.b), the rates are normally independent of loan duration. The uniformity of interest charges not only aggravates the moral hazard problem but also results in adverse selection of borrowers, a "lemon" problem.

Under the Bretton Woods system, the aim of maintaining stable exchange rates was used to justify cheap IMF credits. Many IMF borrowers, however, especially during the Bretton Woods era, were perfectly capable of acquiring foreign exchange via the market.

If, however, a member government is not creditworthy, the question becomes why it should be granted loans at all. There are two possible answers: to overcome imperfections of the capital market or to provide development aid. With imperfect information, the capital market would function imperfectly as well. However, if the IMF really has better information than potential private lenders about the true creditworthiness of its member governments, it could try to improve the market's information rather than to extend credit itself. Surely the fund has an obligation to make such information public for the protection of other lenders. Alternatively, subsidized IMF lending is a poor form of development aid since the IMF's criterion for extending credit (i.e., balance of payments difficulties) is not a suitable indicator of need.

Moreover, the interest rate subsidy creates an incentive to delay adjustment once a credit has been obtained =mArticle V, Section 7.b of the Articles of Agreement specifies that each member is normally expected to repay its credits (even before maturity) "as its balance of payments and reserve position improves." That runs directly counter to the objective laid down in Article I.vi that the fund should "shorten the duration... of disequilibrium in the international balances of payments of members."

The interest rate subsidy might be regarded as an insurance benefit against economic instability, but "premiums" do not differ according to risk. From 1960 to 1982, for example, forty-two member countries accounted for 78 percent of all standby and extended credits from the IMF. That is not an outcome to be expected if members had been hit by random accidents. In fact, cross-sectional regressions by Lawrence Officer and Peter Cornelius showed that, between 1974 and 1980, the flow of IMF credits to member governments tended to be significantly correlated with the outstanding stock of previous IMF credits. Richard Goode presented a list of twenty-four countries that have obtained fund credits for more than ten consecutive years. The maximum is twenty-seven years (Chile and Egypt). He also reported that, in 1974 =n1984, drawings from non-oil-producing countries accounted for 85 percent of fund credit.

In short, the IMF is a continuous provider of aid, in the form of subsidized insurance, to a limited group of member governments. That raises four questions:

- Why do donor governments grant this form of aid?
- Why do they give the largest subsidies to the most negligent members?
- Why is the insurance offered to governments rather than to individuals?
- Why is the subsidy confined to insurance with an international public monopoly, the IMF?

The government treasury origins of the IMF are indicative. As John Makin has noted, the IMF serves the interests of the treasuries of its member governments by flexibly accommodating their borrowing and debt-servicing "needs" at minimum cost. By charging low and uniform interest rates, the IMF protects its members against market judgments and helps insure them against the electoral damage that a visibly poor credit standing might otherwise cause. The policy conditions imposed by the IMF may also be unpopular, but political leaders have occasionally made them scapegoats for unpopular economic reforms. The IMF at least provides politicians with a choice between high-risk premiums (lack of creditworthiness) in the private capital market and the IMF's policy conditions. The IMF's professional staff also has a vested interest in subsidized, uniform interest rates. Low rates increase the demand for IMF credits. Uniform rates help avoid conflict with potential borrowers. For similar reasons, national social insurance systems and public insurance schemes for export credits and foreign investment do not usually charge premiums according to risk. Moreover, paying larger subsidies to the least creditworthy allows the fund, like national social insurance schemes, to justify its activities on humanitarian grounds. As is well known from social insurance economics, however, the poor are often not the worst risks. The debt crisis of the 1980s is a case in point: The governments of the richer developing countries, such as Mexico, proved to be the least creditworthy.

THE MORAL HAZARD OF IMF EXPANSION

Mr. Speaker, today the President called for a further expansion of the International Monetary Fund. He repeated his audacious request that Congress provide $18 billion to the IMF with no conditions and without first requiring IMF reform.

It's time for some presidential accountability--in this area as much as others. We need to recognize that it was the Clinton Administration's own policies that accelerated the financial collapse overseas that is threatening the US economy today.

For Congress to simply endorse those policies through the full funding of an unreformed IMF would be recklessly irresponsible. If the President will not--or, as yet another consequence of his diminished leadership, cannot--bring about real changes in international financial institutions--then Congress must supply leadership in his place.

The IMF proposal actually serves to illuminate a major policy departure that has developed largely unnoticed by Congress, press, and public--unnoticed, that is, until it was too late. I call it the Clinton Doctrine.

It is a policy under which virtually any groupings of bankruptcies anywhere in the world is eligible for a bailout by American taxpayers. This has inflamed what economists call "moral hazard." By covering bad investments, the

Administration has encouraged irresponsible behavior. The financial disasters overseas are in large part a direct consequence of this.

To make matters worse, once the financial collapses occurred, the IMF--presumably with the President's blessing--imposed catastrophic contractionary policies on the affected countries. Even Keynesians know that you don't raise taxes in a recession, and yet that's exactly what the Clinton-guided IMF often proposed. As Larry Lindsey put it, these policies have become our own era's equivalent of the Smoot-Hawley Tariff.

In fairness to the President, he did not initiate this policy of global bailout, which we've been drifting towards for some time. His role has been to sanction it, legitimize it and take it to new and unprecedented levels.

Beginning with the 1995 bailout of Mexico, continuing with the multiple bailouts of Asia, and reaching its inevitable culmination in the farcical bailout of Russia this summer, the Administration has undermined market discipline and helped to create the very crises it was ostensibly trying to prevent.

The IMF under the direction of the Clinton Administration helped cause the problem. Then the IMF made it worse. Now it is making it more difficult for the world to recover.

The IMF has the Midas touch in reverse--virtually every country it tried to help has become worse off from the experience.

In Korea today, children made homeless by the continuing recession are bitterly referred to as "IMF Orphans." Our friends in Korea know, as many in the Clinton Administration do not, that the IMF is largely responsible for their continuing economic difficulties.

Congress must reverse this Clinton Doctrine that has helped bring the world economy to its current state.

A positive step would be to restrain the IMF by deferring a decision on providing the huge $14.5 billion quota increase. This is essentially the House position contained in the Foreign Operations Appropriations bill. Delaying a decision on the IMF money would allow us time to hold an international conference and other meetings to improve the world financial system. The disasters we see overseas are clear evidence that the current arrangements have failed. Rather than pump more money into them, we need to redesign them. We need nothing less than a New Bretton Woods conference. Only then can we make an informed decision on giving away $14.5 billion of our taxpayers' money for these purposes.

Now, many--including many in this House--say that we should give the IMF money upfront in exchange for "real IMF reforms." What they don't understand is that the Administration and the IMF are adamantly against any US-imposed reform. As the French director of the IMF arrogantly put it last week, "The US must bring its contribution and no country is entitled to impose conditions." The most the Administration and other IMF supporters will accept are weak suggestions from us. The reform provisions in pending IMF bills, for instance, are little more than sense-of-Congress resolutions.

So--if Members are serious about doing a money-for-reform trade, I suggest they adopt this principle to start with:

No IMF reform is real IMF reform unless the IMF adopts it before it receives any additional money from the US.

This, in my judgment, is plain common sense. We don't give away $18 billion of our taxpayers money on the strength of a promises or assurances. Any reform provisions that don't meet this principle should be rejected out of hand.

What should those reforms involve? If our aim is to reverse the destabilizing influence that the IMF has on the world's financial system, we should insist on these:

1. *Real Transparency Requirements*: This will allow us to open the IMF books and judge the value of its advice and the effectiveness of its programs.
2. *A Ban on the IMF Offering below Market Interest Rates*: This will address the moral hazard problem. Countries that need liquidity would still be able to get loans from the IMF, but they would not be able to get them at heavily subsidized rates.
3. *A One-year Limit on all IMF Loans*. This will return the IMF to its original role as a lender of last resort and

will move it away from restructuring entire economies. Countries facing currency exchange problems will still be able to get needed cash. But the IMF will no longer offer five-year plans full of Herbert Hoover economic policies.

I'm not naïve, Mr. Speaker. I can count votes and I know this is an uphill fight. But it's one we must make even in the waning days of this Congress.

In the end, Mr. Speaker, it comes down to first principles. My Party believes in Freedom and Responsibility. Guided by those values, we have resisted the statist temptation and instead led America into this era of limited government and broad prosperity. How can we then acquiesce in a plan to vastly expand an international agency that covers other peoples' bad debts and undermines free market processes the world over?

CRISIS IN EMERGING MARKET ECONOMIES

In a world that becomes more global everyday, in a world where private business everyday plays an increasingly dominant role in innovation, investment, financing, and ultimately human progress, let me tell you how much I appreciate the opportunity to address this transatlantic business council. Of course the timing of your meeting could not have been more appropriate.

We are witnessing wave upon wave of tensions in global financial markets, turbulence that spreads like wildfire from one part of the world to another. Have economic fundamentals changed so suddenly, so substantially, and simultaneously throughout the world? Or is the loss of confidence that was understandable in some, I repeat, some countries, being transferred indiscriminately to all markets, emerging and established alike?

In this volatile situation, calm analysis is more important than ever, remembering that not all markets, not all economies, not all crises, are the same. Nor will the path to recovery, where recovery is necessary, be the same in each case. Market participants-and we all-need to be discerning, capable of discriminating among economies, aware that when risks turn to reality in one economy, the same course of events does not need to unfold elsewhere, but that all countries, all institutions must read the markets' messages properly.

Let me start by observing that not all the news of the day is gloomy. Although downside risks have increased in recent weeks in so many places, it should be remembered that the fundamentals of the European and North American industrial economies remain sound. The growth of the U.S. economy is continuing in 1998 without inflationary pressure. A recovery in continental Europe has gained momentum, aided by the imminent birth of the euro.

These economies offer a powerful message to the rest of the world, which remains valid even in turbulent times. Fiscal discipline, supported by a responsive monetary policy within a sound financial system, works. In North America, long-standing budget deficits are turning to surplus, while in Europe the self-imposed discipline of the convergence criteria under the Maastricht Treaty have brought down deficits, many of which seemed entrenched at much higher levels only a short while ago.

By recognizing yesterday that the balance of risks has shifted from inflation to slowdown in demand, the President of the United States here in New York and ministers of finance and central bank governors of Europe and North America, in the context of a G-7 declaration, have indeed pledged their commitment to preserve or create conditions for sustainable domestic growth and financial stability, so critical in today's world environment. So we are at a moment when a credible pro-growth strategy is taking shape-quite a good signal for the world indeed.

Mr. Chairman, you have asked me to focus my remarks tonight on Asia, certainly not because we should downplay the difficult conditions in other parts of the world, but because Asia offers the first rays of hope for resolving the economic crises that now threaten so many countries. In Asia, we find the first countries to experience crisis in 1997, the first to respond, and, although it is not yet widely recognized, the first to be showing some positive results, however tentative and incomplete. The experience of these countries holds out clear hope that serious problems can be avoided in most countries and that seemingly intractable problems in other countries, even Russia, can be resolved given commitment, sound policies, and a steady nerve. This will bring us then to a kind of journey around the world-from Asia to Russia and then to Latin America-concluding by asking ourselves what kind of a new international monetary system could emerge from the present crisis. Asia! The origins of its crisis lie in a complex interplay among domestic macroeconomic, structural, institutional, and political factors, strongly connected with developments in the advanced economies and global financial markets.

Reflection on the pre-crisis situation in the Asian countries in mid-1997 points to the build-up in all countries of serious structural problems in the financial and corporate sectors, and to a varying extent, inadequate macroeconomic policies, perhaps most markedly in Thailand, where the crisis started. Overheating, arising from surging private sector demand, was reflected in real estate and stock market bubbles and, in Thailand particularly, in large trade deficits. Pegged exchange rate regimes had been maintained for too long, encouraging heavy external borrowing, including increasing amounts of short-term credit, which created excessive exposure to foreign exchange risk in both the financial and the corporate sectors. Inadequate prudential rules and supervision allowed the quality of banks' loan portfolios to degenerate quickly.

It would not be appropriate, nevertheless, to attribute the financial crisis in Asia, or indeed in other regions, solely to their policy shortcomings. Conditions in international markets are also highly germane. Private investors were attracted by the high returns in these countries, and there perhaps less inclined to assess carefully the risks, as the track record of these countries seemed to make them less risky than most. This led many to lose sight of the fact that the steady appreciation of the dollar against the Japanese yen from mid-1995 was contributing to a loss of export competitiveness in countries whose currencies were tightly linked to the U.S.

dollar. Then the Thailand crisis blew up and its depth led the markets to reassess emerging markets' risks-a major factor in the broadening of the crisis. The IMF was called for help...always too late indeed.

The policy programs to respond to crisis in Asian countries had to be speedily designed, to put the proper emphasis on the immediacy of macroeconomic adjustment, and to recognize the sheer magnitude of the structural reforms that had to be initiated from the outset. As a matter of fact, the importance of the structural element is the hallmark of these programs. Within these programs, we can discern three tiers of recovery:

- *The First Tier is to Restore Stability*: As usual, immediate action is needed for countries faced with sudden acute pressure on their balance of payments;
- *The Second Tier is to Improve Soundness*: Lost confidence, especially in domestic financial and corporate systems, has to be restored through fundamental institutional changes;
- *The Third Tier is to Boost Efficiency*: The approach of "managed development" underlying economic policy, characterized by mechanisms that interfered with market allocation of resources, has become increasingly out of tune with the rigorous demands of our globalized economy. Basic changes in the approach to policymaking, allowing market forces to operate more freely, will be essential. This tier perhaps has been the more controversial due to many misunderstandings on what were at an earlier stage the parameters of the "Asian miracle," and more than that, due to the fact that questioning this approach was tantamount to challenging many vested interests.

Let us take stock of the major programs supported by the IMF in Korea, Thailand, and Indonesia in terms of these three tiers of recovery. First, with respect to the initial stabilization, as so often is the case, it is the bad news that attracts the headlines. There have been setbacks. Economic activity has contracted sharply, more so than was expected at first. This has been the consequence of a sharp drop in investment as financing has been constrained and unprofitable or inefficient projects had to be cut back. A second factor was the "wealth effect" following sharp declines in stock market prices and exchange rates. A third factor was the fall-off in intra-regional trade, especially with Japan, where stagnation has turned to recession during 1998. This crisis at the heart of the region has been of course central to the difficult process of recovery.

With these contractions have come the social costs: an increasing incidence of poverty, rising unemployment, and steeply rising food prices. But programs have been adapted in response. Let me put some emphasis on this point. These programs have not relied primarily on "traditional" prescriptions of budgetary austerity.

Except in Thailand, the initial fiscal adjustment called for was quite small, particularly in order to leave room for financial sector restructuring. Moreover, where necessary we have been perfectly ready to alter-yes, to relax-targets to allow room within public expenditure for targeted programs of poverty alleviation and to stimulate the economy. Indeed in more than one country, the IMF actually had to question the budgetary zeal of the authorities, exhorting them to make more room for social expenditures.

With respect at least to Thailand and Korea, behind these dark clouds, the beginning of a silver lining can be detected. Several developments point to the return of more stable financial conditions that are essential prerequisites for resumed growth, although undoubtedly new risks arise from recent weakening of the external environment:

- *The External Position has Strengthened Decisively*: Current accounts have swung sharply from unsustainable deficit to large surplus and international reserves now exceed pre-crisis levels. The main factor has been a steep fall in imports. But exports have also played a large part and the improvement would have been greater if commodity prices had not fallen steeply, and demand from within the region, especially Japan, had not fallen off.
- *Currencies are Rebounding*: After the initial precipitous depreciation, all the currencies of the crisis-ridden

countries have shown some appreciation. Even Indonesia, where the decline was steeper and lasted longer, has seen a pronounced appreciation since the depths of its crisis in mid-June. And in Korea, some questions are even being asked about whether the won is appreciating too quickly.

- *Interest Rates are Easing*: In Korea, Thailand, and the Philippines, interest rates have declined notably as currency pressures have eased. As monetary conditions ease, the prospects for recovery in demand and output are improving.
- Inflation has not risen as much as had been feared. Although this reflects very weak demand conditions and a decline in real wages, it means that inflation is unlikely to represent an obstacle to resumed growth.

The objective of the second tier of recovery for which we are working in close cooperation with the World Bank and the Asian Development Bank is to promote the changes that would justify renewed confidence in the soundness of both financial and corporate systems.

In the financial sector, banks were brought under greater scrutiny, with the weakest being closed or restructured, sometimes with public funds. Prudential regulations are being strengthened; so too are standards for accounting, auditing, and disclosure. A more liberal attitude is being taken to foreign banks. The list of changes could be much longer.

PROBLEMS OF THE FINANCIAL SYSTEM

The problems of financial systems were in very large measure an outgrowth of fundamental weaknesses in the corporate sector, especially the excessively close relationship between banks, corporations, and the state. This led to an unsustainable situation. So concepts such as transparency, governance in both public and private sectors, and the fight against corruption, have come to center-stage. Early on, steps have been taken to work out the massive debt obligations of corporations in a way that is fair to both domestic and foreign creditors. The next stages, already under way, will consist of liberalizing domestic markets, lowering trade barriers, privatization, easing restrictions on entry by foreign investors, and strengthening bankruptcy laws and procedures. But again, time and steadfast implementation will be necessary for results to become evident.

The third tier of recovery will be to increase overall economic efficiency or productivity. For years the Asian tigers' growth was driven significantly by the massive flow of investment, supported by the impetus from an expanding, and increasingly educated labor force. Looking to the future, we can be quite certain that it will not be back to "business as usual." True, many familiar features will still be there: the dynamism, the skilled work force, the traditional Asian propensity to work and save. Nevertheless, capital may well be less abundant or more costly, so that to restore growth to sustainable levels, investment will have to become much more efficient.

Where are we now? Despite the sharp decline in output, there are promising signs of a good start to the "first tier" of policies. Indeed, if the IMF's mandate were interpreted in a very narrow, traditional sense, as some have suggested it should be, could we not count our task as largely complete? After all, external reserves have been rebuilt, exchange rate stability is being restored, and inflation is at quite low levels. But to stop at this point would not discharge our responsibilities to the countries in crisis or to the world. Only by implementing policies at the second and third tiers, structural and institutional reforms, will it be possible to ensure that the prospects for sustained high-quality growth are restored, that sound institutions and practices are in place, that the external position remains viable in the medium to long-term: in a word, that the job is done. The Asian countries in crisis have understood that and the IMF has been willing to offer such large financial assistance precisely because they were willing to adopt policies that went far beyond simple stabilization. This is still a matter of some controversy. You will hear perhaps that we are too ambitious; I will suggest to you that it would be illusory to believe that there could be any other way to solve these deeply rooted problems in a sustainable fashion.

I will dwell no more on these first three victims of the crisis and our three tiers of strategy for them. But let me turn more briefly to a number of other countries or regions that have been the subject of particular concern in recent weeks as financial pressures have intensified. Japan first, as it must be central also to the solution of the Asian crisis. Japan, as the second largest industrial economy, plays a pivotal role in the world economy, especially in supporting recovery in Asia. At present, we see an economy that is wracked with financial and corporate sector problems, not so different either from those elsewhere in Asia. But its current recession stands in contrast with the imbalances created by years of fever-pitched activity in the Asian "tigers." In that sense its task is clearer: prompt, resolute action to get its financial system into order is the first urgent order of business. That confidence-building step is essential to underpin the strong fiscal action it may, and indeed should, take simultaneously to stimulate its economy, while pushing its agenda for deregulation, openness and structural reform.

In Russia, the problems are profound; they have origins far beyond the purely economic domain. In economic terms, the principal causes of the Russian crisis relate to domestic fundamentals; contagion from crises elsewhere-including the impact of lower oil and gas prices-is only part of the story. As a matter of fact, even if in a totally different context, the problems of Russia at the beginning of 1998 were strikingly similar to those which at that very moment were destroying Asian prosperity.

Let me tell you here a sad anecdote. In early 1998, back from one of my many trips to Asia, I stopped in Russia to confer with President Yeltsin, and others in economic leadership, to share with them some of the lessons that were already emerging from our experience in East Asia. I told them that a firm monetary stance might well go a long way in stabilizing exchange markets, but that it was neither desirable nor feasible to rely on monetary policy alone for any extended period of time. It was urgent to tackle decisively in Russia the three factors of the "Asian syndrome" that it was also suffering from: continuing macroeconomic deficiency-in Russia, particularly in fiscal policy-weakness in the banking sector, and the pervasiveness of "crony capitalism." It was another way, using the Asian experience, of restating the priorities we had been insisting on for six years. Now, six months later, the markets have delivered their harsh judgment on Russia's failure to address any of these critical issues with sufficient effectiveness. Yes, programs have been ambitious and comprehensive; but implementation fell short.

The path to recovery in Russia will need programs at least as comprehensive as those in Asia, containing elements from all three tiers of policies. Russia's path to recovery is likely to be quite difficult, since Russia needs to restore confidence severely weakened by its decision to unilaterally restructure its domestic debt obligations. Nevertheless, if Russia, like Asia, can begin again to help itself, and do so convincingly, then we stand ready to help. Russia has achieved a lot during the last six years; by far most of the basic elements of its transformation are still in place. Let us hope that the new government will be able soon to start building on these foundations and assembling in the State Duma and in public opinion the broad support that the needed changes will require.

In the meantime, we must continue to shelter the other countries in transition against contagion phenomena. This applies particularly to Ukraine, where despite deteriorating conditions in neighboring Russia, the authorities are showing themselves willing to act, committing to significant reform, and adapting their policies in response to changing conditions. Their recent commitments convinced the IMF that it was appropriate to proceed with a new lending program to support Ukraine's reform program. A three-year arrangement was approved a few days ago, with commitments from our side of more than $2 billion.

Let's now cross the Pacific Ocean. Emerging markets in Latin America have been particularly affected by market turbulence after the Russian crisis. This region had responded strongly to the Mexican crisis in 1995, and made significant progress with structural reforms, especially in the area of public finance, and the financial system. In many cases, their economic performance, with a return to low inflation-often in the single-digit range-and stronger external positions, attest to the success of these policies. The region had generally been coping well with the contagion that followed the Asian crisis in 1997. But with global market volatility in recent weeks, coincident with declining oil and primary commodity prices, a number of these economies have come under renewed pressure.

The countries' response to these developments illustrates two points: first, their determination to undertake appropriate policies; and second, the role that the IMF can play in assisting countries on a regional basis through its policy advice, even before any kind of financial assistance. At my invitation, building upon earlier regional meetings, finance ministers and central bank governors from key countries in the Western Hemisphere attended a regional surveillance meeting in Washington ten days ago. While stressing that they were not seeking additional financial assistance, the authorities attending the meeting reaffirmed that they were committed to sustaining growth through the pursuit of macroeconomic stability, maintaining open capital markets, and deepening reform efforts. As market pressures intensified in subsequent days, these countries took courageous steps to defend their economies.

I need hardly say that these are not the statements or actions of countries about to reverse the positive direction of economic policies. Nor are they the statements of countries that pursue irresponsible economic policies assuming that they will be "bailed out" by the IMF. Nevertheless, it is proper to add that, as I declared last Friday with the unanimous backing of the IMF's Executive Board, the IMF already has financial arrangements with several countries in Latin America, and according to its mandate, it stands ready to strengthen its financial support and broaden it to other countries, if necessary, to back strong economic programs.

In contrast with this policy stance, I must recognize that there are still, from time to time and from place to place, voices to recommend to countries confronted by a difficult external environment, to yield to the temptation of superficially attractive, populist options, such as unilaterally restructuring debt, imposing new payments restrictions, increasing government intervention in markets, or trying to stimulate expansion by printing money. We know too much, alas, where such a retrograde approach leads: it would reverse years of progress toward more open economic management, and will quickly undermine countries' capacity to reap the benefits of the global economy.

This being said, it is quite remarkable to see how limited is the impact of these so-called "alternatives" or experiences. The growing majority of countries is striving in the opposite direction, to implement more promising programs based on sound money, budget discipline, state restraint in its economic intervention, structural adjustment, strengthening of financial systems, and promotion of good corporate and public sector governance, in a context of orderly integration in the world economy. These are the only programs we, of course, support. You will be interested to know that more than 80 countries at this very moment are implementing such programs or negotiating them actively with us. These are emerging countries, transition countries and countries among the poorest, particularly in Africa. Let's salute their courage and wisdom.

As you can see, we are far from being a moribund institution, preoccupied with questions about our future. What concerns us is the future of the international monetary system. And this is why, while being so busy with our work as a fire brigade for the world economy, we are devoting attention to detailed reflection on the global or systemic issues that allowed crisis to develop.

Thus, looking to the longer term, we have been working with our member governments on proposals to strengthen the architecture of the international financial system, identifying steps that can be taken to minimize the risks of further such crises in the future. This work aims to create a global system that is stable, sound, open, transparent, and fair. This is a tall order. We are working intensely, within the IMF itself, and with other international fora and member governments, to make these ideas operative as soon as possible.

The agenda, a complex one indeed, brings together roles, rights, and obligations for the different constituents of the global economy: governments, citizens, private corporations, and international organizations. Let me give you a snapshot of the work that is in progress at present:

- Strengthening the IMF's surveillance of its members policies, especially with respect to financial sector issues and capital flows;
- Improving the soundness of financial systems through widespread adoption of consistent standards and practices for regulating and supervising banking systems, securities markets, and other financial institutions;
- Strengthening the financial infrastructure through more uniform standards for auditing, accounting, bankruptcy procedures, and payments systems;
- Making the golden rule of transparency prevail, by providing for timely and accurate information in the form of both data and more open communication to the markets about economic policy formulation and results;
- Defining the principles of good governance in both the public and private sectors;
- Continuing firm but orderly progress with freeing capital flows, recognizing that it is a long-term goal for many countries, to be set in the context of properly sequenced financial reform and of a strengthening of macroeconomic balances. As you know, this is a domain for which we received a very clear mandate in Hong Kong to go for freedom and orderly dismantling of capital controls. If anything, contrary to the confusion which seems to have emerged lately, the present crisis encourages us to persevere in this direction;
- Developing ways of involving the private sector in forestalling financial crises and in resolving them if they do occur, a domain, I hope, where the private sector will volunteer suggestions, and in which they will not hesitate, if needed, to take action even before more formal or far-reaching arrangements are put in place;

- And, the bottom line, promoting a permanent dialogue with governments, aiming to ensure that economic and social policies contribute to improve opportunities for all citizens to participate in and benefit from economic progress. This is the ultimate aim of all our efforts.

Even as the architecture is being reinforced, one urgent task needs attention to enable us to continue with our work: it is a question of resources. The IMF's tasks are, simply stated, to offer policy advice to all members, and to provide financial support to those members that need it and are prepared to make the necessary policy changes. It is evident that with increased global market turbulence, the Fund needs to be able to remain an effective partner with its members as they confront these challenges. This has a name: it is the increase of our quotas-namely our capital base-a decision involving our 182 members. It is still pending particularly in the United States. I have no doubt that this decision will be taken promptly, as has always been the case in our history, so enabling the Fund not to save the world-this is not its mission-but to help effectively those who strive to save themselves.

Mr. Chairman, these remarks have been too long. Let me hope that they may be of some help for this attentive audience in evaluating what this crisis is all about, what is the right track toward recovery, and what kind of new financial architecture we should put in place, so as to hit the ground running as we emerge from this crisis.

EAST ASIA: THE TRUE MORAL HAZARD

In 1996 international investors poured perhaps $100 billion into East Asia, as East Asia's economies were the darlings of the world capital market. Now capital is flooding out of East Asia at perhaps $150 billion a year, as investors from Frankfurt to Los Angeles to Jakarta try to get their money out the door before what they fear will be a worse crash.

This sudden shift--impelled much more by the herd instincts of Wall Streeters than by any change in the fundamentals of East Asian economic development--means that demand for hard currency to purchase imports (and to finance capital flight) is suddenly much greater than the supply of hard currency earned by East Asia's exports.

When demand exceeds supply, prices rise--the values of East Asian currencies fall. As currencies fall, the resulting financial disruptions and bankruptcies throw people out of work. Government attempts to boost exchange rates by raising interest rates help on one hand by reducing financial turmoil, but hurt on another as higher interest rates discourage investment and throw more people out of work.

East Asia faces a severe depression--like the U.S. after 1873, like Argentina after 1890, like the whole world after 1929--unless the IMF and others loan East Asian governments the hard currency they need to make the process of adjustment slower, steadier, and more manageable.

"But," say many critics of the IMF, "bailing out the governments and the banks this time will only encourage them to overspeculate more in the future. If they know that making overoptimistic speculative mistakes is costless, they will make more such mistakes in the future. We must make them--East Asian governments, New York banks, hedge funds--suffer." To loan to East Asian governments is to encourage "moral hazard."

Supporters of the IMF have had a hard time countering this argument in short soundbites, because it is not completely false. But it is largely false, for three reasons:

First, moral hazard cannot exist unless the bailout is a true bailout--a true payment of public funds to defaulters that is never repaid. The U.S. bailout of the Savings and Loan industry was a true bailout: the U.S. government did not get repaid: instead, the Treasury issued a fortune in bonds to finance the rescue of depositors. The IMF very much intends to get repaid. The IMF is in the business of getting repaid. The IMF is being tough on East Asian countries--requiring that East Asian countries adopt policies to rapidly generate an export surplus even if they raise unemployment--because the IMF knows that if it does not get repaid its survival as an institution is at risk.

If the IMF gets repaid--as it almost surely will--then no moral hazard: moral hazard requires that the IMF pay out of its own pocket and never get repaid. Second, almost everyone involved in the wave of capital flowing into East Asia already has suffered. East Asian governments have certainly suffered. Anyone who bought East Asian government bonds has seen their money dwindle as exchange rates have depreciated. Investors in East Asian stock markets either directly or through emerging markets funds have seen large chunks of their money disappear. Hedge funds that were long in East Asia have suffered. Investment banks have suffered--look at J.P. Morgan and Company's earnings report for the fourth quarter of 1997.

"But," say critics of the IMF, "one class of investors has not suffered: New York bankers who loaned to East Asia and demanded that their money be repaid in dollars have not yet suffered. It's not enough the governments, hedge funds, investment banks, mutual funds, equity investors, and national-currency debt investors have suffered. We must make everyone suffer!"

And it is at this point that I question the sanity--and the goodwill--of opponents of the IMF's actions. The difference between the severe depression in East Asia that threatens and the mild depression that will occur if the IMF programs succeed is some 20 million jobs. Is it worth throwing 20 million more East Asians out of work just to make sure that there is not even a possibility of encouraging "moral hazard"? Especially when the IMF's mind is already perhaps a little too focused on making sure that it gets repaid, in which case by the definition of "moral hazard" there can be none?

To try to seek political advantage and to delight in making East Asia's forthcoming depression as deep as possible seems to me to be the true moral hazard.

7

Recent Changes in International Monetary Fund

Much about the international economy has changed since the end of World War II. In addition, much of what the IMF has done has resulted in failure. The IMF remains ineffective because

IMF lending is more likely to create long-term dependency than to act as short-term assistance. IMF lending, as defined by its articles, is supposed to be short term. But according to economist Doug Bandow, most countries actually become long-term users of IMF loans. A review of IMF lending activities reveals an increasing reliance on the fund by less-developed countries.

For example, between 1965 and 1995, 137 countries received loans from the IMF. For 81 of these countries, the number of times they borrowed from the IMF between 1981 and 1995 increased an average of nearly 50 percent over the number of times they borrowed between 1965 and 1980. Only 44 countries reduced the number of times they borrowed during the same periods; 12 maintained activities at similar levels. This means the IMF is extending loans to more countries with greater frequency than it has in the past, thereby involving greater total amounts of assistance than was the case before 1980. Thus, the IMF has not been able to ensure that its loans to less-developed countries are indeed in the short term. Instead, these loans have been more likely to create long-term dependence.

The IMF has failed to help less-developed countries improve economically. In addition to weakening much of the world economy generally, IMF lending has hurt less-developed countries specifically. For example, a review of IMF loan recipients indicates that most are no better off economically today (measured in per capita wealth) than they were before receiving these loans. In fact, many are poorer: Forty-eight of the eighty-nine less-developed countries that received IMF money between 1965 and 1995 are no better off economically than they were before; thirty-two of these forty-eight countries are poorer than before; and fourteen of these thirty-two countries have economies that are at least 15 percent smaller than they were before their first IMF loan or purchase.

The economies of some recipient countries have performed especially poorly.

For example:

1. From 1968 to 1995, Nicaragua received approximately $185 million in IMF loans. In 1968, per capita gross domestic product (GDP), measured in constant 1987 U.S. dollars, was $1,821; in 1993, it was only $816, or 55 percent less than it had been before Nicaragua received any loans.
2. From 1972 to 1995, Zaire received approximately $1.8 billion in IMF loans. In 1972, per capita GDP, measured in constant 1987 U.S. dollars, was $683; in 1993, it was only $317, or some 54 percent less than it had been before Zaire received any loans.

The inescapable conclusion is that IMF efforts to encourage economic growth have been dismal failures. Whether this has been caused by the recipient countries' poor adherence to IMF policy prescriptions or by flaws within these prescriptions themselves does nothing to alter this conclusion. Harvard economist Jeffrey Sachs believes both may be at fault: "Countries that comply with IMF/WB [World Bank] programs seem to outperform countries that do not. At the same time, however, even countries in compliance with IMF/WB programs experience poor to mediocre growth performance."

ELIGIBILITY FOR IMF CREDITS

Even with today's flexible exchange rates, eligibility for IMF credits continues to depend on the state of the balance of payments. Article V, Section 3.b.ii, of the IMF's Articles of Agreement states the following:

A member shall be entitled to purchase the currencies of other members from the fund... subject to the condition [that] it has a need to make the purchase because of its balance of payments or its reserve position or development of its reserves.

That condition is regarded as fulfilled if, for example, the country's gross hard currency reserves have declined. But a drop in foreign exchange reserves can be deliberately induced--in the case of fixed exchange rates, by increasing the domestic component of the monetary base, and in the case of adjustable parities, by revaluing the domestic currency. Neither choice of economic policy indicates an emergency situation.

In fact, there is considerable evidence that IMF borrowers are largely responsible for their own balance of payments problems. Sebastian Edwards's study of twenty-three developing countries under fixed exchange rates in 1965-72 confirms that excess supply of money tended "to result in international reserves dropping below desired levels." An unpublished IMF study conducted in 1981 even concluded that, in 1964-73, overexpansionary demand policies were the principal cause of balance of payments problems in borrowing countries, while exogenous factors were least important. A study by Thomas Reichmann shows that overexpansionary demand policies were the major factors in fifteen of twenty-one developing countries that had standby arrangements with the IMF during 1973-75.

An analysis by Mohsin Khan and Malcolm Knight concluded that over the whole period of 1973-80, the budget deficit (relative to gross domestic product) was the second most important factor, after their terms of trade, in explaining developing countries' current account balances. An internal IMF working paper by Donal Donovan demonstrated that overexpansionary monetary and fiscal policies also contributed to a country's debt-servicing problems. In the five years before the debt crisis of the 1980s, the rescheduling countries shared the following characteristics:

- Considerably higher rates of net credit expansion to government (13.4 percent annually) than the nonrescheduling countries (5.9 percent annually)
- Considerably higher rates of M_2 monetary expansion (31.9 percent annually) than the nonrescheduling countries (22.8 percent annually)
- Not surprisingly, considerably higher consumer price inflation (23.8 percent annually) than the nonrescheduling countries (14.3 percent annually)

If it is true that the IMF wants to maximize its lending and supervision, it cannot be interested in legal restrictions on eligibility that might effectively bar potential borrowers. The criterion of balance of payments need is not an effective barrier. The IMF admits that "the requirement of need is in the nature of a portmanteau concept. It is a term of art rather than of law.... Reliance on judgmental factors is unavoidable." The governments of the typical borrower countries obviously share an interest in lending conditions that are as easy as possible to meet. But that arrangement is also advantageous for the influential creditor countries since it permits them to use IMF lending in pursuit of their own foreign policy objectives, as the United States did in 1982 when the debt crisis caused the Reagan administration to reverse its opposition to an IMF quota increase.

THE MACROECONOMIC EFFECTS OF FUND-SUPPORTED ADJUSTMENT PROGRAMS

A question that is frequently raised in connection with fund-supported programs is whether such programs have been effective in achieving their macroeconomic objectives. Some writers have argued that, at best, fund programs do little in the way of improving the economic picture, while others have gone as far as to say that programs worsen the situation by inducing stagflation. Providing a clear-cut answer to this question turns out to be no easy task. There is at present little agreement in the profession either about how to estimate the macroeconomic effects of programs or about what impact past programs have actually had on the principal macroeconomic variables the fund typically is concerned with. Although there have been a number of studies on the subject over the past decade, one cannot say with certainty whether programs have "worked" or not.

Before turning to a discussion of the alternative methodologies used in the evaluation of programs, it is important to define how the effects of programs ought to be measured. At the most general level, it has been argued that macroeconomic performance under a program should be compared to the "counterfactual"--defined as the macroeconomic performance that would have taken place in the absence of a program. The counterfactual is perhaps the most appealing yardstick against which to assess program performance and the standard most widely employed in economics to measure the impact of government policy interventions.

What would have happened in the absence of a fund-supported program is by no means the only standard against which to judge the outcomes of programs, but in many cases it is the most appropriate one. However, the counterfactual cannot, by definition, be observed and must be estimated or approximated. The various approaches used in evaluation studies should thus be judged in terms of how good they are in providing estimates of the counterfactual.

The literature suggests that four distinct approaches have been applied to the evaluation of fund-supported adjustment programs: (1) the before-after approach, which compares macroeconomic performance during a program and performance prior to the program; (2) the with-without approach, which compares macroeconomic performance in countries with programs and performance in a "control group" of countries without programs; (3) the actual-versus-target approach, which compares actual macroeconomic performance under the program and the performance specified in its targets; and (4) the comparison-of-simulations approach, which compares the simulated performance of fund program-type policies and simulated performance with some other set of policies.

In the discussion that follows, the studies are grouped according to the approach that was employed by them.

Before-after Approach

In the literature on the effects of fund-supported programs, the before-after approach has been the most popular. The first study to use this approach was by Reichmann and Stillson (1978). These authors examined a total of seventy-nine fund-supported programs implemented during 1963-72 and compared the behavior of the balance of payments, inflation, and growth during the two-year periods before and after the implementation of the program. Using nonparametric statistical tests, they found that there was a significant improvement in the balance of payments in only about one-fourth of all programs. In a majority of cases (over 70 percent) there was no significant change in the balance of payments. Of the twenty-nine programs involving countries with high inflation during the program period, the rate of inflation fell in six of eleven programs for which there was a notable deceleration in the rate of domestic credit expansion; in the nine programs involving a devaluation, there were five in which inflation was higher. Finally, growth performance was examined for seventy programs, and it was concluded that, on balance, fund-supported programs did not exert adverse effects on growth rates. In 40 percent of programs the growth rate declined after the inception of the program relative to the previous two years' average rate of growth, but at the same time growth was higher in 47 percent of the programs.

A similar procedure was followed by Connors (1979), who examined a total of thirty-one programs in twenty-three countries that were adopted during the 1973-77 period. He compared periods of one year before and after the programs. Also using a nonparametric rank test, Connors concluded that fund programs had no discernible effects on the ultimate targets--growth, inflation, and the current account deficit--or on important intermediate targets, such as the ratio of the fiscal deficit to gross domestic product (GDP).

The relationship between fiscal variables and fund program performance was examined in more detail by Kelly (1982). The methodology was primarily of the before-after variety, and in order to take into account possible lags in adjustment, comparisons were made over both one-year and three-year periods. In a sample of seventy-seven programs (covering thirty-three countries) during 1971-80, Kelly observed that when a one-year comparison was used, the fiscal deficit was reduced in 56 percent of the cases and that the current account and fiscal deficits moved in the same direction in 62 percent of the programs examined. This last result was also supported by regression analysis that showed a positive and statistically significant relationship between changes in the ratio of the fiscal deficit to gross national product (GNP) and changes in the ratio of the current account to GNP. Furthermore, in about half the cases there was a decline in the average growth rate over a three-year period and an increase or no change in the other half.

A study by Killick (1984) also attempted to capture the effects of lags by comparing the behavior of the balance of payments, the current account, growth, and inflation a year before the program with the behavior both one and two years after the program. Killick employed nonparametric statistical tests to gauge the effects of thirty-eight programs covering twenty-four countries during the period 1974-79. In contrast to other studies, Killick found that the balance of payments and the current account deteriorated irrespective of the time period over which the comparison was made. However, the difference between the preprogram and postprogram values of these variables was not statistically significant. Inflation was reduced, but the effects on growth were ambiguous. In the first year after the program the rate of growth was higher, but by the second year the positive effect had eroded and the net effect was zero.

Zulu and Nsouli (1985) also constructed before-after measures of program effects in their study of thirty-five programs implemented in 1980-81 for twenty-two African countries. They found that growth was lower or the same in the year after the program in about 60 percent of the cases. For the current account and inflation targets, the split was even--with as many programs showing an improvement in the current account and inflation performance as those showing a worsening or no change. The most recent study using the before-after approach was that by Pastor (1987) for eighteen Latin American countries during 1965-81. Using one-year comparisons and on the basis of alternative statistical tests, Pastor concluded that fund programs led to a significant improvement in the balance of payments but that apparently there was no effect on the current account, inflation, or the rate of growth of nominal GDP.

With-without Approach

The with-without approach is designed to overcome the inability of the before-after approach to distinguish between program and nonprogram determinants of macroeconomic outcomes. The basic reasoning behind this approach is as follows. Assume countries with and without programs are subject to the same nonprogram determinants--that is, they face the same external environment. Then, so the argument goes, by comparing before-after changes in outcomes in program countries to those in the control group of nonprogram countries, the effects of nonprogram determinants will cancel out--leaving the difference in group performance to reflect only the effects of fund-supported programs. Put in terms of the counterfactual, the idea is to use the observed performance of nonprogram countries as an estimate of what the performance of program countries would have been in the absence of a fund-supported program.

The with-without group approach was first used in two studies by Donovan (1981, 1982), which analyzed a sample of programs implemented from 1970 to 1980. The control group of countries without programs was taken to consist of all nonoil developing countries, and the comparisons were carried out over one-year and three-year time horizons. In the first study (Donovan 1981), which covered a sample of twelve programs (for twelve countries) implemented during 1970-76, the improvement in the rate of growth of exports was consistently higher for program countries than for all nonoil developing countries. The increase in the rate of inflation for program countries was about half that of the control group during the first year, and although it rose when three-year comparisons were undertaken, it was nevertheless well below the average increase in the rate of inflation of all non-oil developing countries. The outcome for growth was not as clear-cut. In the one-year comparison there was a sharp improvement in growth in program countries relative to the control group, but in the three-year comparisons growth in countries fell by more than it did in nonprogram countries.

In Donovan (1982) the sample of programs was expanded to seventy-eight, covering the period 1971-80, and the same analysis as in the first study was undertaken. The balance of payments and the current account positions of program countries were found to improve relative to the control group in both the one-year and three-year comparisons. The increase in inflation in program countries was about half that of nonoil developing countries in the one-year comparisons and fell to one-third in the three-year comparisons. However, in contrast to the results of the first study, the rate of growth of real GDP fell by more than the average decline experienced by nonoil developing countries in the one-year comparisons but by less in the three-year comparisons.

Loxley (1984) applied the same types of tests as Donovan (1982) to a group of thirty-eight least-developed economies (defined as countries with per capita incomes of $690 or less in 1980) that had programs with the fund during 1971-82. His results, however, were less definitive than those obtained by Donovan, in that the least-developed countries with programs did no better, on average, in terms of current account, balance of payments, and growth performance relative to other least-developed countries without programs, the program countries examined by Donovan, and all nonoil developing countries. The improvement was statistically significant only in the case of inflation and then only in the three-year comparisons.

Gylfason (1987) also used a version of the with-without approach in his study of thirty-two programs implemented during 1977-79. The reference group included the developing countries that had experienced balance of payments difficulties during 1975-77, and nonparametric statistical tests were used to determine if the behavior of the macroeconomic variables for program countries over a three-year period was significantly different from that of the reference group. First, there was an improvement in the balance of payments in program countries relative to the outcomes in the control group. Second, inflation in program countries did not fall but rather remained approximately the same as the average rate of inflation in the group. Third, the growth rate was not significantly affected by the program.

This pattern of results was basically replicated by Pastor (1987) for Latin American countries. Employing the same statistical methodology as Gylfason, Pastor also found that the balance of payments performance of program countries was significantly better than that of nonprogram countries and that the differences in inflation and growth performance were not statistically significant.

While the with-without approach copes with some of the problems of the before-after approach, it is by no means ideal. The problem is that program countries differ systematically from nonprogram countries prior to the program period, and this difference matters for performance evaluation. In short, program countries are not randomly selected. Instead, they are adversely selected in the sense of having relatively poor economic performance prior to the program period. This is not surprising since, after all, a basic requirement for fund financial support is that the country have a balance of payments need. This requirement alone suggests that program countries would be expected to have weaker than average external positions when the program was implemented.

In any case, nonrandom selection of program countries means that simple with-without estimates of program effects may be biased. Intuitively, the bias occurs because, under nonrandom selection, the with-without estimator attributes differences in outcomes exclusively to program status, when in fact the difference in starting positions itself is a cause of differences in subsequent performance between the two groups. Furthermore, the direction of the bias can go either way. If past economic difficulties signal less-serious current difficulties, even in the absence of a program, then the with-without approach will overstate the beneficial effect of a fund-supported program.

Conversely, if past difficulties signal even more serious present difficulties, then the effect of programs will be understated. There are ways, however, as discussed by Goldstein and Montiel (1986), to modify the with-without approach to reduce some of the biases.

Goldstein and Montiel (1986) applied the generalized evaluation estimator to a sample of sixty-eight programs for fifty-eight developing countries implemented during 1974-81. These authors found that program countries systematically demonstrated weaker performance--that is, higher inflation, slower growth, and larger current account and overall balance of payments deficits--than nonprogram countries in the preprogram period. Adjusting for these preprogram differences in performances and taking into account the effects of policy instruments on targets, Goldstein and Montiel used regression analysis to estimate the program effects.

Two interesting sets of results emerged from this study. First, there were no statistically significant effects of programs on the current account and balance of payments, on the rate of inflation, or on the growth of real output. Second, the estimated program effects under the generalized evaluation estimation were quite different from those obtained with the standard with-without estimator. The latter indicated an improvement in the current account, a slight worsening of the balance of payments, a reduction in inflation, and a rise in the growth rate associated with programs. When the generalized evaluation estimator is used, the improvement in the current account ratio disappears, the deterioration in the balance of payments ratio is magnified, and the favorable outcomes for inflation and growth are reversed.

Actual-versus-targets Approach

Another strand in the literature on program effects compares actual outcomes for certain key macroeconomic variables to the targets for such variables specified by the authorities and the fund at the inception of the program. This approach has not been as frequently used as the other two approaches. Reichmann (1978), for example, studied twenty-one programs for eighteen countries that were in effect during 1973-75 and compared the outcomes to targets for the balance of payments, inflation, and growth. He found that the balance of payments targets were met or exceeded in nearly two-thirds of the programs. The targets for inflation were, however, exceeded in over half the programs. Greater success was achieved in the case of the rate of growth, with 62 percent of programs meeting the targets.

In a similar vein, Beveridge and Kelly (1980) surveyed the fiscal content of all 105 programs supported by the fund that were approved during 1969-78. Their focus was on intermediate targets--domestic credit expansion, government revenues and expenditures, and deficit financing--rather than on the final macroeconomic objectives. Nevertheless, the results for the intermediate targets are informative since achieving these is generally a necessary condition for meeting the ultimate targets for the balance of payments, inflation, and growth.

Beveridge and Kelly showed that almost all programs contained government revenue and expenditure forecasts and that both actual expenditures and revenues tended to differ from these forecasts. A shortfall in revenues occurred in about 40 percent of the cases, while expenditures were above projected values in nearly 60 percent of the programs. Consequently, the overall fiscal deficit targets were achieved in only about half the programs, as were the domestic credit ceilings. Finally, governments were more successful in meeting domestic nonbank financing limits than foreign financing targets. The former were satisfied in almost 70 percent of the programs, but foreign financing of the fiscal deficit exceeded the target in over 60 percent of the cases.

Zulu and Nsouli (1985) also analyzed actual outcomes and targets in their study of programs in African countries approved in 1980-81. They found that the current account targets were met in 38 percent of programs, and the inflation targets in about 48 percent of the cases, but growth targets were only achieved in less than 20 percent of the programs.

Provisions of Financing Programs

Preconditions are actions taken by a country before the IMF executive board will authorize a program.

Performance criteria are benchmarks that, if violated by a country, lead to suspension of further loan disbursements by the fund until a new agreement is reached.

Policy understandings are actions that a country agrees to take but that do not have any explicit sanction associated with nonperformance.

Typical IMF Financing Preconditions and Performance Criteria:

- General commitment to cooperate with the IMF in setting policies
- Reducing government spending, budget deficits, and foreign (external) debt
- Reducing the rate of money growth to control inflation
- Ending government monopolies (i.e., privatization)
- Deregulating industries and reforming the banking sector
- Redirecting domestic credit from the public to the private sector
- Ending government wage, price, and interest-rate controls and government subsidies
- Raising real interest rates to market levels
- Removing barriers to export growth
- Lowering tariffs, ending quotas, and removing exchange controls and discriminatory exchange rates
- Maintaining adequate levels of international reserves
- Devaluing the currency for countries in "fundamental disequilibrium".

BRIEF HISTORY

In 1944, the IMF was jointly established by forty-four member nations in an effort to promote international monetary stability and to facilitate the expansion and balanced growth of world trade. Article I of the fund's charter called on the IMF to make financial resources available to members, on a temporary basis and with adequate safeguards, to permit them to correct payments imbalances. In 1952, the principle of conditionality was implicitly incorporated into the fund's lending policies. Conditionality was conceived to encourage policies that would make it more likely for a member country to be able to cope with its balance of payments problem and to repay the fund within three to five years.

The inception of the practice of conditionality accompanied the birth of the "standby arrangement." In its infancy, the standby arrangement was intended to be a precautionary device to ensure access on the part of members who had no immediate need for such resources in the near future. The standby arrangement, however, matured quickly into a device for linking economic policies to financial assistance. The standby arrangement can be described as a "line of credit outlining the circumstances under which a member can make drawings on the fund" (Guitian 1981, 14). On 20 September 1968, the fund decided to incorporate the practice of conditionality explicitly into its charter. Before this date, the concept of conditionality had generally been referred to in a vague manner. The amendments to the fund's Articles of Agreement in 1968 ended this confusion by introducing, for the first time, clear language that outlined the fund's position with respect to conditionality.

Until the mid-1970s, the typical conditions placed on the use of fund resources involved policies that influenced the level and composition of aggregate demand. During this period, excess demand was perceived as the most important cause of inflation, currency overvaluation, and ultimately payment difficulties. The expeditious elimination of excess demand was viewed as an essential condition for restoring payments equilibrium. This position has often been referred to as the.

The monetarist approach views excess demand as the root cause of inflation and exchange-rate disequilibrium. Its goal is the rapid alleviation, typically in one year or less, of inflation and the restoration of exchange-rate equilibrium vis-...-vis policies that alter the size and composition of aggregate demand. Monetarist policies generally call for

1. Control of the money supply

2. Reduction of the government deficit
3. Exchange-rate devaluation
4. Deregulation of prices
5. Reduction of consumer subsidies
6. Elimination of tariff and non-tariff trade barriers

In the mid-1970s, the monetarist strategy gave way to a more structural, longer-run approach. The introduction of this new approach to payments adjustment was precipitated by the growing recognition, both within and outside the fund, that payment imbalances could no longer be expected to be corrected within one year. In response to this recognition, the fund increased its support for programs that called for adjustment over a longer period. In 1974, the fund established the "extended fund facility," which was designed to provide members with up to three years of financial support. In addition, the fund decided in 1979 to allow standby arrangements to be extended for up to three years.

This development was accompanied by growing support for more comprehensive programs designed to affect the balance of payments through changes in supply as well as in demand. These programs continued to rely on the typical monetarist instruments but in a more gradual manner. In addition, they called for more-structural, supply-oriented policies such as reducing the size of the public sector, channeling resources away from the public sector and into the private sector, creating financial intermediaries, promoting savings, and discouraging wasteful investment by increasing real interest rates. To facilitate the success of these enlarged programs, the fund increased by six times the amount of resources that member countries were allowed to borrow. The "enlarged access policy" of 1981 authorized members to accumulate a maximum of up to 600 percent of their donation (quota) to the fund.

NEW CONDITIONALITY GUIDELINES

The Executive Board of the IMF has approved new guidelines on the design and implementation of conditionality in Fund-supported programs. The guidelines represent the culmination of a comprehensive and far-reaching review of conditionality launched two years ago with the purpose of enhancing the effectiveness of Fund-supported programs. They also represent the first revision of the IMF's conditionality guidelines since 1979. The process of revising the IMF's approach to conditionality was initiated by Managing Director Horst Köhler, after taking up his position in May 2000, and received the firm backing of the Board of Governors at the September 2000 Prague Annual Meetings. The new guidelines were developed by the Fund after seeking input from civil society and public forums held in several countries. The Executive Board discussed a series of staff papers on the topic over the past two years before considering the actual guidelines.

The review and the guidelines it produced were undertaken with the aim of streamlining and focusing conditionality so as to enhance the success and effectiveness of Fund-supported programs and to promote national ownership of reforms. Thus, an important purpose of the guidelines is to improve the interaction between the Fund and borrowing countries as they work together to promote sustainable growth and development.

The guidelines emphasize the need to focus conditionality on policies that are critical to achieving the macroeconomic objectives of Fund-supported programs. They also aim to establish a clearer division of labor with other international institutions, especially the World Bank. The guidelines are based on an increasing recognition of the importance of several interrelated principles, including national ownership of policy reforms; parsimony in the application of program-related conditions; tailoring of programs to the member's circumstances; and clarity in the specification of conditions.

The new guidelines introduce specific criteria for deciding whether conditions are appropriate in each case. Structural conditionality is regarded as an important element of Fund-support programs, as long as it is critical to achieving the macroeconomic objectives of the program. The guidelines also spell out the roles of different types of program-related conditions, including performance criteria, structural benchmarks, and prior actions. A note by IMF staff providing additional explanation and context for the conditionality guidelines was released along with the guidelines. An essential aspect of the IMF view of conditionality is that the member country should take primary responsibility for its own policies, and that documents setting out the country's reform agenda should be drafted as much as possible by the authorities rather than by Fund staff. The Executive Board agreed during the course of its review that properly designed conditionality can complement and reinforce national ownership.

CONDITIONALITY OPERATIONS

Once the IMF has determined the balance of payments need of a member and its eligibility to draw on resources under one or more facilities, the IMF must be satisfied that the member can meet its repayment obligations to the IMF. It therefore provides financial resources to members on certain conditions designed to encourage appropriate economic adjustment and ensure that the member's use of IMF credit is temporary and that it will have the capacity to repay the IMF on time. These conditions are meant to reduce a member's balance of payments deficit to a manageable size while fostering economic growth, employment, and financial stability and eliminating restrictions on international trade and payments.

Consequently, policy benchmarks and performance criteria, often referred to as conditionality, represent a crucial element in the use of IMF resources by members. Conditionality seeks to ensure that the member's policies are adequate to achieve a viable balance of payments position and sustainable economic growth over a reasonable period; that steps are taken toward structural adjustment, as necessary; and that, in addressing balance of payments and structural problems, financing and adjustment work in tandem.

The IMF's guidelines on conditionality, which are reviewed periodically, stipulate that the IMF, in designing adjustment programs, is required to pay due regard to the domestic social and political objectives of member countries and to their economic priorities and circumstances. In its most recent review in July 1994 of the experience with conditionality in IMF-supported adjustment programs, the Executive Board concluded that the guidelines on conditionality adopted in 1979 continued in general to provide an appropriate basis for IMF policies on the use of its resources.

Conditionality may vary with individual programs, as well as with the types of policies or facilities used; it is not a rigid and inflexible set of operational rules. For example, a lower degree of conditionality is associated with the financing of strictly temporary shortfalls in members' export receipts under the Compensatory Contingency Financing Facility than under upper credit tranche arrangements. The guidelines also provide for the incorporation of review and consultation clauses, the inclusion of performance clauses, and the phasing of purchases in Stand-By Arrangements that go beyond the first credit tranche and in Extended Arrangements.

Performance during the period of a Stand-By or Extended Arrangement in support of a member's adjustment program is monitored by means of performance criteria. The conditionality guidelines specify that performance criteria should be limited to those economic variables necessary to ensure that the objectives of IMF-supported programs are met. Performance criteria are normally confined to macroeconomic variables and to those necessary to implement specific provisions of the IMF's Articles or policies adopted under them. Performance criteria may also relate to other (microeconomic) variables when these have a bearing on the effectiveness of the member's adjustment program because of their macroeconomic impact.

The broad objective of balance of payments adjustment policies as embodied in IMF-supported programs is to achieve a current account position that can be sustained by normal capital flows, without resort to restrictions on trade and payments or payments arrears. In response to the substantial changes in the nature and magnitude of economic disequilibria facing members, IMF-supported programs have for several years placed more emphasis on structural reform and the achievement of sustainable economic growth. More recently, the financial crises of 1994-95 and 1997-98 have resulted in an increased focus on (1) the soundness of countries' financial sectors and the need for strengthening banking supervision, prudential norms, and/or regulation, and (2) the role of the globalization of financial markets in external crises and the need for IMF involvement in supervision and management of orderly capital account liberalization.

GUESS WHO CALLS THE TUNE AT IMF?

How can we IMF staffers have a "wrinkle" ("The IMF Wrinkle," Review & Outlook, 10 April 1998) if we're "faceless bureaucrats." Obviously your editorialists continue to grasp at straws in a vain effort to persuade the public that IMF policy prescriptions are invented by wayward, ignorant, and coddled staff members. How else could they fail to prescribe tax cuts anywhere and everywhere all the time without regard to yawning budget deficits? How else to explain their occasional support for currency devaluations (presumably in lieu of deflation, exchange controls, and unlimited lender of last resort bailouts of currency traders)?

But truth be told, staff views don't matter very much. What you seem to have difficulty accepting is that the country representatives on the IMF board--where the United States and other hard currency countries wield the most votes--call the tune. They, not anonymous staff, decide which tax policy and exchange-rate recommendations are preferable. So long as most national leaders and their IMF directors do not share fully Robert Bartley's [editor of the Wall Street Journal] confessional, it's hardly fair to blame IMF staff.

But there must also be a reason why you pretend to believe the proposed IMF quota increase is the personal project of IMF managing director Camdessus rather than the consensus of 182 national governments. Probably it's just too hard to face up to the necessity for backing serious international monetary cooperation with serious lines of credit, just in case global markets don't always work right. That's enough to furrow the editorial brow, indeed.

THE IMF WRINKLE

Michel Camdessus, who's asking the U.S. taxpayer for a fresh $18 billion for the International Monetary Fund, personally takes home $224,650 a year as head of that august body. A fund station chief, say the guy in Djakarta telling President Suharto what hoops to jump through, makes roughly $120,000. The average professional staff member makes $94,341.

The president of the United States is paid $200,000. A congressman voting on the IMF package makes $136,673. The highest-paid--not average--congressional staff members make $123,000. The IMF staff, though, has a wrinkle. The president, the congressmen, and the Capitol Hill staffers have to pay taxes out of their salaries. The folks at the IMF don't.

U.S. nationals working for the IMF at its Washington headquarters, for example, of course must file tax returns and pay Uncle Sam. But what happens next is a bureaucrat's dream. The IMF compensates its employees--wherever they work--for income taxes paid. There is also a generous bundle of perquisites and allowances that ensures that IMF staff under their tax-exempt umbrella can live in tasteful quarters abroad and send their children on an IMF ticket to assorted private schools and universities.

What all this means is that IMF staffers, in prescribing policies for the world at large, do not have to live with their own medicine. They are personally shielded from many of the very policies they like to inflict on others worldwide. From their Washington headquarters they roam the globe, prescribing tax hikes for Thailand, devaluations for Indonesia, and bailouts they describe as costing nothing but for which U.S. taxpayers bear the risk of lending money to a growing list of sinking economies. When the working day's done, however, and it's time for take-home pay, IMF staff can count on steady salaries in U.S. dollars, net of taxes.

It's a point that just might help clarify matters in a debate over IMF funding that has left many members of Congress bored or simply baffled by the intricacies of Mr. Camdessus's many projects. Mr. Camdessus is looking for a 45 percent increase in funding and hopes to have at his command a capital base of some $285 billion; his $18 billion sailed through the Senate on an 84-16 vote. House majority leader Dick Armey has tried to get some debate started in that chamber, complaining about "mission creep" as the IMF goes from a lender of last resort to running all the world's economies and even governments. Representative Spencer Bachus promises to explore what the IMF is doing in hearings in a subcommittee he heads.

The amounts involved in asking IMF employees to pay taxes like anyone else may be small relative to Mr. Camdessus's dreams, or even the hundreds of billions the fund has been tossing around these past few years to bail out places like Mexico and East Asia.

And the policies these billions leverage out of client nations, such as Indonesia, affect mainly the faraway folks who have to pay for their daily bread in devalued rupiah and render up higher taxes under IMF programs for Djakarta. But a good look at IMF staff taxes could give the average congressperson a good glimpse of the mentality of the place.

Indeed, if only IMF policy shapers had some of their own pocket change at risk, they just might prove more cautious about pushing for things like higher taxes and bigger bailouts. Happily, there may be help on the way. Representative Ed Royce (R., Calif.) tells us he is prepared to add to the IMF funding bill an amendment instructing the U.S. Treasury to demand that the IMF scrap its practice of "compensating IMF employees for taxes paid in their home countries." A modest proposal but one that would remind IMF staffers, as they tinker with tax policies around the globe, that there is such a thing as the real world.

FOSTERING A SUSTAINED POLICY IMPLEMENTATION

When it provides financial support to a member country, the IMF must be sure that the member is pursuing policies that will ameliorate or eliminate its external payments problem. The explicit commitment that members make to implement remedial measures in return for the IMF's support is known as conditionality. This commitment also ensures that members are able to repay the IMF in a timely manner--which allows the IMF's limited pool of financial resources to revolve and be available to other members with a balance of payments problem.

IMF financing, and the important catalytic effect it has in securing other financing, enables the country to adjust in an orderly fashion, without resort to measures that would be inimical to its own or other countries' prosperity.

Conditions for IMF financial support may range from general commitments to cooperate with the IMF in setting policies to the formulation of specific, quantified plans for financial policies. IMF financing from its general resources in the "upper credit tranches" (that is, where larger amounts are disbursed in return for implementation of remedial measures) is phased. The IMF requires a "letter of intent," which outlines a government's policy intentions during the period of the adjustment program; policy changes to be taken before approval of the arrangement; performance criteria, which are objective indicators for certain policies that must be satisfied on a quarterly, semiannual, or in some instances a monthly basis for drawings to be made; and periodic reviews that allow the executive board to assess the consistency of policies with the objectives of the program.

CONDITIONALITY IS FLEXIBLE

Although IMF conditionality employs specified performance criteria, it does not rely on a rigid set of operational rules. The executive board's guidelines on conditionality:

- Encourage members to adopt corrective measures at an early stage
- Stress that the IMF pay due regard to members' domestic social and political objectives, as well as economic priorities and circumstances
- Permit flexibility in determining the number and content of performance criteria
- Emphasize that IMF arrangements are decisions of the IMF that set out--in consultation with members--the conditions for its financial assistance

CONDITIONALITY IN PRACTICE

The IMF takes a pragmatic approach to helping members formulate economic reform programs, recognizing that no one model suits all members. Each IMF-supported program is designed by the member country in close collaboration with the IMF staff. The process involves a comprehensive review of the member's economy, including the causes and nature of the balance of payments problems and an analysis of the policies needed to achieve a sustainable balance between the demand for, and the availability of, resources.

IMF-supported programs emphasize certain key aggregate economic variables--domestic credit, the public sector deficit, international reserves, and external debt--and crucial elements of the pricing system--including the exchange rate, interest rates, and, in some cases, commodity prices--that significantly affect the country's public finances and foreign trade and the economy's supply response.

During a standby or extended fund arrangement or during an arrangement under the enhanced structural adjustment facility, a member's reform program is monitored by the IMF through performance criteria selected according to the economic and institutional structure of the country, the availability of data, and the desirability of focusing on broad macroeconomic variables, among other considerations. Performance under IMF-supported reform programs is also monitored through periodic reviews by the IMF executive board.

GROWTH ORIENTED ADJUSTMENT

While macroeconomic policies designed to influence aggregate demand continue to play a key role in IMF-supported adjustment programs, it is widely recognized that measures to strengthen the supply side of the economy are frequently essential to bring about a sustained return of external viability and sound growth. IMF-supported policy adjustments by member countries to enhance the growth potential and flexibility of their economies include measures to remove distortions in the external trade system and in domestic relative prices, measures to improve the efficiency and soundness of the financial system, and measures to foster greater efficiency in government spending. Structural reforms in these areas have been particularly important in programs under the extended fund facility and the enhanced structural adjustment facility.

Given the emphasis on structural reforms in IMF-supported programs, close collaboration with the World Bank has been important.

TRADE RELATED CONDITIONALITY

In October 1997, the board considered a staff report on trade reform in medium-term IMF-supported programs. Directors felt that trade liberalization should play an important role in IMF-supported programs. They agreed that, in addition to promoting efficient resource allocation, trade reform was important in fostering transparency and good governance and in reducing the scope for administrative discretion, incentives to lobby for protection, and opportunities for rent seeking. The analysis of countries' trade policies in the report was based on an index of trade restrictiveness, which directors generally welcomed as a valuable tool for classifying the relative restrictiveness of trade regimes.

Many directors supported front-loaded liberalization measures and the use of prior actions, performance criteria, structural benchmarks, and reviews to monitor implementation of trade reforms. Other directors cautioned that trade-related conditionality should be applied flexibly and should take into account each country's initial conditions, the degree of political support, and the authorities' own commitment to reforms. For trade reform to succeed, directors remarked, it should be broadly based and should initially replace non-tariff barriers with tariffs, while eliminating customs duties exemptions and trade-related subsidies, all of which would tend to strengthen the government's fiscal position or at least avoid revenue losses.

SOCIAL SAFETY NETS

Adjustment programs typically have an impact on income distribution, employment, and social services. While sound macroeconomic policies and effective structural reforms promote sustained growth and employment, the adjustment process itself may involve short-term social costs for vulnerable groups. Measures built into IMF-supported programs address these costs. In collaboration with the World Bank staff, the IMF staff analyzes the social implications of reform measures and advises the authorities on how best to design social safety nets and target them to assist the neediest groups.

PROBLEMS WITH CONDITIONALITY

There are several problems with IMF lending, though the organization makes it hard to judge its activities. Jeffrey Sachs, director of the Harvard Institute for International Development, for instance, has complained about IMF secrecy that "makes it extremely difficult for outside observers to prepare a serious quantitative appraisal of IMF policies." The details of IMF standby agreements are not reported, and the organization refuses to release audits of its loans. Ultimately, however, the best test of the IMF's achievements is whether borrowers seem to be making progress as a result of the fund's activities. Alas, the fund appears to flunk that test, for several reasons.

Inappropriate Conditions

The IMF has often focused on narrow accounting data, causing its advice to have perverse consequences. As a condition for a loan the IMF will, for instance, demand that a nation reduce its current account deficit--so the borrower restricts imports. Insistence that a country cut its budget deficit may cause the government to raise taxes, slowing growth. In fact, the IMF has explicitly lobbied for higher levies, pushing the administration of Argentina's president Carlos Menem to increase the value-added tax, for instance, and advocating that Mauritius adopt "a series of new taxes." Even where the budget deficit does not actually grow as the economy shrinks, the fund has succeeded in reducing the budget deficit only by reinforcing the very borrower policies, such as high taxes, that block growth.

There are obviously some cases in which the IMF does push for sensible reform. However, the "toughness" of the fund's conditionality has varied over time. Economist John Williamson reported that analysis showed "enormous variation between one program and another." Among the factors causing the fund to vary its conditions was, admitted Williamson, pressure "to lend money in order to justify having it."

Moreover, even setting some useful conditions may have little impact if other policies still cause serious distortions in the borrowing country. Observed Raymond Mikesell, who in 1983 estimated that more than half of the less-developed countries were following self-destructive interventionist economic policies, "The continued existence of these conditions [such as price controls] in a substantial proportion of the [less-developed countries] suggests that not enough attention is being given to policy reform in the negotiation and implementation of the IMF conditionality programs."

Lack of Enforcement

Moreover, the IMF, like the World Bank, does not do enough to enforce its conditions. If a country violates its agreement with the IMF, the organization may simply grant a waiver, modifying the offending conditions. Or the fund may suspend the loan, only to later negotiate a new agreement. Money will start to flow again, the borrower will violate the new conditions, the IMF will hold up payments, the loan will be renegotiated, and the process will begin anew. How else can one explain seventeen different arrangements with Peru between 1971 and 1977, eight separate standby programs for Brazil between 1965 and 1972, decades' worth of credit for Zaire, and so on? In fact, the largest Third World borrowers between 1947 and 1987 were India, Brazil, Argentina, Mexico, and Yugoslavia, all of which maintained state-managed economies throughout the period despite the fund's loan conditions.

The IMF seems to measure success by making loans. The assumption is that financial input into poor countries automatically translates into growth output; thus, to not extend credit is to fail. Members of President George Bush's administration obviously had a similar view; Treasury secretary Nicholas Brady, for instance, proposed a new World Bank fund supported by the IMF. President Bill Clinton, a fervent backer of increased aid for Moscow, appears to share the same credit-equals-growth assumption. Yet shoveling more money into essentially insolvent states that have squandered billions in prior loans makes no sense. IMF conditionality would likely be more effective if the fund's refusal to make new loans were based on factors other than a country's inability or unwillingness to repay past IMF loans.

Statist Subsidies

As noted earlier, however sensible the IMF's conditions, they mean little when a nation's overall policy climate is badly askew. In general, the fund asks countries to take too few of the steps necessary to promote growth; nevertheless, the left still regularly attacks the fund for allegedly advocating capitalism. But John Williamson [senior fellow at the Institute for International Economics] has defended the IMF against the criticism that it is too market oriented.

It has also been charged that the Fund is biased against socialism. That the Fund welcomes those governments that are willing to work with market forces cannot be doubted. At the same time, the Fund clearly does not have an evangelical zeal for spreading "the magic of the market" parallel to that of, say, the Reagan administration. Its attitude, it would claim, is non-ideological: it seeks to promote economic rationality, and it just happens that under a wide range of circumstances the readiest means to that end involves harnessing, instead of fighting, market forces.

What is surely true is that the Fund does not refuse to provide financial assistance to members with left-wing governments. On the contrary. [In 1982] some 16.5 percent of IMF credit was directed to the six communist member countries (China, Kampuchea, Laos, Romania, Vietnam, and Yugoslavia...) and Michael Manley's Jamaica was at one stage the heaviest per capita borrower from the Fund.... Moreover, the Fund continued to give the Allende government [of Chile] the benefit of the doubt in drawing from the Compensatory Financing Facility.

The IMF similarly disclaims a bias against collectivist systems: "The fund has had programs in all types of economies and has worked with their authorities, identifying the best way to achieve external balance or exercising its function of surveillance over the payments and exchange system.... In many instances, fund-supported programs have accommodated such non-market devices as production controls, administered prices, and subsidies." Yet how is a country with such policies going to achieve self-sustaining economic growth?

It is hard to take seriously an organization's claim to be "prodevelopment" when it regularly pours large sums of money into the worst economic systems on earth.

One friend of the fund has argued "that to the extent that programs succeed in their objective of establishing macroeconomic stability in the economy, they can be expected to have a positive impact on growth in the longer run." But how often has the IMF been able to transform those policies that are bad in almost every way?

In an assessment of lending to communist states, for example, Valerie Assetto wrote that "Romania's economic reforms were superficial and actually worked to increase the power of the state.

The ensuing economic crisis quickly eclipsed the `reform' movement, and it quietly expired. Fund and [World] Bank support of the Romanian development effort continued throughout this period." Similarly, she found that the "Yugoslav authorities actually retreated slightly from the market orientation of the 1960s" despite generous assistance in following years.

As late as 1990 Michel Camdessus, managing director of the IMF, lauded the fact that the IMF remained engaged in Yugoslavia, supporting "a comprehensive and bold program to stop inflation in its tracks and to reform the economy over the medium term." Yet economists Jeffrey Sachs and David Lipton blamed the fund's conditions--particularly its commitment to continued devaluations--for helping to "cause Yugoslavia to drift from high inflation to hyperinflation."

At times it would appear that the more perverse the policies, the more generous the IMF. The problem is not just the former Soviet bloc, but the many Third World regimes that followed statist economic policies for decades. For instance, India collected more money than any other developing state from the IMF, which acted more as a lender of first rather than last resort, during its first forty years. Yet while India was borrowing prodigiously from the IMF (and other multilateral institutions), it was pursuing a Soviet-style industrialization program. Catherine Gwin of the Carnegie Endowment for International Peace observed the country's economic orientation:

India's economy is continental in scope; highly industrialized and extremely poor; centrally planned--some would say overly planned; administratively encumbered and rampant with corruption; caste-bound and socialist-inspired; determinedly self-reliant; and, though guided by principles of social democracy, protective of the interests of politically powerful, propertied groups.

India has also devoted a large portion of its budget, well supplemented by foreign aid, to its military. In the fall of 1981, for instance, India was simultaneously negotiating with France for a $2 billion Mirage jet deal and with the IMF for a $3.6 billion loan.

In the 1970s, the Mexican government was destroying its economy even as it was a regular IMF customer. When Mexico's threatened default on its vast international obligations essentially set off the debt crisis in 1982, the IMF came to the rescue, a role extolled by the fund.

Yet the loans did little to improve Mexico's economic performance; that nation did not begin making major market-oriented reforms until the end of the decade after squandering billions more of foreign money on counterproductive state-led development schemes.

The IMF has some thirty-two programs operating in Africa, yet nowhere have national economic policies been worse or past lending more misguided.

In 1974, for instance, the IMF negotiated a loan to Tanzania, which agreed to adopt a package "of compromises that might be called socialist realism," in the words of one observer. But the government, which had ruined the economy through such policies as forced agricultural collectivization (the ujaama program), refused to cut spending, and the IMF terminated the program, having done no more than subsidize the leading example of "African socialism." In 1983, Reginald Herbold Green, of the Institute of Development Studies, concluded that "IMF influence on Tanzanian action has, to date, been fairly modest. Direct impact since 1976 has, arguably, been negative. Indirect effects are hard to assess."

Kenya, which borrowed roughly $130 million in 1988 and owed more than $380 million total at the end of 1989, was then building a sixty-story, $200 million office building--complete with a larger-than-life statue of President Daniel arap Moi--in Nairobi. Earlier lending programs to Kenya also proved disappointing. In his analysis of IMF lending to these two African states, Stanley Please of the World Bank was particularly critical of Tanzania's failure to review programs that were not working. In his view, Kenya suffered from some of the same difficulties, and, he concluded, "the problem of the inadequate use of pricing and the overextension of the public sector" was "a pervasive one in Africa."

Only after its Marxist revolution did Ethiopia begin borrowing from the IMF, yet it was the government's collectivization of agriculture that dramatically worsened the famine during the mid-1980s. The loans to Ethiopia exhibited another damning aspect of IMF lending.

The fund underwrites any government, however venal and brutal. Naturally, the loans are not earmarked for repression. But the IMF extends credit directly to governments, and money is fungible. Whether Ethiopia took its IMF cash and directly bought bombs for use against Eritrean rebels or shifted its accounts around in Addis Ababa first made no real difference; in either case, the fund (as well as other lenders, such as the World Bank) was an accomplice to murder.

Another good IMF customer was Nicolae Ceausescu's Romania, which, in contrast to so many other poor nations, regularly paid its debts. China owed the fund $600 million as of the end of 1989; in January 1990, just a few months after the blood had dried in Beijing's Tianamen Square, the IMF held a seminar on monetary policy in the city. Other clients include or have included Burma, Pinochet's Chile, Laos, Nicaragua under Somoza and the Sandinistas, Syria, Vietnam, Zaire, and so on--the IMF has rarely met a dictatorship that it didn't like.

CONDITIONALITY IN PRACTICE

Why Discretionary Ex-Post Conditionality?

The fund imposes its conditions after the member country has gotten into trouble. The requirements are supposed to prevent borrowers from hanging on to their subsidized IMF credits longer than necessary. But the fund could more effectively accomplish its goals if the conditions addressed the causes of the crisis. Nations that have negligently, or even deliberately, created a difficult situation should be barred from receiving IMF credits at all. Ex ante conditions could, for example, include a requirement that domestic credit expansion may not exceed the growth of production potential, that the budget deficit may not exceed a certain percentage of the gross national product, that the rules of the General Agreement on Tariffs and Trade must be strictly observed, and that there may be neither controls on capital movements nor expropriation of investors.

Of course, such "ex ante conditionality" would greatly limit the number of member countries entitled to borrow from the IMF. It would reduce the power of fund officials. Such reform, moreover, would be in the interests of neither borrower governments inclined toward negligence nor lender governments that like to use the IMF to promote foreign policy goals or satisfy domestic interest groups.

Even in the case of purely ex post conditionality, moral hazard could be reduced if the IMF would at least issue--and apply--strict rules for its conditions. The governments of typical debtor countries would then have no hope of getting away with weak conditions thanks to good relations with IMF officials or special negotiating skills. At present, however, the IMF practices ad hoc conditionality, or a case-by-case approach. Fund officials oppose strict rules about the application of IMF conditions because they limit the fund's discretionary power. Influential lenders and borrowers feel the same way.

Why is the IMF's Conditionality not more Transparent?

If the IMF adjustment programs are justified on the grounds that they constitute "new knowledge" and thus an international public good, their terms should be made known. Publication might also increase the probability of the fund and its borrowers adhering to their programs, which seem to be less and less effective.

Why are agreements not published? Secrecy helps a borrower government that does not intend to meet the stipulated conditions save face.

If a borrower intends to fulfill the conditions, secrecy enables it to make the IMF a scapegoat for additional reform measures the IMF did not demand. IMF officials avoid unwanted public supervision and a serious assessment as to the effectiveness of IMF programs. Broken conditions suggest that the fund is ineffectual. If, by contrast, the fund's conditions are minimal and therefore easy to fulfill, it would become evident that the IMF has little impact on borrowers' policies.

Monitoring by the IMF, the banks, and the general public would also be easier and more effective if policy conditions were simple and few.

But the fund seems to prefer a multitude of policy conditions. Moreover, policy targets, to be effective, must relate to easily controllable variables--either policy instruments or close intermediate economic targets.

Otherwise, it is not clear whether a violation is due to policy failures or unforeseeable disturbances. Without controllability, there can be no responsibility. Targets for relatively uncontrollable variables are not only likely to be missed, as IMF experience shows, they are also unlikely to exert much influence on the conduct of economic policy.

The fund's policy targets, however, tend to include remote, endogenous variables, such as the current account balance, that depend heavily on any number of uncontrollable factors. A public choice perspective suggests that the IMF staff prefers those sorts of requirements because they reduce potential outside control and criticism of the fund's effectiveness. Further, a multiplicity of conditions, without weights attached to them, makes it difficult to evaluate the efficiency of any program, raises the cost of monitoring for external observers, and permits the fund to attribute the low degree of successful program implementation to target conflicts.

The fund's desire to protect itself against outside monitoring may also explain why it prefers highly variable ad hoc conditions to simple rules. Once more, the customary borrowers and the most influential lenders share the IMF staff's interest. The choice of remote endogenous target variables can serve a similar purpose. Missing a target can almost always be attributed to unforeseeable disturbances. In that way, the debtor governments can conceal their noncompliance and the IMF staff can conceal the ineffectiveness of its conditions.

Why are Conditions Procyclical?

Several authors have noted that IMF conditionality varies procyclically: It is stricter when the world is in a recession than when there is a boom. The period from 1979 to 1982 is a particularly good example. There is also econometric evidence that tightening of conditionality reduces the volume of IMF credits.

One need not be a Keynesian to criticize the procyclical effect of such variations in conditionality. Why does the IMF reinforce the cycle? Fund officials have a vested interest in lending extensively and imposing strict economic policy conditions because both constitute an exercise of power and a source of prestige.

At a time of worldwide recession, when the demand for IMF credits increases, fund officials can maximize their authority by tightening lending conditions but not more than is compatible with some increase in credit volume. In boom times, in contrast, the decline in demand for credits leads to eased conditions--as exemplified by the structural adjustment facility and the enhanced structural adjustment facility.

Varying conditionality thus becomes a substitute for altering interest rates since the rates the IMF can charge are fixed in advance. If that explanation is correct, it follows that Richard Cooper's 1983 proposal for countercyclical use of IMF conditionality is not feasible because it runs counter to the bureaucratic interest of the IMF staff.

Major IMF Financing Programs, 1995-99

Compliance with Conditionality for Thirty-four Programs Approved in 1983 (pe/centage of countries that comply)

Member Country`	Date Agreement Approved by IMF Executive Board	Amount of IMF Financing (billions of U.S. dollars)	IMF Financing Facility
Mexico	1 February 1995	17.8	SBA
Russia	11 April 1995	6.8	SBA
Pakistan	13 December 1995	0.6	SBA
Russia	26 March 1996	10.1	EFF
Philippines	18 July 1997	1.1	EFF
Thailand	20 August 1997	3.9	SBA
Pakistan	20 October 1997	1.6	EFF and ESAF
Indonesia	5 November 1997	10.2	SBA but replaced by EFF 25 August 1998
South Korea	4 December 1997	21.0	SBA
Philippines	27 March 1998	1.4	SBA
Indonesia	15 July 1998	1.3	SBA
Russia	20 July 1998	11.2	EFF, SRF, and CCFF
Brazil	2 December 1998	18.1	SBA and SRF

Mugabe Says Zimbabwe Might Soon Cut Ties with IMF

Harare--President Robert Mugabe said on Sunday that Zimbabwe might soon cut ties with the International Monetary Fund, which he accused of being a tool to force political changes in countries unpopular with the West.

Mugabe--under pressure at home to quit over an economic crisis blamed on his 19-year-old government--also said he would take to the U.N. forum his charges that the United States and former colonial power Britain were interfering in Zimbabwe's internal affairs.

The Zimbabwean government last week denied reports in the state media that it was severing ties with the IMF and the

World Bank, but Mugabe told the official Sunday Mail he was considering this although relations with the bank might survive.

In an interview with the newspaper on Zimbabwe's 19th independence anniversary, Mugabe said the IMF was denying his southern African state balance-of-payments support although the government had met its conditions.

"Why should we continue to plead. The money is a loan and if you are going to go down on your knees and confess, as if to the Almighty, for your sins and they will say okay you have done wrong and can you now do this and that in the future," he said. "For goodness sake, we are a sovereign country and we must not humiliate ourselves to that extent," Mugabe said.

A few weeks ago Mugabe also accused the IMF of trying to impose tough decisions on Zimbabwe and hinted ties could be cut. "They are being political but of course we want to allow some time to advance before we actually come to a definite decision," Mugabe said on state television.

The IMF has withheld $53 million in aid to Zimbabwe since last August, demanding transparency in government policies. The fund says it is mainly worried about Mugabe's threats to seize mostly white-owned farmland to resettle landless blacks, paying only for developments but not for the land, which he argues was "stolen" by British colonists in the 1890s. The IMF has also questioned government spending on the war in the Democratic Republic of the Congo, where Mugabe has deployed over 6,000 troops to support President Laurent Kabila against rebels backed by Rwanda and Uganda.

Other Western donors have indicated resumption of IMF aid to the southern African country will unlock their own funds, which are seen vital to reviving a flagging economy. Analysts and government officials say although Mugabe--who is battling an economic crisis partly manifesting itself in record inflation and interest rates and regular violent street protests--could not afford to dump the IMF and World Bank, he could do it out of frustration.

Mugabe, 75, told the Sunday Mail he was ready to turn his back on the IMF because he believed it had lost its orientation, but he said he would stick with the World Bank "unless it proves to be exactly like the IMF monstrous creature." "Let that monstrous creature get out of our way. Unless I am prevailed upon to see things otherwise, not just by way of arguments, but I would rather, by something concrete that the IMF is doing or will be doing, I will lead my government in the direction where we dismiss the IMF as an institution that we can relate to, and that is coming very soon," he said.

What we can conclude from the above observations may be summarized as follows:

- The IMF's core conditionalities do not address the basic economic development policy problems of the country;
- In the absence of a determined effort to tackle the country's fundamental policy problems, many of the IMF's core and less emphasized conditionalities such as credit restriction, deregulation of fertilizer prices, privatization, increasing rents on government-owned houses and raising water and electricity charges, all of which have actually been implemented have given rise to widespread public resentment without any prospect of recompense in the foreseeable future in terms of real improvements from fundamental reforms.
- The government has been more willing to implement RAF conditionalities that promise to raise its revenue than those with the potential to effect basic economic transformations. Hence, the general outcome so far has been that the IMF's terms and conditions have not succeeded in exerting the necessary pressure on the government to affect fundamental economic reforms. In fact, the vacillating nature of the Fund's policy stance has at times emboldened the Ethiopian authorities to treat it with lack of seriousness. IMF experts and negotiators working on the Ethiopian economy often congratulate themselves on having helped formulate an economic policy in Ethiopia that has brought about reasonably high GDP growth, price and exchange rate stability and sustainable fiscal and current account

deficits and the like. In reality however, several of these claims are statistical figments of the imagination fed into computers.

Confronted with such counterarguments, RAF experts respond with a stiff upper lip: "It could have been worse!" The point is, it could have been a lot better!

What to do? Simple. Let the IMF and World Bank work together more closely than is the case at present to include in the core IMF conditionalities issues related to the following:

- creation of a land market
- restitution of nationalized houses and other properties to former owners or their legal heirs, and paying adequate compensation where this is not possible for technical and other reasons;
- abolition of politically affiliated business enterprises, particularly those with monopoly and quasi-monopoly influences;
- a significant reduction in the exorbitant increases in government-owned houses made by the Addis Ababa Administration;
- a reduction in the rental-income and capital-gains taxes
- the removal of incompetent and unqualified persons from key positions in the civil service and their replacement by more efficient personnel.
- allowing foreign participation in the banking and insurance sub-sector.

THE IMF AND THE ASIAN ECONOMIC CRISIS

Although the Asian financial crisis is over, countries like Indonesia will feel its effects for years. Unfortunately, critics say, the policies imposed by the International Monetary Fund (IMF) during this tumultuous time worsened the situation--causing exactly the consequences that have brought globalization under attack.

- There is little doubt that IMF and U.S. Treasury policies contributed to an environment that enhanced the likelihood of a crisis by encouraging--in some cases insisting on--rapid financial and capital-market liberalization.

- The IMF misdiagnosed conditions in East Asia, failing to realize the problem was not excess demand for goods and services, but insufficient demand--thus dampening demand could only make matters worse.
- Second, if firms have a low level of indebtedness, high interest rates can be absorbed--but with high levels of indebtedness, imposing high interest rates is like signing a death warrant for many firms--and for the economy.

The failure of the IMF to recognize the important interactions among the policies pursued in the different countries was hard to fathom, analysts say. By continuing to advocate contradictory policies, the IMF exacerbated the spread of the downturn from one country to the next.

IMF critics offer the following suggestions for handling the crisis:

- Maintain the flow of finance and halt existing debt repayment.
- Create a special bankruptcy provision that would allow for a relatively quick reorganization of a firm, rather than liquidation.
- Strong intervention of the government aimed at financial restructuring-establishing clear ownership of firms, enabling them to re-enter credit markets.

The way the IMF approached the crises has left a legacy of private and public debt, critics conclude.

FLOATING RATE

Under a floating rate, there cannot be and never has been a foreign exchange crisis, though there may well be internal crises, as in Japan. The reason is simple: Changes in exchange rates absorb the pressures that would otherwise lead to crises in a regime that tried to peg the exchange rate while maintaining domestic monetary independence. The foreign exchange crisis that affected South Korea, Thailand, Malaysia, and Indonesia did not spill over to New Zealand or Australia because those countries had floating exchange rates. As between the alternatives of a truly fixed exchange rate and a floating exchange rate, which one is preferable depends on the specific characteristics of the country involved. In particular, much depends on whether a given country has a major trading partner with a good record for stable monetary policy, thus providing a desirable currency with which to be linked. However, so long as a country chooses and adheres to one of the two regimes, it will be spared foreign exchange crises and there will be no role for an international agency to supplement the market. Perhaps that is the reason why the IMF has implicitly favored pegged exchange rates.

The present crisis is not the result of market failure. Rather, it is the result of governments intervening in or seeking to supersede the market, both internally via loans, subsidies, or taxes and other handicaps and externally via the IMF, the World Bank, and other international agencies. We do not need more powerful government agencies spending still more of the taxpayers' money, with limited or nonexistent accountability. That would simply be throwing good money after bad. We need government, both within the nations and internationally, to get out of the way and let the market work. The more that people spend or lend their own money, and the less they spend or lend taxpayer money, the better.

WINNERS AND LOSERS

Building support for change is an important element in ensuring a reform program can be implemented successfully. Ideally, one would be able to identify the winners and losers of any reform process; make sure the winners realized who they were; and then seek ways of countering the opposition.

But it is usually difficult to identify winners and losers with any great certainty. Some short-term losers might recognize that they are vulnerable-protected domestic industries facing the prospect of greater foreign competition might have good reason to worry. But not always. One of my favorite stories concerns Mexican refrigerators. A major refrigerator manufacturer in Mexico was strongly opposed to NAFTA because he reckoned that opening up trade would enable American manufacturers to make significant inroads into the Mexican market.

This turned out to be a misjudgment. A big weakness with Mexican-made fridges was the poor quality of compressors previously available to the fridge-makers. NAFTA made it possible to import and use higher quality US-made compressors in Mexican fridges and so enabled the manufacturer in question to become a leading player in the American refrigerator market for smaller models.

In the short-term, though, predicting such outcomes is difficult and beneficiaries do not recognize their prospective gains. It takes time for the full effect of reform measures to work through the economy. Removing subsidies and moving to a flexible exchange rate regime will help export-oriented firms increase their overseas markets, for example: but it is unlikely to do so overnight.

And in the meantime, people are uncertain and afraid. You cannot know that you will be hired by an expanding exporting firm: but you can guess that your job-or your profits-are threatened by greater import competition.

Better understanding of the reform process can dampen some opposition. The removal of agricultural export subsidies is often opposed without recognition that exchange rate change can confer bigger benefits.

Winners will become evident as a reform program progresses; and then they can be enlisted to support further reforms. In the short-term, though, it is not possible to identify the firms and workers who will start up or expand businesses as reforms take hold. Ending protection and freeing up trade makes it easier for new firms to compete successfully-but the identity of those firms and those workers who get the jobs they create will only become apparent later.

Losers are similarly difficult to identify in advance, but their identity might become apparent more quickly as firms lay off workers, or go out of business, in response to more competitive pressures.

It is clearly important that reforms that are introduced do not create vested interests that might then oppose future reforms. Establishing preferential trade agreements that create trade diversion can make further trade liberalization more difficult. A mis-guided regulatory framework could also make it difficult to deepen financial markets at a later stage.

COMPREHENSIVENESS

The main focus here has been on trade and labor market reforms-in deference to the audience here this evening. But similar considerations apply in many other areas. A successful reform program means tackling problems on a wide front.

Major areas of reform include governance issues and the establishment of secure property rights and predictable legal systems; better government expenditure management; the move to less distortionary tax systems; pension system reform; and the privatization of state owned enterprises, among others.

COMMITMENT AND FOLLOW-THROUGH

The importance of commitment and perseverance cannot be overstated. Too many reform programs have lost momentum because policymakers lost their appetite for change, or were overwhelmed by opposition, or because uncertainty on the part of economic actors led to a slow response that helped engender political opposition. The lack of follow-through can have a significant economic cost, and it can also be politically painful for governments whose enthusiasm for reform faded at the wrong moment. The cost of failed or partially implemented reforms can be high.

Look at Argentina, an economy still recovering from the impact of the crisis in 2001. Yet in the 1990s, Argentina's reform program was, initially, seen as a model.

After the experience of the 1980s, when the Argentine economy had contracted by about half a per cent a year, while inflation had soared-to a peak in the late 1980s of 3,000 per cent-the 1991 Convertibility Plan was seen as the centerpiece of reform. The aim was to deliver high growth and low inflation, based on disciplined macroeconomic policies and market-oriented structural reform. The Argentine government wanted to escape from past inflationary failures: and at the start the government showed every sign of a readiness to take the difficult steps needed to deliver macroeconomic stability.

Central to the convertibility plan was its guarantee of peso convertibility with the dollar at parity. Having a fixed exchange rate system was seen as crucial for building up the anti-inflationary credibility that the government needed. A quasi-currency board was established in order to underpin the system and so reinforce the government's commitment. The early results were promising. For such a plan to work in the longer term, however, fiscal restraint is required.

In the first two years of the plan, Argentina experienced real annual GDP growth of over 10%, and more than 5% in 1993-94. Inflation was down to single digits by 1993. There was a huge surge in capital inflows. The loss of confidence in emerging markets that followed Mexico's so-called Tequila crisis of 1995 seemed to do little more than interrupt performance improvements temporarily. Argentine growth rebounded in 1996-97.

But this apparently impressive performance masked structural weaknesses that weren't confronted. The convertibility plan was only sustainable if there was fiscal discipline and sufficient flexibility in the economy to adjust to shocks. However, fiscal control was undermined by off-budget expenditures; and it was too weak to prevent growing reliance on private capital flows to finance government borrowing. The estimated structural fiscal position went from rough balance in 1992-93 to a deficit of about 2.75% of GDP in 1998. In addition, there was persistent off-budget spending, mainly as a result of court-ordered compensation payments after the social security reforms of the 1990s, and arrears to suppliers. This raised the government's average new borrowing requirements to more than 3% of GDP a year over this period. In 1996, for example, when off-budget spending is included, the total deficit was 4% of GDP. The problem was made worse by overoptimistic assessments of the economy's growth potential. There were more temporary factors at play than was realized at the time. This, of course, meant that the authorities had less room for maneuver on the fiscal front than they believed. The decentralized system of government in Argentina made fiscal control particularly difficult. The provinces, for example, had little incentive to improve revenue performance or constrain expenditure growth: and this important weakness in the fiscal structure was not tackled.

Exports grew, but nowhere nearly as rapidly as imports. By the late 1990s, there was an uncomfortably high debt to export ratio: it was 455% in 1998, and jumped, unexpectedly, to 530% in 1999.

Added to all this was the fact that the pace of structural reforms lost momentum in the mid-90s; indeed, some reforms were reversed. Perhaps the biggest weakness here was the labor market which was heavily regulated in Argentina. Individual workers have long enjoyed considerable protection, with high barriers to dismissal and the guarantee of generous fringe benefits. Yet a fixed exchange rate regime required labor market flexibility to enable the economy to respond to shocks.

Some labor market reforms were introduced in the 1990s. In 1991, for example, there was some modest improvement in flexibility. In 1995 came equally modest steps that made it easier to hire temporary workers and introduced more flexible working hours. But these improvements did not go far, and reform in this area quickly lost momentum. To make matters worse, Congress diluted a further government attempt to increase labor market flexibility-so much so, in fact, that the final outcome promoted further centralization of collective bargaining. The result of all these lukewarm changes was predictable: unemployment rose, to 12% in 1994; and productivity growth fell to zero in the second half of the 1990s.

These structural rigidities were all the more problematic in the light of the fixed exchange rate regime. It became increasingly clear during the 1990s that successful operation of the quasi-currency board required much better fiscal control than the government was able to deliver. Since the collapse, of course, there has been much debate about whether the pegged exchange rate regime was ever appropriate as a long-term policy instrument.

The arguments over the exchange rate regime have ensured a plethora of different explanations of the eventual crisis in 2001. Both the then government and the IMF have been criticized, most recently by the Fund's own Independent Evaluation Office, in a report published last month. But it is clear that the impact of the crisis would at least have been mitigated if the original reform program had been more ambitious-specifically if it had included serious reform of the labor market and if it had tackled the problem of fiscal relations between central and provincial governments; and if this more ambitious program had been fulfilled.

Effective implementation of fiscal, labor market and structural reforms could have meant that the economy was robust and flexible enough to cope with unanticipated shocks and thus could have avoided the economic collapse that resulted from the abandonment of the convertibility plan.

WHAT, WHEN AND HOW

So what have we learned about the best way to implement reforms, and when? Of course, the specific reform measures will depend on the circumstances of individual countries, and so too will the most appropriate timing. But it is clear that some general principles appear to hold good.

But it is also clear that trade and exchange rate reforms should be an early priority. The more rapidly an economy is opened up to the rest of the world, the better. This is partly because opening brings considerable economic benefits, as I mentioned earlier; and partly because the more open the economy the more difficult it will be to reverse the reforms.

Fiscal discipline has to be a key component of any sound economic reform program. Its absence helped undercut the Turkish reforms of the 1980s and was clearly a major factor in Argentina's more recent crisis.

Fiscal rectitude is difficult in countries that have pressing social needs and serious shortcomings in infrastructure that can impede growth. But better targeted spending-to those most in need-can help. So can more efficient tax collection which will boost tax revenues, and a widening of the tax base.

Beyond identifying winners and losers and building support for change, it seems clear that political leaders need to be ready to confront their opponents. How this is done can be critical. In Britain, Margaret Thatcher successfully took on the miners in 1984: but the Heath government failed when it confronted the same group in 1973-74. Confronting opponents is partly a matter of picking fights that are winnable-and luck plays an important part here-and it is partly a matter of having the courage to see the battle through to the end.

Effective reform also requires good communication, so that citizens know what the aims are and what the potential ramifications are. Transparency is also important because it is an important means of building support.

THE IMF'S ROLE

The IMF has an important role in all this. The Fund's principal objective, as it always has been, is the maintenance of international financial stability. That gives the Fund an important role in crisis prevention and resolution. Reform is, in a very broad sense, the Fund's business. Article IV surveillance on our member countries provides an annual assessment of economic policies, along with recommendations for reform, as appropriate. This applies equally to the largest industrial economies, emerging market countries and the poorest countries. This evening I have referred mainly to the reform process in emerging market countries. But the Fund also regularly recommends reform in our richest members: we recently made recommendations relating to the fiscal situation in the United States.

The Fund's role in the reform process under surveillance is an advisory one. This is partly in order to respect the sovereignty of member governments. But it also reflects the recognition that national policymakers are those who have to adopt reforms and try to ensure their success. It is they who have to secure the support of civil society and the various economic actors involved and whose response will contribute to the success or otherwise of the reforms.

But for countries receiving financial assistance from the Fund as they try to resolve crises, such assistance is provided on a conditional basis, with payments provided in installments against agreed benchmarks.

The terms of such assistance are agreed with member countries, the government must "own" the reform programs that are undertaken. The Fund's role is to be assured that the program has a reasonable prospect of success.

There is a third way in which the Fund assists countries implementing reforms: technical assistance. This can be more important than is often realized. On a wide range of policy issues, from tax administration to budget accounting, from financial sector regulation to the development of commercial codes, the Fund has amassed considerable expertise and experience that can benefit governments seeking advice on formulating and implement such measures. It is clear from the wide range of governments that seek technical assistance from the Fund that this expertise has become a valuable and valued resource.

Currently, for example, the Fund is actively supporting banking reform in Turkey, providing technical advice for budgetary reforms in China and encouraging trade reform in Africa. The Fund has actively supported countries adopting floating exchange rate regimes and pension reforms.

CONCLUSION

Let me briefly conclude by re-iterating that reform is obviously important-and often urgently needed. Many countries need to implement change if they are to continue to grow, or are to achieve sustained growth. But well-judged and effectively implemented reform is also important-and difficult. Mis-guided or overly timid reforms can undermine the reform process and make it difficult to muster support for future reform programs.

Perseverance is crucial. Reforms have to be followed through. There is no scope for talk of `reform fatigue'. Reforms bring the flexibility that is essential for economies to adapt successfully to changes in the global economy.

Finally, there is one ingredient alien to economists-luck. We do not like admitting that there are things that we do not know and, more importantly, can not know. But the reform process is, inevitably, something of a mystery. We cannot predict the exact outcome. But by proper and effective implementation we can increase the prospects of success.

8

Present Scenario

Financial crises are the defining moments of the problems that confront policy makers. This section reviews and interprets the recent history of crises, and the factors that are alleged to have produced them. The list of problems includes (1) fundamental policy-design flaws in banking systems and in international assistance programs that subsidize risk and foment fundamental bank and government insolvency, and (2) inherent problems of financial systems that aggravate those shocks through four different channels (which are referred to collectively as "liquidity" problems).

The last twenty years, and particularly the last five years, have witnessed an unprecedented wave of financial collapses. The magnitude of the losses incurred by banks during these collapses is staggering. The negative net worth of failed banks in the U.S. for the years 1931-1933 was roughly 4% of GDP. Nearly a hundred crises with losses of this or higher magnitude have occurred over the past two decades. Twenty of those crises have resulted in losses in excess of 10% of GDP, and ten have produced losses in excess of 20% of GDP.

Another novelty of the new crises has been the simultaneous collapse of banks and fixed exchange rates. Exchange rate collapses historically were sometimes associated with banking system collapses, but historically the two occurred together much less often than today, and the historical exchange rate collapses were less severe.

What is driving these crises? The literature has produced a number of explanations, which are not mutually inconsistent.

Since the purpose of this paper is to devise solutions (not just for the sake of devising them, but also in the hope of fostering change) I do not pre-judge the weights that should be attached to the various views. For a proposed set of reforms to the global financial architecture to attract supporters, it must encompass a broad spectrum of views.

Problem 1: Counterproductive financial bailouts of insolvent banks, their creditors, and debtors by governments, often assisted by the IMF, have large social costs. Bailouts are harmful for several reasons. First, they entail large increases in taxation of average citizens to transfer resources to wealthy risk-takers. Tax increases are always distortionary, and serve to accentuate the unequal wealth distribution. Second, by bailing out risk takers local governments and the IMF subsidize, and hence encourage, risk taking. Moral-hazard incentive problems magnify truly exogenous shocks that confront banking systems. Excessive risk taking by banks results in banking collapses and produces the fiscal insolvency of governments that bail out banks, leading to exchange rate collapse. Banks willingly and knowingly take on more risks-especially default risks and exchange risks-than they would if they were not protected by government safety nets.

Risk taking often follows a two-stage process. Initially, macroeconomic shocks (e.g., a decline in the terms of trade) reduce bank capital and raise the possibility of currency devaluation. That changes both the incentives for banks to take risks and their opportunities to do so subsequently. The incentives to take risk rise both because bank capital is lower and because banks seek to protect their loan customers (who sometimes also own the bank) from the effects of the adverse macroeconomic shock. The opportunity for taking on risk during a downturn is higher both because of increases in the credit risk of borrowers and because of increased exchange rate risk. Furthermore, a rising risk of depreciation lowers the relative cash flow cost of borrowing dollar-denominated funds, which can make borrowing in dollars attractive to distressed firms and banks. Banks that borrow short-term dollar-denominated funds economize on the current cash flow cost of those borrowings, but take on a large risk of capital loss if the exchange rate peg collapses. In the absence of safety net distortions that encourage risk taking, macroeconomic shocks would encourage the opposite behavior-a reduction in bank risk exposure to reassure bank debt holders. But overly generous protection of banks insulates them from market discipline and makes them willing to increase their asset risk in the wake of adverse shocks. Banks are willing to do so because potential losses will be borne by taxpayers through government-sponsored bailouts of the banking system.

The risks in these banking systems constitute an off-balance sheet liability of their governments, since governments either explicitly or implicitly guarantee to bail out banks that fail. Thus bank risk and fiscal risk grow together and explain the simultaneity of banking and exchange rate collapses. The differences between emerging market financial crises of the last two decades and historical crises-the larger size of current banking system losses, and the coincidence of banking system and exchange rate collapses-are attributable to the new link between private risk taking and public financing of the losses produced by those risks.

Banks are not the only entities protected by government safety nets. Large, politically influential firms other than banks often receive implicit protection from the government on their debts, which encourages a similar tendency to bear exchange risk and to rely on short-term dollar-denominated funds, particularly in the wake of shocks that raise the risks of devaluation.

The moral hazard problem also can exacerbate the extent of devaluation during exchange rate collapses. Domestic banks that bet against devaluation prior to the exchange rate collapse (by borrowing dollars or entering forward exchange contracts) can magnify the extent of the collapse by adding selling pressure to the market once the collapse begins. As banks experience initial losses on their open exposures to exchange risk, they may be forced to sell their positions suddenly, which magnifies short-term devaluation pressures. In Mexico, this process of unraveling excessive bank (or non-bank) exposures to exchange risk (in the form of dollar-denominated borrowings and derivative positions) contributed to the severity of the exchange rate collapse in 1995. Garber (1997) argues that the dumping of derivative positions and the scramble for cash by Mexican banks in response to large losses on those positions led banks not only to liquidate their long peso positions, but also to dump their short-term government securities (tesobonos) on the market, which put added pressure on the peso in early 1995 and contributed to government problems in rolling over maturing treasury debt.

In addition to the immediate economic costs associated with bailouts (tax increases and moral hazard), there is also a longer term cost from the way bailouts affect the political process domestically and internationally. Domestically, bailouts encourage crony capitalism in emerging market economies and thus help to stunt the growth of democracy and reform. Bailouts also undermine democracy and economic competition in industrialized countries. Bailouts (whether channeled through the IMF or the ESF) are often a means for the U.S. Treasury to provide subsidies to international lenders and foreign governments without Congressional approval under the guise of liquidity assistance.

IMF policies exacerbate all these problems. The IMF's role in bailouts is threefold. It provides a small wealth transfer (via the interest subsidy on its loan). Second, and more importantly, it pressures countries to bail out international lenders who are often complicit in excessive risk taking. Third, the IMF helps to ensure that domestic taxation (to finance the bailout) will occur, by lending legitimacy to the bailout and by requiring increased taxation as a condition of IMF assistance.

So far I have argued that moral hazard is the key villain in the recent, unprecedented wave of financial system collapses. That is not to say that all the costly consequences of financial crises are an unavoidable consequence of moral-hazard-induced fundamental bank insolvency and its fiscal consequences.

If the only costs of financial system collapse were the direct costs of fundamental insolvency-that is, the amount of wealth lost directly through the actions of protected banks and borrowers-then the only threat to the global financial system would be safety net protection itself. In that case, the simple solution to redesigning the IMF arguably would be simply to abolish it, as Schwartz (1998) suggests. The argument for reforming the IMF, rather than abolishing it, revolves around the view that there are important indirect costs attendant to "liquidity problems" that magnify the direct costs to fundamental bank and government solvency. The potential importance of these indirect costs, and the potential for the IMF to mitigate them, underlies the argument for preserving the IMF. Concerns about liquidity costs can be divided into four additional problems, which are discussed separately below.

Problem 2: Asymmetric information about the incidence of observable shocks within the financial system, especially when combined with short-term debt finance can magnify the economic consequences of fundamental shocks by leading to a liquidity crisis. The historical evidence on banking panics in the U.S. and elsewhere suggests that panics resulted from observable economic shocks with unobservable consequences for individual financial intermediaries. The vulnerability of financial intermediaries to crises reflects the fact that the value of their assets are hard to observe (loans are not marked to market) and their debt is very short term (often demandable). Those characteristics are intrinsic to the value-creating functions of banks, but they also make banks vulnerable to crises. Small fundamental shocks to aggregate banking system solvency can promote widespread disintermediation from banks, leading to a contraction in credit, a decline in economic activity, price deflation, and "fire sale" losses as banks and their loan customers scramble to gain liquidity.

Asymmetric-information-induced runs on banks prompted by fundamental shocks to bank asset values characterized the panics of 1873, 1884, 1890, 1893, 1896, and 1907. The weeks and months prior to these banking panics witnessed uniquely adverse combinations of the growth of business insolvencies and declines in equity prices. Previous and subsequent financial panics, in and outside the United States, have been similarly traced to observable fundamental shocks with unobservable consequences for individual banks and bank borrowers.

Because bank panics result from bank vulnerability to asset value shocks, bank diversification can be extremely useful in forestalling panics. The peculiar propensity for banking panics in the U.S. reflected the fragmentation of U.S. banks by location, which made bank loans less diversified than in other countries. That observation suggests that an important ingredient in reducing banking risk in today's global economy is to encourage banks to operate branches throughout the world, and to hold an internationally diversifed bundle of securities in their portfolios. Lack of bank diversification has been shown to be a major contributor to bank instability in emerging market economies in recent times, as Caprio and Wilson (1997), Wilson, Saunders, and Caprio (1997), and Kane (1998) emphasize.

Problem 3: The expectations of speculators can exaggerate the effects of adverse shocks, and can even precipitate self-fulfilling financial collapses when weakened financial systems are also illiquid. Current IMF assistance is inadequate to deal with this problem because it offers too little assistance, and attaches too many conditions to that assistance at the time of the loan request, which delays the availability of funds. There is a "Sachs version" of this alleged liquidity problem, and a "Mahatir version." The Sachs version (outlined in Sachs et al. 1996, Cole and Kehoe 1996) recognizes that economic fundamentals still drive crises to some degree (which, for example, explains why Singapore has not come under speculative attack in the recent crisis). The Mahatir version, predictably, sees speculative attacks as conspiracies that victimize the innocent.

My own view is that the evidence does not support placing much weight on multiple-equilibria explanations of current financial crises. The Mahatir version has been contradicted by recent empirical studies of the behavior of hedge funds and other institutional investors. The Sachs version is also very weak on empirical support. As a general theory of crises it should apply not only to the current wave of disasters, but to historical cases as well. But the evidence cited above on the history of financial crises, contrary to Radelet and Sachs's (1998) claim, does not support the view that historical crises are explicable as bad equilibria within the context of the

Diamond-Dybvig (1983), or the Sachs, models of multiple equilibria. In other words, a model that would explain the current wave of crises as bad equilibria must also explain (as these models do not) why these purported bad equilibria are new. The moral-hazard approach can do so (since safety net protection and the quasi-privatization of risk are relatively new phenomena); it is not clear whether the multiple-equilibria approach can.

Furthermore, Sachs and others search for multiple equilibria explanations mainly because they find little evidence of extreme fundamental weakness in macroeconomic flow indicators (e.g., conventional measures of government deficits or current account deficits). But, as argued above, they are simply looking in the wrong place for evidence of fundamental weakness. Expectations of future government expenditures often drive crises, not current expenditures. Financial sector imbalances (expected government costs of a bank bailout, or the bailout of an underfunded pension system) produce fiscal imbalance through the off-balance sheet contingent liabilities of the government, not through measured flows that show up in today's current account balance or current taxes and expenditures. In a world where banking sector collapses often produce fiscal costs in excess of 20 percent of GDP, and where government expenditures move smoothly compared to changes in off-balance sheet liability exposures of governments (since banking system losses can occur very quickly), a focus on macroeconomic flows as measures of fundamentals leaves the prince out of the play.

Despite these objections, there surely is something to Sachs's argument if rephrased as the simple claim that a country with very low international reserves is more vulnerable to speculative attacks on its exchange rate or banking system than are others. Furthermore, as Garber (1997) points out, it is very hard to reject rational-expectations multiple-equilibria explanations econometrically. For these reasons, for the purposes of developing my proposed reforms I will assume that the Sachs and Mahatir views have some validity, and that it would be desirable for a global safety net to address the potential for self-fulfilling financial crises to emerge from a combination of small fundamental weaknesses and low liquidity (i.e., low bank and central bank reserves relative to short-term obligations).

Problem 4: "Contagion" across countries in securities and loan markets. Correlations in asset returns are much higher across emerging market countries during crises than at other times, and even government bond yields move together to an unusual degree during financial crises. There are several explanations for this "contagion." One is irrationality on the part of investors. A second is rational portfolio rebalancing by international investors; if portfolio investors (like banks) target a given default risk on the debt they issue, then they will endogenously shrink asset risk in one country in response to capital losses or exogenous increases in asset risk in another country. A third explanation revolves around linkages in international trade that can transmit economic decline, which is then reflected in asset prices. A fourth explanation revolves around multiple equilibria (either through changes in speculators views about the probability of bad equilibria, or through reductions in central bank liquidity following a global flight to quality). To the extent that cross-country contagion reflects irrational speculation or multiple equilibria, policies that would solve those problems would also eliminate cross-border spillover effects.

Problem 5: Government debt management sometimes leans too much on short-term debt. There are good reasons (incentive compatibility) for governments to shorten their debt maturities during times of fiscal uncertainty. Indeed, governments have been doing so for centuries. But doing so might promote self-fulfilling attacks on currencies (following the multiple-equilibria reasoning of Cole and Kehoe 1996, and Sachs et al. 1996). Mexico's financial crisis is often held up as an example of such a problem. While I have argued that these authors likely overstate the empirical evidence in support of that view (particularly in Mexico, where weak fundamentals in the banking system and in central bank policy were clearly present by late 1994, and persist to the present), there is a version of this view that is reasonable: A short term structure of government debt probably aggravates liquidity problems that have their origins in other fundamental shocks (fiscal risks associated with banking system collapse), as in Mexico during the tesobono sell-off of 1995. There is another reason to be concerned about the short term structure of government debt. Governments suffer a moral-hazard problem with respect to the maturity structure of their debts because IMF protection removes the cost of taking illiquidity risk through the shortening of government debt term structure. In an environment where the IMF cannot credibly say no to bailing out governments who abuse its protection, the IMF may be encouraging financial fragility by not penalizing government debt structures that rely excessively on short-term obligations.

From the perspective of these five challenges to financial system stability, current IMF policies are woefully inadequate, and indeed, are part of the problem. When a country suffers a banking system-cum-exchange rate collapse, its government protects politically influential domestic stakeholders by bailing out banks, their debtors, and their creditors, all at the expense of taxpayers. IMF loans to countries suffering financial collapse serve as bridge loans to permit the rescheduling of debt. The conditions imposed by the IMF along with its financial support help to ensure that tax increases to finance the bailout will be forthcoming, making the IMF an accomplice to the transfer of wealth from taxpayers to domestic oligarchs and global lenders. Banking reforms, promoted by the IMF as a condition for assistance, are inadequate and there is no credible mechanism for ensuring that "mandated" reforms will be carried out.

Furthermore, IMF assistance is provided only after an agreement is reached, and funds are released in limited amounts over several months. That way of providing assistance is not effective in solving liquidity problems, which require large amounts of funds to be available on very short notice. Thus current IMF assistance is a non-starter, both from the standpoint of limiting moral hazard problems and reducing the risks of liquidity crises.

We can do much better. Public policy cannot eliminate unavoidable shocks to the financial system. But thoughtful policy can reduce the five avoidable risks listed above, which magnify the costs of exogenous shocks that buffet banking systems and government finances.

Principles on which to Build a Global Financial System

In light of Section II's discussion, the central two-fold objective of policy is to avoid moral-hazard problems that give rise to imprudent banking practices while also protecting against the four "liquidity" problems that can magnify fundamental shocks. A careless approach to providing liquidity assistance results in excessive and counterproductive assistance-a tendency to "throw money" at fundamental problems, which aggravates problems of imprudent banking and encourages unwise fiscal, monetary and debt management policies.

Finding the right balance between liquidity assistance and market discipline is the crux of the policy problem. A financial system safety net will not achieve that balance by making it impossible for banks to fail or for exchange rates to collapse. A system that would eliminate the possibility of collapse would also encourage poor management of private and public affairs. Banks should sometimes fail, exchange rates should sometimes depreciate, and governments should sometimes have trouble rolling over their debts. While finding the appropriate balance requires care, I will argue that constructing a balanced safety net does not pose an intractable economic dilemma. It is not the case that policy makers confront an inevitable dismal trade-off between higher incentive costs from the safety net and greater benefits from safety net protection against liquidity crises. It is possible to capture the benefits of legitimate "liquidity insurance" without suffering the costs of moral hazard.

How can financial system safety nets provide systemic insurance against illiquidity without engendering moral hazard? To achieve that goal credible ex ante rules must be devised that properly allocate ex post losses to private agents, local governments, and international agencies. A global financial safety net, therefore, must define more than the IMF's lending policy, it must define the "tranches of risk" that are credibly assumed by parties other than the IMF, as well as the risks the IMF assumes.

This goal is not new. In fact, it underlay Walter Bagehot's (1873) classic policy prescriptions for domestic central banking: to lend freely at a penalty rate on good collateral. Bagehot argued an elastic and immediate supply of liquidity was essential to an effectively structured lender of last resort, and that appropriate loss sharing rules in the form of collateral requirements and penalty interest rates would discourage abuse of the safety net.

Successful lenders of last resort historically have had in common an ability to set credible rules for defining the sharing of risk that minimize moral hazard while maximizing the ability of the system to provide liquidity during crises. In the United States prior to the Civil War, three states (Indiana, Ohio, and Iowa) successfully operated mutual insurance systems for member banks, which revolved around that principle (Calomiris 1989, 1990, 1993). These were imitated by the New York Clearing House, and by other private clearing houses (Cannon 1910, Gorton 1985). Member banks were constrained by rules and credible monitoring arrangements that limited the riskiness of their debts. Insolvent banks were ejected from coalitions that provided liquidity protection for solvent banks. Enforceable rules requiring the pooling of risks during crises to solve liquidity problems ensured sufficient collective protection. These systems provide examples worthy of imitation today. All successful historical safety net systems revolved around credible arrangements for limiting moral hazard by clearly defining how losses incurred by members would be allocated.

Defining the allocation of risk for the global safety net requires a segmentation of risk into three tranches: the private tranche (exposures to loss incurred by private claimants of individual financial institutions), the domestic government tranche (exposures to loss assumed by local government bank safety nets, and hence, local taxpayers), and the IMF tranche (exposures to loss assumed by the IMF). The other key design feature of the global safety net is determining how the IMF's financial positions are financed (how risks taken by the IMF will be passed on to other parties).

The role of financial system regulations, which include IMF membership criteria and the rules for IMF lending, is to clearly define when and how the IMF lends, and how losses are allocated within the financial system to maximize the effectiveness of protection against illiquidity, while minimizing the moral-hazard costs of protection. To be effective, those rules not only have to make economic sense, but must be transparent and credible. In other words, the rules governing the global safety net have to qualify not only as economically sensible, but also as politically robust.

A New Institutional Structure for Credible Loss Sharing

Without a credible "first tranche" of private loss, moral hazard will plague any attempt to provide liquidity, either from domestic governments or the IMF. What is needed is a set of transparently credible rules that impose a margin of private loss on bank claimants, which limits the exposure of taxpayers to bailou costs ex post, and in so doing, limits banks' willingness to undertake risks ex ante. Putting those safeguards into place should be a requirement of membership in the IMF. Members would then be eligible for IMF liquidity protection-loans from the IMF that are specifically designed to resolve liquidity problems, not to bail out insolvent banks.

By setting these clear, credible criteria for IMF membership, and devising rules for IMF lending that guard against liquidity problems without providing bailouts (that is, without absorbing bank solvency risks), the IMF and its loan programs would help to stabilize global financial markets. What sorts of rules would work to accomplis these objectives? The rules divide into three types: (1) domestic regulations required as a condition for IMF membership, (2) rules governing IMF lending to members, and (3) rules defining the way IMF loans are financed.

CREDIBLE BANK REGULATION: SUBORDINATED DEBT, LIQUIDITY, INSURANCE, AND FREE ENTRY

The bank regulatory requirements that should be mandatory for IMF members include four components: (1) capital requirements (including, in particular, a subordinated debt requirement as part of the capital requirement), (2) "reserve" requirements (minimum ratios of assets in cash and in "global securities"), (3) the explicit insurance of bank deposits, and (4) "free banking" (unlimited chartering of banks conforming to common regulatory standards, and unlimited investment by foreigners in banks, conforming to the same standards as domestic investors).

A key function of capital regulations is to provide a credible first tranche of private loss by ensuring that uninsured bank claimants (stockholders and subordinated debt holders) will lose wealth when banks suffer adverse shocks to the values of their risky assets. Minimum cash reserve ratio requirements serve a similar function (effectively ensuring a margin of protection for insured debt), and also enhance bank liquidity. A minimum amount of "global securities"-domestic and foreign marketable instruments-adds to the transparency of bank balance sheets and helps to diversify bank risk. Thus restrictions on asset holdings and on the composition of bank liabilities provide crucial buffers that ensure the privatization of bank losses, and thus make it easier for local governments and the IMF to provide liquidity protection cost effectively. These regulatory requirements are a first line of defence that reduces the risk of bank failure, the potential for costly bank bailouts, and the liquidity risk that banks face.

Free entry into banking by foreign investors provides an important source of capital (to meet regulatory capital requirements). It also helps to diversify both the ownership base of banks and their asset portfolios (since foreign banks naturally hold more globally diverse portfolios), which makes banks more resilient in the face of adverse domestic shocks. Finally, foreign banks provide important competitive pressure that improves the quality of domestic bank management (Demirguc-Kunt and Levine 1998, Kane 1998).

Because of the importance of credibility and transparency, bank capital and portfolio regulations must be designed carefully. Credibility and transparency require a reliance on market discipline to enforce bank regulations (Keehn 1989, Wall 1989, Flannery 1998, Berger et al. 1998). In capital standards, the devil is in the details. A key flaw in the Basle capital requirements to date has been their emphasis on government supervisory standards when measuring capital. Book value equity is measured by supervisors who often have little skill, and even less incentive, to report bank asset losses accurately. Second, the Basle standards imply an arbitrary link between their measure of asset risk and book value capital, while the true asset risk of the bank can differ from the Basle measure of "risk-weighted assets." The mandated 8% capital requirement is not sufficient if banks assume very high asset risk, and the measurement of risk-weighted assets under the Basle standards leaves much room for bank manipulation of risk.

The Basle capital requirements can be substantially improved by incorporating into the Basle framework a minimal (say, 2%) subordinated debt requirement, as a means to ensure a credible relationship between capital and asset risk via market discipline. This approach was first proposed by the Chicago Federal Reserve Bank (Keehn 1989) and the Atlanta Federal Reserve Bank (Wall 1989) in response to the U.S. S&L and banking crises of the 1980s. The approach outlined here is a modified version of the Chicago Fed plan.

As part of the existing 8% tier 1 and tier 2 Basle capital requirement, banks would be required to issue at least 2% of risk-weighted assets (as defined under the Basle standards) in the form of a new class of subordinated debt. That debt would be subordinated to (that is, junior to) other bank debts. Unlike equity holders, subordinated debt holders do not benefit from "asset substitution" (increasing asset risk in order to exploit the implicit put option value of deposit insurance). Thus subordinated debt holders would be a conservative force for restricting bank risk taking, and protecting relatively senior bank deposits. Because subordinated debt is easy to measure (unlike the book value of equity), a minimal subordinated debt requirement avoids the problems of relying on domestic bank supervisors to measure compliance with equity standards. Furthermore, the yields on the debt are observable, which provides a continuous and transparent market opinion about bank risk.

To be successful, however, subordinated debt issues should be restricted in several ways. To ensure that it serves its role as a source of market discipline, subordinated debt must be held at arms length, and therefore, cannot be held by any willing purchaser. I recommend that the debt be non-tradable, and held only by a group of approved and registered holders (which would differ for each issuer). Each bank's group of qualified holders would be a subset of, say, 50 institutions pre-approved by both the domestic regulator and the IMF as reputable foreign financial institutions with no other financial transactions with the issuing bank. Placing subordinated debt in the hands of well-diversified foreign institutions also helps to ensure that subordinated debt holders will not be bailed out, which is necessary for subordinated debt to serve as a source of market discipline.

It is also essential that a subordinated debt requirement specify how increased bank risk (visible in the yields of subordinated debt) would be penalized by bank regulators. Perhaps the simplest procedure is to set a maximum yield spread over comparable maturity treasury instruments (say, 5%) and require that subordinated debt not be issued at yields in excess of that maximum spread. Banks that fail to roll over their debts at or below the mandated yield spreads eventually would have to contract their risk-weighted assets to remain in compliance with the 2% subordinated debt requirement.

The maturity of subordinated debt should reflect the right balance between enhancing market discipline (by requiring that the debt be rolled over sufficiently frequently) and limiting the amount of rollover that can occur over short intervals (to avoid the risk of sudden illiquidity). For example, requiring that subordinated debt be issued in the form of 24 overlapping generations of two-year debt-one-twenty-fourth of which mature each month-would be a reasonable way to achieve discipline without leaving banks vulnerable to liquidity crises. That arrangement would limit the rate of decline of subordinated debt to roughly 4% per month. Given the required minimum ratio of subordinated debt to risk-weighted assets, that would also limit the maximum monthly decline of risk weighted assets mandated by the requirement to 4%.

The subordinated debt requirement is designed to encourage prudent behavior by banks ex ante (since, on the margin, they are always subject to market discipline), and to encourage appropriate adjustment of asset risk to adverse shocks ex post. Unlike many banks currently, banks subject to a subordinated debt requirement would not purposely increase risk in the wake of losses. Instead, banks would have strong incentives to reduce asset risk and cut dividends (or find alternative ways to raise capital) in the face of losses, much as banks did before safety nets changed their incentives to react appropriately to shocks.

Because subordinated debt holders bear risks that come from both on-balance sheet and off-balance sheet asset risks, they discourage attempts by banks to avoid regulatory capital standards by placing transactions off banks' balance sheets. Subordinated debt holders also encourage banks to develop clear reporting procedures and effective tools for risk management.

A banking system governed by a credibly uninsured subordinated debt requirement is self-equilibrating. Banks may have difficulty rolling over subordinated debt in response to severe shocks (given the proposed yield spread limit on subordinated debt). The failure to roll over subordinated debt mandates a contraction of risk weighted assets (e.g., a contraction of loans). That contraction itself reduces asset risk, eventually allowing the market spread on subordinated debt to fall within the prescribed limits of the regulation.

Restrictions on bank asset composition are also desirable, both to promote liquidity for the system as a whole, and to provide a transparent safeguard against bank default risk in addition to requiring subordinated debt. Argentina's high reserve requirements were extremely useful in helping Argentine banks to weather the tequila crisis in early 1995. Argentina has also shown creativity in the way it allows banks to meet those reserve requirements. Banks are encouraged to hold up to 50% of their reserves offshore in private commercial banks, and may hold much of their reserves in the form of standby arrangements with foreign commercial banks (for which the Argentine banks pay a fee) rather than in the form of actual dollar deposits. Like a subordinated debt requirement (also a feature of the Argentine system) this arrangement rewards low-risk banks who are able to pay low fees for their standbys.

I propose a similar requirement as part of the mandatory minimum reserve requirement for banks-a 20% reserve requirement relative to bank debt, with half to be held offshore (partly to protect against government confiscation of bank resources). Banks can satisfy the 10% offshore reserve requirement by maintaining standbys in that amount with any AA rated international bank. The "global securities" requirement would also be set at 20% of deposits. At least half of that securities portfolio must consist of foreign hard-currency-denominated (meaning denominated in dollars, yen, or euros) debt securities placed and priced in international public markets, with yield spreads at the date of purchase of less than 3% over the comparable maturity treasury instrument (of either the U.S., German, or Japanese governments denominated in their respective currencies). The other half of the required securities portfolio could consist of any publicly traded debts (including local government and private bonds), so long as their yield spreads were less than 5% over comparable treasury securities at the date of purchase. The securities portfolio requirement serves the dual function of encouraging global diversification and providing an additional liquidity buffer for banks.

The final regulatory requirement is deposit insurance. All bank debt that is not included in subordinated debt should be explicitly insured by the local government. Doing so would eliminate the possibility of banking panics, either due to asymmetric-information problems (Section II's "Problem 2"), or multiple equilibria (Section II's "Problem 3).

The argument for government deposit insurance is primarily a political, rather than an economic, one. Arguably, private methods of protecting against banking panics may be superior to government deposit insurance. But since governments tend to be incapable of credibly committing not to provide insurance ex post, it is not possible to construct effective private systems.

Explicit government insurance is superior to implicit government insurance. While there are some theoretical and empirical arguments in favor of "constructive ambiguity" in deposit insurance that might favor implicit over explicit insurance, those arguments are not convincing. Implicit insurance does not provide as much protection against runs. Also, making insurance explicit allows governments to charge insurance premia for the protection, and helps government actions to conform better to stated government policy (surely a desirable principle in a world where reputation building has value).

In the presence of the other prudential regulations (the subordinated debt requirement and the portfolio requirements), deposit insurance should not be very costly. In a world where market discipline constrains bank behavior, there are likely to be few bank failures, and small losses from insuring banks.

These four regulations-subordinated debt requirements, minimum reserve and securities ratios, free banking, and deposit insurance are a minimal standard, which should be required as a condition for membership in the IMF. I would recommend that countries go beyond that minimal standard when devising their bank regulations, particularly in the areas of insider lending limitations, barriers between commerce and banking, regulations of market risk exposures, and more realistic definitions of risk weighted assets than those found in the Basle standards. For example, risk weighted assets should be defined in a way that is more sensitive to real risk than are the Basle standards. In Argentina, risk weights on loans are determined by the interest rate on the loan, and can be as much as 600% of the book value of the loan for very high interest loans.

While it is desirable to improve bank regulation by including requirements in addition to the four minimal standards, some regulatory standards should vary across countries. Furthermore, a subordinated debt requirement, and the market discipline it brings, arguably subsumes other regulatory standards, and makes additional measures less important. If banks have to satisfy market discipline, markets will informally "impose" safeguards against market risks, insider lending, and other potential problems, since banks will have to satisfy market perceptions about their overall risk profile.

By keeping the list of required regulations short and simple it will be easier for the IMF to credibly enforce the rules it sets. By vigorously enforcing these rules (e.g., ejecting countries from the IMF if they fail to enforce minimal requirements or if they bail out subordinated debt holders when banks experience losses) the IMF will return reason and balance to international banking, and prevent its own protection from being a source of financial instability.

A reformed global banking system will also reduce the riskiness of emerging market securities. Banking systems as a rule have been run inefficiently in emerging market countries, and banks often pursue opportunities more on the basis of insiders' interests than a proper valuation of loans. For that reason there are many viable projects that should be financed by banks rather than via securities issues (that is, projects that require ongoing monitoring and discipline by banks through concentrated local holdings of claims on borrowing firms), but are pushed into securities markets for lack of a local means of bank finance. In a properly functioning global banking system, those projects would be financed by banks, and banks would be more internationally diversified to permit them to deal with the risks that arise from those risky projects.

The four core banking regulations would ensure a properly functioning global banking system. Free entry, competition, and credible market discipline would encourage proper diversification, prudent management of risk, and an efficient allocation of bank capital. It would also make it possible for the IMF to do the job it was chartered to do-providing liquidity insurance-without the destabilizing side effects of moral hazard.

OTHER IMF MEMBERSHIP REQUIREMENTS

Thus far I have focused on the structure of banking systems, and on proposed mandatory bank regulatory requirements for IMF membership. That emphasis is appropriate given the important role banking system losses and moral hazard have played in exchange rate collapses and IMF-sponsored bailouts. But there is more to the global financial architecture than the regulations governing banks.

In addition to the mandatory bank regulations, the IMF should impose restrictions on government recapitalizations of banks (or implicit subsidization of banks through a variety of other means), and set minimal standards for government debt maturity structure, and for a prudent fixed exchange rate policy. It is appropriate for the IMF to set standards for debt management and exchange rate policy, as well as banking practices, since the IMF will provide liquidity assistance to buttress fixed exchange rates or to facilitate debt rollover.

The main purpose of restrictions on government assistance to banks is to ensure that the market discipline brought by the subordinated debt requirement is not undermined by government assistance through channels other than deposit insurance. A detailed discussion of the limits on recapitalization policy are described below under the rubrics of "transition problems" and "large macroeconomic shocks."

As in the case of mandatory banking regulations, the other rules should be as few and as simple as possible, and should be designed to make compliance with them easily observable to the IMF and to third parties. Countries should face a ceiling on the proportion of short-term sovereign debt they issue. For example, members could be required to maintain ratios of short-term debt that were no more than 25% of the previous year's export earnings, and no more than 25% of total sovereign debt.

Countries should not be required to maintain fixed exchange rates, but if a country does peg its exchange rate, then it should be required to meet two additional requirements. First, it should have to maintain a minimum ratio of reserves to high-powered money. Economic theory has little to say about the "right" reserve ratio for a central bank to maintain, except that the right minimal proportion of reserves depends on the confidence the market places in fiscal and monetary policy. Countries operating currency boards maintain ratios of nearly 100%, but there are many examples of countries that have been able to maintain exchange rates for long periods of time with much smaller reserve ratios (the United States prior to 1933, for example). Rather than requiring everyone to hold 100% reserves, or trying to set standards for reserves that depend on hard-to-observe fiscal and monetary fundamentals, I propose requiring a low minimal reserve ratio (25%), and encouraging countries to properly manage their reserve policies by making it clear (by enacting the aforementioned reforms) that the IMF will provide support only to resolve bona fide liquidity problems.

Second, member countries with fixed exchange rates should be required to permit banks to offer deposits denominated in both domestic and foreign currency. Doing so (as Argentina did when it adopted its currency board) helps to insulate banks from the risk of devaluation; funds can flow out of the domestic currency without flowing out of the banks. Bank deposit accounts in both currencies also provide continuous market information about the risk of devaluation. Domingo Cavallo, the Argentine finance minister, has argued that observing interest rates in both currencies gives domestic policy makers a valuable signal of market perceptions of government policies that bear on the maintenance of the exchange rate (Cavallo 1999).

Observing interest rate differentials prior to a speculative attack also gives the IMF valuable information which may be useful in judging the causes behind a speculative attack. If the perceived risk of devaluation (reflected in the interest rate differential) rises gradually over a matter of months, while the government makes little effort to diffuse market concerns through increases in reserves or fiscal reforms, then it is hard to blame the speculative attack on multiple equilibria or irrationality. In some cases, as discussed below, the IMF might wish to withdraw its support for an exchange peg that so obviously ignores market concerns over long-term fundamentals.

I do not include any membership requirements with respect to capital controls or devaluation policy. It would be too difficult to devise general rules to cover these areas; moreover, the appropriate policies with respect to capital controls and the appropriate circumstances for a devaluation should be left to governments to decide for themselves.

Many economists have rightly argued that the proper alternative to bailouts is a functioning bankruptcy code that can distribute loss according to clearly specified rules. I agree with that point of view, but do not attach it here as a condition for IMF membership for two reasons. First, it would be hard to specify the terms of that bankruptcy code in an uncontroversial way (the Swedish code is my personal favorite). Second, it is probably not necessary to add bankruptcy reform as an additional requirement of IMF membership. A banking system that is responsive to market discipline will be a powerful force for creating bankruptcy reform endogenously. The same can be said for the endogenous reform of commercial law, collateral registration procedures, and accounting standards.

I also omit any discussion of fiscal policy targets. It is too hard to design useful, credible, uniform rules about fiscal policy-for example, off-balance sheet exposures are often crucial to long-term fiscal health and are very hard to measure.

IMF GOALS, LENDING POLICY, AND SOURCES OF FUNDS

Thus far, I have outlined the criteria for membership in the newly constituted IMF. IMF membership depends on satisfying four bank regulatory requirements (free banking, market-based capital standards, reserve and securities requirements, and deposit insurance), and three additional policy requirements (limits on short-term government debt, and two additional rules for fixed-exchange-rate economies: a minimal central bank reserve requirement, and the requirement that banks be permitted to offer accounts denominated in both domestic and foreign currency). Countries that do not satisfy these seven requirements would be ejected from the IMF; there would be no room for discretion in bending those rules.

Now I turn to the question of what function the IMF would serve, and how it would achieve its objectives. The goal of the IMF would be to mitigate problems of illiquidity that may arise when a country is pegging its exchange rate. Note that most of the problems listed in Section II are addressed by IMF membership requirements. Problems associated with bailouts, and banking panics resulting either from asymmetric information about bank loan portfolios or multiple equilibria, are addressed by the requirements that limit abuse of the safety net and by mandatory insurance of bank deposits. Problem

5 (government debt rollover risk) is addressed by limiting short-term sovereign debt issues, which also prevents governments from free riding on IMF insurance against liquidity risk.

The systemic risk that remains to be addressed is the possibility that central bank illiquidity could produce a speculative attack on the exchange rate peg caused either by multiple exchange rate equilibria or irrational speculators, rather than by fundamental fiscal and monetary policy weakness. Preventing such attacks was the clear intent of the IMF's founders who sought to provide a safeguard against unwarranted currency depreciation that might result from sudden pressures on the balance of payments.

To provide liquidity protection I propose that the IMF operate a discount window to lend to central banks. The proposed discount window lending policy is based on Bagehot's (1873) rule: lend freely during crises on bona fide collateral at a penalty rate. By penalty rate I mean a rate higher than the preexisting market clearing rate, but not as high as the rate would be if no protection were offered. Bona fide collateral is defined as any government debt instrument held by the central bank that is priced in the market, so long as at least 25% of the amount of the collateral offered is in the form of foreign government securities.

To be concrete, a government that is a member in good standing would be able to have its central bank borrow dollars from the IMF for a short period of time (say, 90 days) if it posts 125% of the borrowed amount in securities. Collateral securities would be valued using prices from one week prior to the request. The borrowing interest rate would be two percentage points above the value-weighted yield on that bundle of securities one week before the request. Thus, since the bulk of collateral will consist of the borrowing countries' sovereign debt, by setting the interest rate at a fixed amount above the lagged yield on the sovereign debt, IMF lending can successfully provide an elastic supply of liquidity, and can short-circuit a "bad equilibrium" in which self-fulfilling expectations produce a collapse in the value of government debt. To ensure that bank regulatory protections remain in place, central banks would not be permitted to post as collateral securities they borrowed or purchased from their local commercial banks. IMF loans should not be rolled over for an additional 90 days without some form of special approval (say, a large supernumerary majority of IMF members voting in favor of extending the loan).

To avoid abuse of IMF protection, it may be desirable for the IMF to retain the option to turn down a request if it could provide evidence that the fundamentals driving the value of the collateral securities had deteriorated precipitously in the week before the request. For example, if yield spreads between bank accounts denominated in local and foreign currency had widened dramatically in response to political events that weakened fundamentals, then the IMF might reasonably refuse assistance. Russia's experience during August 1998 is an example of such a precipitous fundamental deterioration.

The 125% collateralization, along with the requirement that 25% of the collateral take the form of government securities issued by foreign governments, and-perhaps most importantly-the banking reforms that limit member government fiscal exposure to bank losses all serve to limit the default risk suffered by the IMF and encourage central banks to maintain foreign government securities holdings in addition to cash reserves, which bolsters the credibility of the exchange rate. The collateral requirements, the short duration of the loan, and the penalty interest rate together limit the size of the credit subsidy received by the borrowing central bank, which discourages frivolous use of the IMF discount window. Countries that default on IMF loans should be barred from borrowing for some time (say, 5 years), and should not be permitted to re-enter as members until they have repaid their debts in full (including accrued interest).

The new IMF discount window would provide significant protection against short-term liquidity problems. Governments would be able to convert large amounts of their bonds into cash on short notice, provided that they also maintained sufficiently large holdings of foreign government securities to meet the 25% collateral requirement. Assistance would be available on short notice, and no conditions (other than membership) would be attached to it. Of course, this discount window would not protect a country against persistent balance of payments outflows, and it should not attempt to do so. Persistent outflows, which would lower central bank holdings of hard currency and hard-currency-denominated securities, would be a sure sign of fundamental weakness. IMF lending should not try to lend to prop up unsustainable currency pegs. It should lend freely, however, to ensure that sudden "self-fulfilling" speculation does not undermine an otherwise sustainable peg.

It is worth emphasizing that a Bagehotian lender of last resort cannot provide much protection against banking panics that are caused by asymmetric information about bank loan quality, since lending against securities collateral makes the value of deposits more, rather than less, susceptible to declines in the value of bank loans. That is why it is necessary to combine a Bagehotian lender of last resort (like the reformed IMF discount window envisioned here) with credible protection against asymmetric-information problems in the banking sector. Deposit insurance eliminates depositors' incentives to run banks when they become concerned about the value of loan portfolios. Credible market discipline (through a subordinated debt requirement and asset portfolio requirements) reduces the incidence of such asymmetric-information problems and provides strong incentives for banks to control loan risk, which eases the funding burden of providing deposit insurance protection, and fosters deposit insurance credibility. Thus the IMF's ability to provide liquidity protection against speculative attacks on exchange rates will only be effective if combined with those other regulatory requirements.

How would the IMF finance its lending to central banks? The IMF would borrow cash from the central banks that issue it (in the U.S., Germany, or Japan). IMF borrowings from central banks would be fully collateralized by the government securities of the hard-money country of issue. Those collateral securities would be contributed by all IMF members, and held by the IMF to be used as needed. For example, if the IMF were borrowing dollars from the Fed, it would post 100% collateral in the form of U.S. government securities. IMF members would share the financial burden of supplying that collateral, and therefore would share the risk of the borrowing country defaulting on its IMF loan. IMF lending would not imply an increase in the aggregate supply of hard currencies, since the Fed, the Bank of Japan and the European Central Bank would all be free to sterilize the effects of their loans to the IMF.

Transition Problems

Some of the world is very far from meeting the conditions specified above for IMF membership. How difficult would it be for countries to satisfy the seven membership requirements, and what transitional policies could facilitate that process?

The central bank reserve requirement, the limits on government debt maturity, and the requirement that banks be permitted to offer accounts in domestic and foreign currency would be relatively easy to satisfy. The main difficulty is transforming the banking systems of many countries (including those in some Western European countries, as well as the vast majority of those in developing economies) into competitive, market-oriented systems. The problem is not mainly an economic one; if governments opened their banking systems to foreign entry and imposed the regulations suggested above, efficient banking systems would develop quickly. The problem, however, is the politics of banking-the resistance of entrenched special interests to reforms that would erode the rents they currently enjoy. The challenge reformers face is to find a way to placate that political opposition.

The resistance to market discipline can be found even in relatively efficient banking systems (like that of the United States), where only recently some of the largest banks have begun to call for subordinated debt requirements to eliminate "too-big-to-fail" protection. Those banks consistently opposed such measures over the past decade, predictably preferring to maintain the implicit subsidy from the taxpayers. But now many of them (and, notably, The Bankers Round-table, which represents the largest 150 U.S. banks) are calling for reform because they see credible market discipline, and a subordinated debt requirement in particular, as a means of permitting an expansion of bank powers (The Bankers' Round-table 1998). Deregulation is one way of buying support for market discipline, but in many developing economies (where banks already enjoy broad powers, and where bank owners would have great difficulty in meeting market-enforced capital standards), it may be necessary to buy support more overtly through a government-financed recapitalization of existing banks. That recapitalization would make it easier to swallow the pill of market discipline, and if a one-time subsidy would set the stage for credible regulatory reform (on the lines described above), it would be well worth the cost.

Such a recapitalization must be carefully designed, however, so that it is cost effective, and does not undermine market discipline in the future. One approach to providing government subsidization of bank recapitalization without undermining the effectiveness of market discipline is proposed in Calomiris (1998b, 1999). Assistance would take the form of subsidized government purchases of bank preferred stock for a short period (say, five years). Those purchases would occur on a matching basis with arms-length public offerings of new common stock. To qualify banks would have to agree to other provisions, including the suspension of dividend payments on common stock during the period in which the government holds preferred shares. The one-time recapitalization subsidy is designed automatically to target assistance toward the relatively strong, and to help make subordinated debt requirements feasible.

The World Bank, and other development banks, could help during the transition process in two ways: by providing financial assistance to encourage countries to implement credible market discipline (and thereby qualify for IMF membership), and by offering advice on how to structure complementary institutions and laws (including commercial laws, accounting codes, and bankruptcy laws). Too often World Bank loans have crowded out private lending and removed incentives for countries to adopt the fundamental reforms of property rights on which private lending depends. World Bank loans to China are the clearest example of such misdirected lending. But in some cases the World Bank successfully has targeted its assistance to encourage privatization of financial institutions and the creation of credible market discipline. Its loan subsidies to Argentina to help pay for the privatization of provincial banks are an example. The World Bank and other development banks could help ensure broad based membership in the new IMF by redirecting loan subsidies toward government programs that restructure banking systems to encourage adherence to market discipline.

LARGE MACROECONOMIC SHOCKS

No matter what the stated commitment to market discipline, time inconsistency problems will tempt governments to provide assistance to banks during severe macroeconomic downturns. Banking systems that respond properly to market discipline will necessarily magnify recessions by curtailing the supply of loanable funds when they experience losses on their loan portfolios. Governments will be tempted to relax market discipline to prevent the aggravation of cyclical downturns.

A better approach is to maintain market discipline through the subordinated debt requirement, but subsidize private bank recapitalization (using the preferred stock matching subsidy described above) to counteract especially severe economic downturns. I am not arguing that bank recapitalization is desirable economically; rather, I am arguing that if government intervention into the banking system is politically inevitable, it is better to intervene to help banks meet the standards of market discipline, rather than simply repealing those standards.

It is also crucial that other forms of bank bailouts be forsworn. In particular, central banks of IMF member countries should not be permitted to operate discount windows that implicitly bail out banks. In the presence of deposit insurance, a private interbank market for reserves, and IMF liquidity assistance there is no need for a domestic discount window to implement monetary policy (Goodfriend and King 1988, Bordo 1990). If central banks insist on operating a discount window, they should be required to restrict potential abuse by employing in their domestic discount window lending the same Bagehotian principles advocated here for the IMF window.

The Political Economy of Financial Reform

Politics poses challenges for any attempt to bring economic reason and market discipline to bear on the regulation of the global financial system. Politicians and regulators are jealous of their power, tend to prefer systems that rely on discretion rather than rules and are more comfortable managing cryptic decision making processes (the proverbial smoke-filled rooms in which IMF policies are determined today) than engaging opponents openly in public fora.

Thus the reforms I advocate-the abolition of the Exchange Stabilization Fund and a sweeping reform of the IMF-will likely not be very welcome in Washington or in the treasury departments or finance ministries of many nations. That does not mean that reform is impossible, but it certainly will be an uphill battle.

Consider, for example, the problem this proposal poses for the U.S. Treasury Department. It has frequently used the Exchange Stabilization Fund (Schwartz 1997, 1998) and the IMF as means to provide foreign aid under the guise of liquidity assistance. These mechanisms have the advantage that they avoid the unpleasant and inconvenient requirement of seeking Congressional approval for such aid. The recent IMF assistance programs for Mexico in 1994-1995, and for Russia in 1998, were among the most unseemly recent examples of pushiness by the U.S. administration.

The political obstacles to rationalizing the current system are formidable. But the distortions in decision making created by those obstacles also are motivating a redoubling of effort in some quarters to reform the system. Simplifying the IMF's role and decision making process by setting simple, meaningful, and publicly observable membership criteria, and placing strict bounds on how and when the IMF provides assistance, would be a welcome means of reducing politically motivated distortions from the process of providing necessary liquidity assistance. These reforms would also remove the IMF from the uncomfortable position of dictating the details of macroeconomic and microeconomic policy to its member nations. Aside from

IMF membership criteria, according to my proposal, no conditions would be attached to IMF liquidity assistance.

The prospect of a world where the power to allocate risk would be less abused, and where political puppeteers would find the strings of the financial system beyond their reach, fires the imagination and invites the effort to see such a project through. The recent failings of IMF-U.S. Treasury policies in Mexico, Asia, and Russia, and the chorus of criticism facing the IMF and the Treasury, provide a window of opportunity for reform. Congress is now poised-for the first time in U.S. history-to thoroughly evaluate the process of decision making within the IMF.

Yet, a deeper question remains unanswered. Assuming that something like this plan did succeed in being passed, and that it would perform as advertised, would the policies be politically credible? The key to credibility is the willingness to enforce market discipline in the banking system-which ensures that first-tranche losses from financial collapse are borne privately by subordinated debt holders. Will member governments do so, and will the IMF be willing to eject members that fail to impose those losses? It is not possible to predict political processes very exactly. At the same time, the subordinated debt plan has been designed to maximize the probability of political survival. Subordinated debt is a very thin sliver of private loss (2% of risk-weighted assets), and would be held (preferably, outside of the country of issue) by large, diversified international financial institutions for whom that sliver of loss should not be devastating. The vast majority of claims on banks are protected from loss by deposit insurance. Subordinated debt also is specifically earmarked ex ante for loss, and governments that do not bail out subordinated debt holders can point to IMF membership requirements that prohibit bailing them out. Furthermore, allowing for stock recapitalization during the most severe macroeconomic crises removes one of the main threats that might otherwise relax market discipline. That said, it must be admitted that no economic plan is foolproof, and that much will depend on how the IMF reacts to attempts by members to undermine market discipline. The more economists and policy makers worry about this issue in advance, the better.

Other details of the plan must also be addressed to make it more politically survivable. Non-bank banks (intermediaries that operate as banks, but do not call themselves banks) and similar evasions of the spirit of the membership requirements must be guarded against. Small banks, who will find it hard to access global subordinated debt markets, and who may possess the political power to block regulatory reform, must be compensated as well. The easiest way to proceed might be to allow small banks (defined, say, as banks with less than $1 billion in assets) to issue their subordinated debt in the form of interbank deposits held by large local banks.

A final political obstacle to reform might be called the "one world syndrome." I propose that the IMF charter prohibit loans to non-member countries. Because membership criteria will not be met by everyone, that implies that some countries will be excluded (by their own actions) from IMF protection. For some, it will be awkward to devise a global safety net and an international lender that excludes countries from membership and protection. But this is necessary for two reasons.

First, restricting access to the IMF helps taxpayers worldwide to limit their own governments' abuse of IMF lending in support of bailouts that transfer resources to influential oligarchs. Policy markers should recognize that without the core institutions of a successful market economy-clear and credible private property rights, competition, and adherence to market discipline to ensure appropriate incentives toward risk taking-quasi privatization of banks and liberalization of capital flows builds a house of cards that will inevitably topple. It is counterproductive for the IMF to assist such economies or to encourage them to enter global capital markets. Helping oligarchs to preserve their power and status at the expense of local taxpayers only makes it harder for economies to build the foundations of successful liberalization.

Second, IMF membership rules are necessary to prevent member countries from abusing the protection offered by other members. As in all successful private and public arrangements that provide liquidity protection, regulations are necessary to prevent free riding. For a mutually beneficial liquidity insurance system to work, membership criteria must be meaningful and membership must be valuable, otherwise the ability to free ride will undermine the willingness to reform domestic banking systems and other policies.

Of course, the U.S. government, and others, would still be able to provide foreign aid to non-member countries for strategic or humanitarian reasons. But that assistance would not flow through the IMF or the ESF.

Conclusion

A global financial architecture can be defined as the set of institutions, contracts, and incentives that determine how financial risks are taken and how losses and gains from taking those risks are allocated. This paper offers an ecumenical proposal for reforming that architecture.

As a working assumption, I have assumed that there is some truth in virtually every argument that is made about the problems facing the global financial system, and have argued that it is possible to design a global safety net that properly allocates risk, eliminates (or at least significantly reduces) problems of moral hazard, and still provides protection against illiquidity problems. I have argued that the imagined system would be simple to operate, and would be more credible politically (more "time consistent") than many alternatives. It would also permit the IMF to provide elastic liquidity assistance to help members defend their exchange rates from unwarranted attacks.

The proposed changes would also avoid IMF micro-management in the midst of crises, which has been criticized as an abuse of power (Feldstein 1998), an ineffectual means of financial system reform, and counterproductive to the provision of rapid liquidity assistance. Focusing the IMF's mission on true liquidity assistance would transform it from an agency that balances political interests to one that solves well defined economic problems, which would do much to rebuild the shattered reputation of the Fund.

Others, no doubt, will find ways to improve this proposal. By being concrete-drafting "blueprints" rather than just outlining broad principles-I do not mean to suggest that mine is the only imaginable way to proceed, but rather I hope to have stimulated specific discussions, and to have pointed to the need to combine economic logic with political pragmatism when designing the rules that govern the global financial system.

Offering a plan for reform does not constitute an unconditional argument for keeping the IMF. Schwartz (1998) is right, in my view, to argue that in its current form the IMF does more harm than good. Abolishing the IMF may be the right policy to pursue if it turns out that the path to reform, including credible IMF enforcement of meaningful membership criteria that limit safety net abuse, is blocked by those with vested interests in preserving the status quo.

9

International Monetary Fund and its Membership

BANK REGULATIONS

- Basle standards (but without restrictions on subordinated debt/tier 2 capital)
- 2% subordinated debt requirement (with rules on maturities, holders, and yields)
- 20% cash reserve requirement
- 20% "global securities" requirement
- Free entry by domestic and foreign investors into banking
- Bank recapitalizations are permitted, but strict guidelines must be met (and must follow preestablished rules, as in preferred stock matching program)
- Domestic lenders of last resort avoid bank bailouts by following Bagehotian principles

OTHER MEMBERSHIP CRITERIA

- Limits on short-term government securities issues
- If fixed exchange rate, 25% minimum central bank reserve requirement
- If fixed exchange rate, banks offer accounts in domestic and foreign currencies

IMF LENDING RULES

- Loans are provided only to members in good standing (those following above rules)

- If a member defaults, it may not borrow for 5 years, and then only after arrears paid Loans are for 90 days
- Supernumerary majority of members required to roll over loans for another 90 days
- Loans are collateralized by 125% of value of loan in government securities
- 25% of the 125% collateral must be in foreign government securities
- The interest rate on the loan is set at 2% above the value-weighted yield on the collateral observed one week before the loan request
- The IMF reserves the right to refuse a loan to a member
- No conditions are attached to IMF loans

IMF FUNDING

- The IMF borrows from the discount windows of the Fed and other central banks
- IMF borrowing from central banks is 100% collateralized by government securities issued by the government of the lending central bank
- Government securities that serve as collateral for IMF borrowing from central banks is lent to the IMF by its member countries

EMERGENCY LENDING

- IMF, World Bank, IDB, and others would make no other emergency lending available
- In implementing such rules, the devil is in the details, hence my emphasis is on "blueprints" (specific concrete proposals) rather than simply on organizing principles. Slight differences in details can make the difference between a reform agenda that achieves both liquidity and proper incentives toward risk taking and one that achieves neither. Before discussing those details, let me review the problems my proposal is meant to address.

WHY WE NEED A NEW IMF

Over the past twenty years, ninety banking crises have occurred in equal or greater magnitude (in terms of banking system losses) to the U.S. banking experience during the Great Depression. In at least ten cases, banking system losses exceed 20 percent of GDP-a staggering and unprecedented set of losses, which are occurring during a time of relatively stable and rapid global growth.

Banking system collapse due to excessive risk taking by banks has been a common feature of all the recent financial collapses. Bank losses precede and cause exchange rate collapses. In other words, banking systems have become the key source of financial instability. Economists have pointed to several core problems that feed that instability. First and foremost are incentive problems that encourage risk taking, particularly in response to adverse macroeconomic shocks.

Before banks were protected by government safety nets, economic downturns produced contractions of bank credit supply and cuts in bank dividends, as banks scrambled to reassure depositors that bank loan losses would not result in losses for depositors. Safety net protection has removed that important disciplinary check on bank behavior. Safety net protection (ultimately, taxpayer protection of banks and their claimants) relaxes market discipline on bank risk taking and subsidizes higher risk in banks. This effect is especially pronounced after banks experience initial losses to the value of their assets. In the wake of such losses, safety net protection encourages banks to consciously increase their asset risk. Those increases in risk often take the form of increased default risk and exchange rate risk after banks have already seen severe depletion of their capital.

Bailouts of developing economies' banks and international bank lenders, orchestrated by domestic governments in cooperation with the IMF and the U.S. Treasury, must stop. Not only do they produce inefficient risk taking, fiscal disasters for domestic governments, and enormous distortionary taxes to pay the costs of the bailouts, they also undermine the core competitive and democratic processes on which successful financial systems depend (by supporting crony capitalism within both developed and developing economies).

The IMF didn't invent bank bailouts, and IMF involvement in bailouts is mainly indirect. Nonetheless, it is quite destructive. The IMF provides only a small wealth transfer to its borrowers in the form of its loan subsidy, and so does not directly pay for much of the cost of the bailout. But the IMF pressures borrowers to bail out foreign bank lenders, and it lends support and legitimacy to domestic bailouts too by requiring government taxation to finance the repayment of IMF loans.

The destruction wrought by these bailouts has led many-including George Schultz and Anna Schwartz-to call for abolition of the IMF. Others argue, however, that liquidity assistance by the IMF could be useful if properly designed. Indeed, IMF liquidity assistance has sometimes been helpful. The most obvious case may be the March 1995 IMF loan to Argentina. Here the IMF lent to a government that had pursued significant, tangible fiscal and bank regulatory reforms and did so with the express goal of financing a defense of the Argentine currency board (not financing a bailout of banks or other government expenditures).

ADDRESSING LIQUIDITY PROBLEMS

The two potentially most important liquidity problems are (1) banking panics that result from temporary confusion on the part of bank debt holders about the incidence within the banking sector of losses attendant to an observable shock and (2) self-fulfilling collapses of fixed exchange rates that result from government illiquidity.

To solve the first problem, I propose a set of banking regulations that together would remove the threat of banking panics including: (1) capital standards founded on market discipline, achieved through a requirement that banks maintain a minimal proportion of uninsured, junior (or subordinated) debt; (2) credible deposit insurance for other bank debt claims; (3) a 20 percent "cash" (or equivalents) reserve requirement (relative to bank assets); (4) a 20 percent "global securities" requirement (relative to bank assets); (5) free entry by domestic and foreign competitors into banking; and (6) limitations on other government assistance to banks (which limit the transfer of bank losses to taxpayers). My plan for designing effective, credible market discipline for banks is largely based on the Chicago Federal Reserve's 1989 subordinated debt proposal, although there are some differences.

It is important to emphasize that a broad consensus has emerged on the need to add some form of subordinated debt requirement to the Basle capital standards. Advocates of some form of such a requirement now include: the Bankers' Roundtable, the U.S. Treasury, several Federal Reserve Banks, at least one Fed Governor, members of Congress, and the Shadow Financial Regulatory Committee.

Last year, the Federal Reserve Board assembled a task force charged with exploring how best to design and implement a subordinated debt requirement. Outside the United States, several countries either have passed or are considering such a requirement.

The combination of domestic deposit insurance and market discipline (which prevents the abuse of deposit insurance) can resolve the threat of banking panics that result either from confusion about the incidence of shocks or from self-fulfilling concerns about the insufficiency of bank reserves.

The IMF's role would be mainly to address the other liquidity problem-liquidity crises that face member governments as the result of unwarranted speculative pressure on exchange rates. This was the original intent of the IMF's founders, and it remains a legitimate objective of IMF policy.

Recent studies that emphasize the value of IMF liquidity protection argue that the current form of IMF assistance is inadequate-it is too little, too late, and with too many conditions and delays to be effective in short-circuiting self-fulfilling runs on currencies or government debt. But how does one provide effective liquidity protection without encouraging counterproductive bailouts of banks and/or governments?

My plan is to replace the current IMF and Exchange Stabilization Fund with a new IMF, which would offer a discount window lending facility. That facility would only be available to IMF members-and membership would require adherence to the aforementioned banking regulations, as well as some additional rules regarding government debt management, a 25 percent minimum reserve requirement for the central bank (if a fixed exchange rate is maintained), and a requirement that banks offer accounts denominated in both domestic and foreign currency.

By restricting access to the IMF window to members in good standing who conform to a few simple and easily verified rules, the IMF avoids free-riding on liquidity protection and the hazard of unwittingly financing bank bailouts in the guise of liquidity protection.

The rules governing the discount window follow Walter Bagehot's classic principles for ensuring liquidity, while avoiding free riding: lend freely on good collateral at a penalty rate. The specifics of membership rules, limits on collateral, and penalty lending rates (described above in "The Calomiris Plan in Brief") encourage member countries' central banks (like their other banks) to diversify their securities portfolios and maintain adequate liquid reserves.

If a member is in good standing, loans are made available on good collateral using one-week-old prices to value collateral. The loan interest rate is set at 2 percent above the value-weighted yield to maturity on the collateral offered. That provides a fast and effective means to short-circuit a self-fulfilling "bad equilibrium."

OTHER FEATURES

Why no additional conditions for loans? For liquidity assistance to be effective, it must be delivered quickly and supplied elastically. Why no more rules for members? There are lots of basic rules countries should meet to build effective domestic financial systems.

These include accounting standards, procedures for registering collateral interests, court enforcement of creditors' and stockholders' rights, a transparent and efficient bankruptcy code, and many more. But these rules are more controversial (for example, I would argue that the Swedish bankruptcy code is far superior to the American) and are hard to specify in a simple way. I have not tried to construct a list of all desirable rules, but rather, a set of minimal rules that are important, simple, and verifiable.

Furthermore, additional rules (accounting, bankruptcy, and commercial laws) will arise endogenously if there is credible market discipline within the financial system, which the subordinated debt requirement and other rules will ensure. Market discipline is a lever for other reforms because it creates a strong constituency of banks and their debt-holders who will seek ways to improve transparency, contract enforceability, and sensible workout procedures.

How will the IMF actually operate the new window? IMF lenders would contribute (that is, lend) bonds to the IMF, which along with borrowers' collateral would be used to access the discount window of the hard-currency central banks (which would lend cash to the IMF collateralized 100 percent by the government securities of that central bank's government). The hard-currency central banks, thus, would lend without risk. They would also be free to sterilize the effects of IMF borrowing on the aggregate supply of hard currency.

To avoid the potential for costly bailouts, other redundant mechanisms would be abolished. That would include not only other IMF assistance, but also the Exchange Stabilization Fund and emergency assistance to banks via the World Bank and Inter-American Development Bank.

Political Feasibility

Having argued that this plan would achieve proper incentives in private banking and in government finance and would also protect against liquidity crises, I now turn to the more difficult question: whether it is politically feasible. Clearly, vested interests have reasons to oppose this approach because it would deprive them of valuable (though socially costly) subsidies. It may be possible, and worthwhile, to "buy off" those vested interests (particularly within developing countries' banking systems) by offering a one-time injection of public funds to help recapitalize banks, and thereby make the pill of market discipline easier to swallow. It is worth considering how domestic governments interested in implementing true reform might be helped by the World Bank and other development banks to achieve membership in the newly constituted IMF.

Too often the World Bank has crowded out private lending and removed incentives for countries to adopt credible market discipline. World Bank loans to China are the clearest example of this problem.

But in some cases (notably in Argentina recently) the World Bank has provided subsidies to make privatization and market discipline more achievable by rewarding cronies (e.g., provinces that control public banks) for giving up their instruments of patronage. More World Bank assistance should be directed toward that end.

A central principle of my proposal is that the functions of the IMF and the World Bank need to be clearly separated. The IMF should focus on liquidity protection for member countries that have achieved sound financial liberalization. The efficacy of that protection would be much enhanced by focusing on achieving that narrowly defined economic objective.

The World Bank would facilitate liberalization and hence help to expand the IMF's membership list. Encouraging bona fide liberalization is a long-term process. The form and pace of assistance required is different from that of emergency liquidity assistance, and it is very counterproductive to confuse the two missions and the two kinds of assistance.

Possibly the greatest obstacle to my proposal will be the likely opposition of the U.S. Treasury to repealing the Exchange Stabilization Fund and focusing the IMF on providing bona fide liquidity assistance. The Treasury has used the Exchange Stabilization Fund and the IMF as slush funds to provide foreign aid (without the inconvenience of seeking congressional approval) in the guise of "liquidity" assistance. Getting the U.S. Treasury to forswear such activities is a formidable challenge-one that may require veto-proof support in Congress.

If all these challenges to reforming the IMF could be overcome, and something like this proposal were enacted, would the IMF abide by the new rules? Obviously, the goal of my plan has been to design rules that are transparent to outsiders and would make it harder for the IMF to "forbear" in enforcing those rules. The more we all talk about ways to further limit such forbearance, the better.

In summary, I think it is economically feasible to restructure the way the IMF does business to promote a more efficient and democratic financial system-one that ensures market discipline while avoiding market chaos. If the G7 chose such a path, other countries would follow: The rewards to participating in an open, market-oriented, and stable global financial system would be irresistible.

The transition process could be facilitated if the funds currently channeled through the World Bank and other development banks could be redirected toward helping countries to qualify for membership in the newly constituted IMF.

The IMF would be more effective in its actions and more legitimate in the eyes of emerging-market countries if it pursued the less ambitious goal of maintaining countries' access to global capital markets and international bank lending.

Its experts should focus on determining whether the troubled country's problem is one of short-term liquidity and, if so, should emphasize that in its advice and assistance. The IMF should eschew the temptation to use currency crises as an opportunity to force fundamental structural and institutional reforms on countries, however useful they may be in the long term, unless they are absolutely necessary to revive access to international funds.

It should strongly resist the pressure from the United States, Japan, and other major countries to make their trade and investment agenda part of the IMF funding conditions.

The IMF should remember that the borrowers and the lending bankers or bondholders should bear primary responsibility for resolving the problems that arise when countries or their corporations cannot meet their international debt obligations. The IMF should provide technical assistance on how the debtors can improve their current account balances and increase their foreign exchange. It should act as a monitor of the success that the country is making in moving toward self-sustainable liquidity, providing its own funds as an indication of its confidence in the country's progress rather than as a bailout of international lenders and domestic borrowers.

If the IMF can focus its attention on this narrower agenda, it can devote more of its scarce staff talent to the problem of crisis prevention. The IMF should work with countries that have not yet reached a currency crisis in order to prevent the large current account deficits or the excess short-term debts that could later precipitate a crisis.

If the fund is seen more as a client-focused and supportive organization than as the imposer of painful contractions and radical economic reforms, it is likely to find that countries will be more willing to invite its assistance when it can be most helpful.

10

Future Prospects of International Monetary Fund

Today's high-level meeting provides a welcome opportunity to take stock of where we stand in meeting the challenges facing the global economy. And there can be no question that the foremost challenge is poverty. The Financing for Development Conference in Monterrey produced an unprecedented common understanding about what it will take to overcome world poverty. First, the basis for everything is self-responsibility. Economic development requires good governance, respect for the rule of law, and policies and institutions which create a good investment climate and unlock the creative energies of the people. Second, on this basis, developing countries can rightly expect faster and more comprehensive support from the international community. What is crucial now is to transform the Monterrey Consensus into concrete action and measurable results. To establish proper accountability, we should identify more clearly the respective responsibilities of poor countries and their development partners-donor countries, international institutions, the private sector, and civil society. I am confident that it will be possible to achieve the Millennium Development Goals, if all cooperate to do their parts under this two pillar approach.

We can all be happy that the doomsday scenarios some predicted after the terrorist attacks of September 11 did not materialize. Thanks in particular to the decisive interest rate cuts and tax reductions in the United States and the supportive policy response in Europe, a recovery of the world economy now appears to be under way. And I think it was also important for confidence that the membership of the IMF came together last November in Ottawa to define a collaborative approach to strengthen the global economy.

To be sure, there are still questions about the strength and durability of the recovery. These relate especially to corporate earnings and investment in the United States, fragilities in financial markets, and regional political tensions. But on the whole, I am confident that the world economy will gain strength in the second half of this year. What is required now is vigilance and a shift from short-term considerations to tackling decisively the underlying economic and financial imbalances in the global economy. This calls for strong leadership of the advanced industrial countries, by taking action to strengthen the prospects for sustained growth in their own economies and through leading by example in the effort to make globalization work for the benefit of all.

Strong US growth in the second half of the 1990s served the global economy well. But this has been accompanied by a widening current account deficit which raises concerns over the sustainability of capital inflows to the United States and the valuation of dollar assets. In this situation, it will be crucial for the US to ensure that the budget remains balanced over the medium term, as part of a strategy for increasing national savings. But the US current account deficit is not just an issue for the United States: what is also needed to strengthen the global economy is more robust, domestic demand-driven growth in other advanced economies. It is clear that it would be possible to raise potential growth rates in Europe to 3 percent a year or even more, if there would be more ambition for structural reform. Similarly, in Japan the return to a growth performance that corresponds to the country's size and potential demands accelerated action to dispose of nonperforming loans, deregulate key industries, and restructure Japan's banking and corporate sectors. The recent improvement in business activity should not reduce incentives for action on these reforms.

Emerging markets and other developing countries should stay the course of sound fiscal and monetary policies and structural reform, which is indispensable to weather the ongoing storm. In this context, there also must be confidence that the international environment will hold opportunities for countries committed to reform.

PRAGUE IMF PROTEST TURNS UGLY

Protests at the annual meeting of the World Bank and International Monetary Fund here started on a festive note Tuesday, but by evening small groups of anarchists, hard-line leftists and vandals were smashing shop windows and tossing Molotov cocktails at police. Officers responded with tear gas.

For a time late Tuesday afternoon, protesters achieved their goal of blocking access to and from the meeting hall for the opening session of the three-day gathering. Delegates eventually left by special subway trains, but evening plans for many were disrupted.

It was an empty victory for the protest's main organizers, who had called for nonviolence from their followers.

The demonstrators--police put the number at up to 9,000--have vowed to halt the meetings, continuing an anti-globalization drive that disrupted trade talks in Seattle last year and prompted violence in London in May.

One thousand police officers were called in from other regions of the Czech Republic on Saturday to supplement the already beefed-up force of 11,000 assembled to cope with the protests, authorities said.

Most of the protesters argue that the IMF and World Bank are worsening the plight of the world's poor and should cancel debts owed by the neediest nations. Others who have latched on to the movement and were largely responsible for the violence go much further, charging that the capitalist system is exploitative and should be destroyed.

Police reported that by late evening, 51 officers and 18 protesters had been hospitalized. Thirty-four people were arrested--11 Germans, two Poles and 21 Czechs. A Japanese delegate to the financial gathering was hit by a stone but declined treatment, and a Russian delegate suffered a cut lip when hit by a bag of sand, police said. In one incident, police officers were hit by a homemade gasoline bomb, and the flames were doused by colleagues wielding a water cannon. After dark, protesters smashed windows at McDonald's and KFC outlets in the city center, as well as many other buildings, and they set cars on fire.

A gala evening for delegates at an opera was canceled after protesters surrounded the building.

Alice Dvorska, a Czech leader of the Initiative Against Economic Globalization, or INPEG, said her umbrella organization for the protests wanted to "disassociate" itself from the violence because it had "organized only the march."

"We're actually very disappointed with everything today," said Chelsea Mozen, 24, an American and INPEG spokeswoman. "We've been organizing completely nonviolently, and we're very frustrated about what's happening on the streets."

Reaction among Czechs appeared to be strongly in favor of the police, who in most cases simply observed as protesters staged illegal but peaceful demonstrations, yet acted firmly when violence erupted.

In a reflection of the local mood, Prague 1 Radio declared Tuesday evening that the rioters trashing Wenceslas Square--the scene of enormous peaceful demonstrations in 1989 that toppled communism--were "professional fighters who did not come here to protest but to destroy."

"We did expect problems, but we did not expect such brutality, especially of the foreign protesters," Prague Mayor Jan Kasl said. Last December in Seattle, thousands took to the streets during a World Trade Organization meeting, leading to clashes between police and giving greater prominence to the issue of globalization.

The protests here Tuesday began with a street-festival atmosphere. Many demonstrators wore outlandish costumes, dressed as everything from the elves of Czech fairy tales to "radical cheerleaders," who wore something akin to paper-strip hula skirts over their jeans.

"They're trying to take control and do as they please, globalizing power for corporate sleaze," went one of the chants, recited by a woman who identified herself as Mary Christmas, an erotic dancer from New York.

"Well, there's poverty and misery all over the land; the situation's gotten out of hand," she continued. "When so few own so much, it's time to take a stand: Take back the power! End corporate greed!"

Asked why she came to demonstrate, the woman replied: "When I found out that my clothes were made by some woman who cannot feed her children, it makes me cry. Also, all our friends are here and it's a great party."

The party atmosphere began to fade as one group of about 1,000 protesters faced off against about 100 police in riot gear, backed by four armored personnel carriers, at a bridge leading to the Prague Conference Center, where the IMF and World Bank meeting opened.

"I think we will try to go through [the police line] because we think the meeting there is illegitimate," said Reko Ravela, 28, a Finnish postman who wore a helmet and foam padding in preparation for a confrontation with police. "That's where the real criminals are, so we will try to go there and stop the meeting." A subway stop was within the police perimeter surrounding the meeting hall, so authorities always had a way to get the delegates out. But to avoid letting protesters get too close, trains did not stop at that station during the afternoon. So in practice, the only way in or out of the center was through lines of police.

Without organized transportation, some meeting participants were stuck inside. Then, late in the afternoon, after driving back a group of protesters that had stormed up a hillside to attack the perimeter of the conference area with stones, police ordered everyone to stay inside while they faced off with the protesters, who had blocked all access roads.

"I've been waiting here since 12:30 to get to my hotel, but there were no buses," Margarita Bringham, the wife of a Finnish delegate, said while trapped in the conference center about 6 p.m. "I wanted to go to the lovely sightseeing tour, and here I am."

The confrontations ended peacefully after protesters learned that special subway trains had taken delegates nonstop to a station on the far side of the city, where they were put on buses and driven to their destinations.

IBRD

What is the World Bank

In 2004 the World Bank provided $20.1 billion for 245 projects in developing countries worldwide, with its finance and/or technical expertise aimed at helping those countries reduce poverty. We live in a world so rich that global income is more than $31 trillion a year. In this world, the average person in some countries earns more than $40,000 a year. But in this same world, 2.8 billion people-more than half the people in developing countries-live on less than $700 a year. Of these, 1.2 billion earn less than $1 a day.

As a result, 33,000 children die every day in developing countries. In these countries, each minute more than one woman dies during childbirth. Poverty keeps more than 100 million children, most of them girls, out of school.

The challenge of reducing these levels of poverty, while the population continues to grow-by an estimated 3 billion people over the next 50 years-is enormous.

The World Bank works to bridge this divide and turn rich country resources into poor country growth. One of the world's largest sources of development assistance, the World Bank supports the efforts of developing country governments to build schools and health centers, provide water and electricity, fight disease, and protect the environment.

Not a bank, but rather a specialized agency. The World Bank is not a "bank" in the common sense. It is one of the United Nations' specialized agencies, and is made up of 184 member countries. These countries are jointly responsible for how the institution is financed and how its money is spent. Along with the rest of the development community, the World Bank centers its efforts on reaching the Millennium Development Goals, agreed to by UN members in 2000 and aimed at sustainable poverty reduction.

The "World Bank" is the name that has come to be used for the International Bank for Reconstruction and Development

(IBRD) and the International Development Association (IDA). Together these organizations provide low-interest loans, interest-free credit, and grants to developing countries.

Some 10,000 development professionals from nearly every country in the world work in the World Bank's Washington DC headquarters or in its 109 country offices.

$9 billion in assistance. The world's low-income countries generally cannot borrow money in international markets or can only do so at high interest rates. In addition to direct contributions and loans from developed countries, these countries receive grants, interest-free loans, and technical assistance from the World Bank to enable them to provide basic services. In the case of the loans, countries have 35-40 years to repay, with a 10-year grace period.

In fiscal 2004 IDA provided $9 billion in financing for 158 projects in 62 low-income countries.

Interest-free credit and grant financing comes from IDA, the world's largest source of concessional assistance. Some 40 rich countries provide the money for this funding by making contributions every four years. The fund was replenished most recently in 2002, with nearly $9 billion from donors and another $6.6 billion from the Bank's resources. At that time, donors agreed on increased use of IDA grants-up to 21 percent of resources-to help address the special difficulties, such as the HIV/AIDS epidemic, faced by the poorest and most vulnerable countries.

IDA credits make up about one-quarter of the Bank's financial assistance. Aside from IDA funds, very little of the Bank's income is provided by its member countries.

$11 billion in loans. Higher-income developing countries-some of which can borrow from commercial sources, but generally only at very high interest rates-receive loans from the IBRD.

Countries that borrow from the IBRD have more time to repay than if they borrowed from a commercial bank-15 to 20 years with a three-to-five-year grace period before the repayment of principal begins. Developing country governments borrow money for specific programs, including poverty reduction efforts, delivery of social services, protection of the environment, and promotion of economic growth that will improve living standards. In fiscal 2004 IBRD provided loans totaling $11 billion in support of 87 projects in 33 countries.

Raising capital. The IBRD raises almost all its money in the world's financial markets-$13 billion in fiscal 2004. With a AAA credit rating, it issues bonds to raise money and then passes on the low interest rates to its borrowers.

The World Bank Group. In addition to IBRD and IDA, three other organizations make up the World Bank Group. The International Finance Corporation (IFC) promotes private sector investment by supporting high-risk sectors and countries. The Multilateral Investment Guarantee Agency (MIGA) provides political risk insurance (guarantees) to investors in and lenders to developing countries. And the International Centre for Settlement of Investment Disputes (ICSID) settles investment disputes between foreign investors and their host countries.

Global goods. Over the past few years, the World Bank has put significant resources into activities meant to have global impact. One is debt relief, and under the enhanced Heavily Indebted Poor Countries (HIPC) Initiative, 26 poor countries have received debt relief which will save them $41 billion over time. The money these countries save in debt repayments will instead be put into housing, education, health, and welfare programs for the poor.

The World Bank, along with 189 countries and numerous organizations, has committed to an unprecedented global partnership to fight poverty. The Millennium Development Goals define specific targets in terms of school enrolments, child mortality, maternal health, disease, and access to water to be met by 2015.

Among numerous other global partnerships, the World Bank has put supporting the fight against HIV/AIDS at the top of its agenda. It is the world's largest long-term financer of HIV/AIDS programs. Current Bank commitments for HIV/AIDS amount to more than $1.3 billion, with half of that for sub-Saharan Africa.

Corruption and fraud. The World Bank works with countries in their anti-corruption efforts and has as well a number of mechanisms in place to prevent corruption and fraud in bank-financed projects. The Department of Institutional Integrity has a 24-hour Fraud and Corruption Hotline: 1-800-831-0463.

The variety of work on the ground. The Bank is currently involved in more than 1,800 projects in virtually every sector and developing country. These are as diverse as providing microcredit in Bosnia Herzegovina and raising AIDS awareness in communities in Guinea, supporting education of girls in Bangladesh and improving health care delivery in Mexico, helping East Timor rebuild upon independence or India to rebuild Gujarat after a devastating earthquake.

In addition, to a small selection of project profiles, the Countries and Projects sections of this website provide details of the Bank's work on the ground.

At the World Bank we have made the world's challenge-to reduce global poverty-our challenge.

Our work focuses on achievement of the Millennium Development Goals that call for the elimination of poverty and sustained development. The goals provide us with targets and yardsticks for measuring results.

Our mission is to help developing countries and their people reach the goals by working with our partners to alleviate poverty. To do that we concentrate on building the climate for investment, jobs and sustainable growth, so that economies will grow, and by investing in and empowering poor people to participate in development. The World Bank is like a cooperative, where its 185 member countries are shareholders. The shareholders are represented by a Board of Governors, who are the ultimate policy makers at the World Bank. Generally, the governors are member countries' ministers of finance or ministers of development. They meet once a year at the Annual Meetings of the Boards of Governors of the World Bank Group and the International Monetary Fund.

Because the governors only meet annually, they delegate specific duties to 24 Executive Directors, who work on-site at the bank. The five largest shareholders, France, Germany, Japan, the United Kingdom and the United States appoint an executive director, while other member countries are represented by 19 executive directors.

The President of the World Bank, Paul Wolfowitz, chairs meetings of the Boards of Directors and is responsible for overall management of the bank. By tradition, the bank president is national of and is nominated by the largest shareholder in the bank, the United States. The President is elected by the Board of Governors for a five-year, renewable term. The Executive Directors make up the Boards of Directors of the World Bank. They normally meet at least twice a week to oversee the bank's business, including approval of loans and guarantees, new policies, the administrative budget, country assistance strategies and borrowing and financial decisions.

The World Bank operates day-to-day under the leadership and direction of the president, management and senior staff, and the vice presidents in charge of regions, sectors, networks and functions.

OPERATIONS

The World Bank's two closely affiliated entities-the International Bank for Reconstruction and Development (IBRD) and the International Development Association (IDA)-provide low or no interest loans and grants to countries that have unfavorable or no access to international credit markets. Unlike other financial institutions, we do not operate for profit. The IBRD is market-based, and we use our high credit rating to pass the low interest we pay for money on to our borrowers-developing countries. We pay for our own operating costs, since we don't look to outside sources to furnish funds for overhead.

So, where does the money come from to operate the World Bank, and how do we use the funds to carry out our mission?

FUND GENERATION

IBRD lending to developing countries is primarily financed by selling AAA-rated bonds in the world's financial markets. While IBRD earns a small margin on this lending, the greater proportion of its income comes from lending out its own capital. This capital consists of reserves built up over the years and money paid in from the bank's 184 member country shareholders. IBRD's income also pays for World Bank operating expenses and has contributed to IDA and debt relief.

IDA, the world's largest source of interest-free loans and grant assistance to the poorest countries, is replenished every three years by 40 donor countries. Additional funds are regenerated through repayments of loan principal on 35-to-40-year, no-interest loans, which are then available for re-lending. IDA accounts for nearly 40% of our lending.

LOANS

Through the IBRD and IDA, we offer two basic types of loans and credits: investment loans and development policy loans. Investment loans are made to countries for goods, works and services in support of economic and social development projects in a broad range of economic and social sectors. Development policy loans (formerly known as adjustment loans) provide quick-disbursing financing to support countries' policy and institutional reforms. Each borrower's project proposal is assessed to ensure that the project is economically, financially, socially and environmentally sound. During loan negotiations, the bank and borrower agree on the development objectives, outputs, performance indicators and implementation plan, as well as a loan disbursement schedule. While we supervise the implementation of each loan and evaluate its results, the borrower implements the project or program according to the agreed terms. As nearly 30% of our staff is based in some 100 country offices worldwide, three-fourths of outstanding loans are managed by country directors located away from the World Bank offices in Washington.

IDA long term loans (credits) are interest free but do carry a small service charge of 0.75 percent on funds paid out. IDA commitment fees range from zero to 0.5 percent on un-disbursed credit balances; for FY06 commitment fees have been set at 0.30 percent. For complete information about IBRD financial products, services, lending rates and charges, please visit the

World Bank Treasury. Treasury is at the heart of IBRD's borrowing and lending operations and also performs treasury functions for other members of the World Bank Group.

GRANTS

Grants are designed to facilitate development projects by encouraging innovation, co-operation between organizations and local stakeholders' participation in projects. In recent years, IDA grants-which are either funded directly or managed through partnerships.

ANALYTIC AND ADVISORY SERVICES

While we are best known as a financier, another of our roles is to provide analysis, advice and information to our member countries so they can deliver the lasting economic and social improvements their people need. We do this in several ways: through economic research on broad issues such as the environment, poverty, trade and globalization and through country-specific economic and sector work, where we evaluate a country's economic prospects by examining its banking systems and financial markets, as well as trade, infrastructure, poverty and social safety net issues, for example.

We also draw upon the resources of our knowledge bank to educate clients so they can equip themselves to solve their development problems and promote economic growth. By knowledge bank we mean the wealth of contacts, knowledge, information and experience we've acquired over the years, country by country and project by project, in our development work. Our ultimate aim is to encourage the knowledge revolution in developing countries. These are only some of the ways our analyses, advice and knowledge are made available to our client countries, their government and development professionals.

CAPACITY BUILDING

Another core bank function is to increase the capabilities of our own staff, our partners and the people in developing countries-to help them acquire the knowledge and skills they need to provide technical assistance, improve government performance and delivery of services, promote economic growth and sustain poverty reduction programs. Linkages to knowledge-sharing networks such as these have been set up by the bank to address the vast needs for information and dialogue about development:

Advisory Services and Ask Us help desks make information available by topic via telephone, fax, email and the web. There are more than 25 advisory services at the bank. Staff members who respond to inquiries add value to the work of our own staff, clients and partners by responding quickly to their knowledge needs. Often, they are the first and possibly the only contact the public at large and the people in developing countries have with the World Bank.

Global Development Learning Network is an extensive network of distance learning centers that uses advanced information and communications technologies to connect people working in development around the world.

World Bank Institute Global and Regional Programs bring together leading development practitioners on-line and face-to-face to exchange experiences and to develop skills.

B-SPAN webcasting service is an Internet-based broadcasting station that presents World Bank seminars, workshops and conferences on sustainable development and poverty reduction.

PROJECTS

At any given moment in locations around the globe, people are engaged in development projects designed to improve living standards and reduce poverty. Last year, the World Bank provided $23.6 billion for 279 projects in developing countries worldwide, with our financial and/or technical expertise aimed at helping those countries reduce poverty.

The bank is currently involved in more than 1,800 projects in virtually every sector and developing country. The projects are as diverse as providing microcredit in Bosnia and Herzegovina, raising AIDS-prevention awareness in Guinea, supporting education of girls in Bangladesh, improving health care delivery in Mexico, and helping East Timor rebuild upon independence and India rebuild Gujarat after a devastating earthquake. Visit these sites to explore in depth how the bank partners with governments, communities and private sector businesses to implement sustainable development:

PROJECT LIFECYCLE

Learn the steps the World Bank goes through to ensure the success of each project.

THE BUSINESS CENTER

Obtain information on how to bid on World Bank financed projects in developing countries.

Each year the World Bank lends between US$15-$20 billion for projects in the more than 100 countries it works with. Projects range across the economic and social spectrum in these countries from infrastructure, to education, to health, to government financial management. The projects the Bank finances are conceived and supervised according to a well-documented project cycle. Documents produced as part of the project cycle can be valuable sources of information for interested stakeholders wanting to keep abreast of the work the Bank is financing and for businesses wishing to participate in Bank-financed projects. Below is a step-by-step guide to the project cycle, the documents that are produced as part of the process, and how to access them.

HOW THE PROCESS BEGINS

The Bank recognizes that many past assistance efforts, including some of its own, failed because the agenda was driven by donors rather than by the governments it was trying to assist. Under its current development policy, the Bank helps governments take the lead in preparing and implementing development strategies in the belief that programs that are owned by the country, with widespread stakeholder support, have a greater chance of success.

In low-income countries, the Bank uses the Poverty Reduction Strategy (PRS) approach which involves widespread consultation and consensus building on how to boost development. Under this process, a national poverty reduction strategy is prepared by the country, creating a framework for donors to better co-ordinate and align their programs behind national priorities.

The government consults a wide cross-section of local groups and combines this with an extensive analysis of poverty in the country's society and its economic situation. The government determines its own priorities from this process and produces targets for reducing poverty over a three to five year period. These are outlined in a Poverty Reduction Strategy Paper (PRSP). The Bank and other aid agencies then align their assistance efforts with the country's own strategy-a proven way of improving development effectiveness.

The Bank's blueprint for its work with a country is based on a Country Assistance Strategy (CAS) which, in the case of low income countries, is derived from the priorities contained in the country's Poverty Reduction Strategy Paper. The CAS is produced in co-operation with the government and interested stakeholders. The preparation of the CAS may draw on analytical work conducted by the Bank or other parties on a wide range of economic and social sectors, such as health, education, agriculture, public expenditure and budgeting, fiscal management, or procurement, among others.

THE IDENTIFICATION PHASE

The Bank's Country Assistance Strategy (CAS) forms the blueprint for its assistance to a country. In low-income countries, the CAS is based on the priorities identified in the country's Poverty Reduction Strategy Paper (as outlined above). The goals outlined in the CAS guide the priorities of the Bank's lending program and are a useful source of information for interested stakeholders and businesses wishing to identify potential future areas of Bank lending.

During the identification phase, Bank teams work with the government to identify projects which can be funded as part of the agreed development objectives. Once a project has been identified, the Bank team creates a Project Concept Note (PCN) which is an internal document of four to five pages that outlines the basic elements of the project, its proposed objective, likely risks, alternative scenarios to conducting the project, and a likely timetable for the project approval process.

USEFUL PUBLIC DOCUMENTS

The Project Information Document (PID) is prepared after an internal review of the PCN and is released publicly through the Bank's InfoShop. It is usually four to five pages long and contains the information mentioned above-the objective, a brief description, etc. It also contains the name of the World Bank Task Manager or Team Lead who is supervising the project, a useful contact for companies interested in bidding for work on the project. The PID is an essential resource for tailoring bidding documents to the project concerned. The Integrated Safeguards Data Sheet (ISDS) is also prepared for the first time after the project's first formal review and made available publicly. It identifies key issues under the World Bank's safeguard policies for environmental and social issues, and provides information about how they will be addressed during project preparation.

THE PREPARATION PHASE

This part of the process is driven by the country that the Bank is working with and can take anything from a few months to three years, depending on the complexity of the project being proposed. The Bank plays a supporting role, offering analysis and advice where requested. During this period, the technical, institutional, economic, environmental and financial issues facing the project will be studied and addressed-including whether there are alternative methods for achieving the same objectives. An assessment is required of projects proposed for Bank financing to help ensure that they are environmentally sound and sustainable (Environmental Assessment). The scope of the Environmental Assessment depends on the scope, scale and potential impact of the project.

The Appraisal Phase

The Bank is responsible for this part of the process. Bank staff review the work done during identification and preparation, often spending three to four weeks in the client country. They prepare for bank management either Project Appraisal Documents (investment projects) or Program Documents (for adjustment operations) and the Financial Management team assesses the financial aspects of the project. The PID is updated during this phase. These documents are released to the public after the project is approved.

The Negotiation and Approval Phase

After Bank staff members have appraised the proposed project, the Bank and the country that is seeking to borrow the funds, negotiate on its final shape. Both sides come to an agreement on the terms and conditions of the loan. Then the Project Appraisal Document (PAD) or the Program Document (PGD), along with the Memorandum of the President and legal documents are submitted to the Bank's Board of Executive Directors for approval. The appropriate documents are also submitted for final clearance by the borrowing government which may involve ratification by a council of ministers or a country's legislature. Following approval by both parties, the loan agreement is formally signed by their representatives. Once this has occurred, the loan or credit is declared effective, or ready for disbursement, after the relevant conditions are met, and the agreement is made available to the public.

The Project Appraisal Document (PAD) presents all the information the Board needs to approve Bank financing of the proposal. Before 1999, this document was called the Staff Appraisal Report. The Program Document (PGD) describes adjustment lending operations, and sets out the Bank's appraisal and assessment of the feasibility and justification for the program.

The Technical Annex supplements a Memorandum and Recommendation of the President for freestanding technical assistance loans, which do not require Project Appraisal Documents.

THE IMPLEMENTATION AND SUPERVISION PHASE

The implementation of the project is the responsibility of the borrowing country, while the Bank is responsible for supervision. Once the loan is approved, the borrowing government, with technical assistance from the Bank, prepares the specifications and evaluates bids for the procurement of goods and services for the project. The Bank reviews this activity to ensure that its procurement guidelines have been followed. If they have, the funds will be disbursed. The Bank's Financial Management Team maintains an oversight of the financial management of the project including periodically requiring audited financial statements.

Report on the Status of Projects in Execution provides a very brief summary of all projects that were active during the previous fiscal year. Previously an internal communication to the Board of Executive Directors, the SOPE Report now is available to the public. Projects that closed during the fiscal year are no longer included in the SOPE, since their Implementation Completion Reports are also publicly disclosed.

The Implementation Completion Report

At the end of the loan disbursement period (anywhere from 1-10 years), a completion report identifying accomplishments, problems, and lessons learned is submitted to the Bank Board of Executive Directors for information purposes.

Implementation Completion Reports review the results and assess an operation on completion of each loan financed by the Bank. Operational staff prepare these self-evaluations for every completed project.

The Evaluation Phase

Following the completion of a project, the Bank's Operations Evaluation Department conducts an audit to measure its outcome against the original objectives. The audit entails a review of the project completion report and preparation of a separate report. Both reports are then submitted to the executive directors and the borrower. They are not released to the public.

Project Performance Assessment Reports rate project outcomes (taking into account relevance, efficacy, and efficiency), sustainability of results, and the institutional development impact. One in four completed projects (or about 70 a year) is chosen for a Project Performance Assessment Report, which takes Operations and Evaluation Department staff about six weeks to produce and normally includes a visit to the project in the borrowing country. Impact Evaluation Reports assess the economic worth of projects and the long-term effects on people and the environment. These "second looks" at projects are performed five to eight years after the close of loan disbursements.

Inspection Panel Reports review claims by affected parties that the Bank failed to follow its operational policies and procedures with respect to the design, appraisal and/or implementation of a Bank-financed operation.

Projects may be dropped at any point in the project cycle from preparation to approval. For these projects, which never achieve active status, Project Information Documents, described above, are effectively the final documents.

Since inception in 1944, the World Bank has expanded from a single institution to a closely associated group of five development institutions. Our mission evolved from the International Bank for Reconstruction and Development (IBRD) as facilitator of post-war reconstruction and development to the present day mandate of worldwide poverty alleviation in conjunction with our affiliate, the International Development Association. Once we had a homogeneous staff of engineers and financial analysts, based solely in Washington, DC. Today, we have a multidisciplinary and diverse staff that includes economists, public policy experts, sector experts and social scientists, and 30% of our staff is now based in country offices.

Reconstruction remains an important focus of our work, given the natural disasters and post conflict rehabilitation needs that affect developing and transition economies. We have, however, broadened our portfolio's focus to include social sector lending projects, poverty alleviation, debt relief and good governance. At today's World Bank, we have sharpened our focus on poverty reduction as the overarching goal of all our work.

INTERNATIONAL BANK FOR RECONSTRUCTION AND DEVELOPMENT

The International Bank for Reconstruction and Development (IBRD) is one of five institutions that comprise the World Bank

Group. The IBRD is an international organization whose original mission was to finance the reconstruction of nations devastated by WWII. Now, its mission has expanded to fight poverty by means of financing states. Its operation is maintained through payments as regulated by member states. It came into existence on December 27, 1945 following international ratification of the agreements reached at the United Nations Monetary and Financial Conference of July 1 to July 22, 1944 in Bretton Woods, New Hampshire.

The IBRD provides loans to governments, and public enterprises, always with a government (or "sovereign") guarantee of repayment. The funds for this lending come primarily from the issuing of World Bank bonds on the global capital markets-typically $12-15 billion per year.

These bonds are rated AAA (the highest possible) because they are backed by member states' share capital, as well as by borrowers' sovereign guarantees. (In addition, loans that are repaid are recycled (relent).) Because of the IBRD's credit rating, it is able to borrow at relatively low interest rates. As most developing countries have considerably lower credit ratings, the IBRD can lend to countries at interest rates that are usually quite attractive to them, even after adding a small margin (about 1%) to cover administrative overheads.

HISTORY

Commencing operations on June 25, 1946, it approved its first loan on May 9, 1947 ($250m to France for postwar reconstruction, in real terms the largest loan issued by the Bank to date).

The IBRD was established mainly as a vehicle for reconstruction of Europe and Japan after World War II, with an additional mandate to foster economic growth in developing countries in Africa, Asia and Latin America. Originally the bank focused mainly on large-scale infrastructure projects, building highways, airports, and powerplants. As Japan and its European client countries "graduated" (achieved certain levels of income per capita), the IBRD became focused entirely on developing countries.

Since the early 1990s the IBRD has also provided financing to the post-Socialist states of Eastern Europe and the former Soviet Union. (IBRD), specialized agency of the United Nations, with headquarters at Washington, D.C.; also called the World Bank. Plans were laid at the Bretton Woods Conference (1944) for the formation of a world bank; it was formally organized in 1945, when 28 countries ratified the agreement; there are now 184 members. The bank not only makes loans to member nations, but, under government guarantee, to private investors, for the purpose of facilitating productive investment, encouraging foreign trade, and discharging burdens of international debt.

All members of the bank must also belong to the International Monetary Fund. The bank is self-sustaining and has maintained a profit on its lending activities. It is controlled by a board of governors, one from each member state. Votes are allocated according to capital subscription. Ordinary affairs are conducted by 22 executive directors, five appointed by the five largest capital subscribers, the United States, Germany, Japan, Great Britain, and France, and 17 elected by the remaining members. Regional vice presidents oversee the bank's operations in five regions: Asia, Latin America and the Caribbean, East Africa, West Africa, and (in one grouping) Europe, the Middle East, and North Africa.

The bank also operates the Economic Development Institute, which offers training in economic development for officials of member countries. Closely affiliated with the bank is the International Finance Corporation (est. 1956), which invests in private enterprises without government guarantee. The bank organized the International Development Association (1960) to extend credit on easier terms, mainly to developing countries.

The group of institutions is known as the World Bank Group. Criticism that the IBRD-financed projects were environmentally destructive led the bank to establish an environmental fund (1990) providing low-interest loans for developing countries. Developing nations have complained that the IBRD imposes the free-market system on them, thereby discouraging planning, nationalization, and public investment.

WORLD ECONOMY IN TRANSITION

To counter the speculative attacks on their currencies in late 1997 and early 1998, a number of Asian countries have tightened monetary policy. Although this approach has been questioned by some, experience shows that a period of tight money may be needed to restore exchange rate stability if policymakers fail to act early and forcefully.

During the second half of 1997 and in early 1998, a series of speculative attacks caused several Asian currencies--notably, the Thai baht, Malaysian ringgit, Indonesian rupiah, and Korean won--to depreciate sharply. Although these currencies may have been overvalued before the attacks, their depreciation was far greater than any "correction" that might have been necessary to restore the export competitiveness of the countries in question. What explains the acuteness and persistence of the crisis?

One key explanation is that policymakers failed to address problems in advance of the crisis and did not act forcefully enough when the crisis erupted. Their reluctance either to tighten monetary policy to bolster exchange rates or to keep it sufficiently tight more than temporarily was a particularly important factor contributing to the erosion of investor confidence in the region. The crisis became self-perpetuating.

It is true that, in the short term, tightening monetary policy may exacerbate the difficulties of economies with weak financial systems. But experience has shown that, during a crisis of confidence, the alternative is likely to be worse. An easy monetary policy, by allowing the domestic currency to continue depreciating, undermines confidence and threatens rapid inflation.

For countries with substantial debts in foreign currencies, like some of the Asian economies, a steep currency depreciation may undermine the solvency of domestic firms and financial institutions as much as--or even more than--temporary increases in interest rates. And if confidence in a currency continues to erode, a larger and more prolonged increase in interest rates may be required to stabilize the situation than would normally be necessary in the early stages of a crisis.

As the Mexican crisis of 199495 and recent experiences in Brazil, the Czech Republic, Hong Kong Special Administrative Region, and Russia have shown, once confidence in a currency has been compromised, a period of sufficiently tight money is necessary, whether to defend a currency peg or to stabilize a flexible exchange rate. How tight varies from country to country.

For example, Mexico, because of its history of macroeconomic instability and high inflation, had to allow nominal interest rates on 28-day Cetes (peso-denominated government obligations) to climb to 7080 percent for a few months. Argentina held to its exchange rate peg during the Mexican crisis; had Argentina abandoned the peg, confidence in its currency would have collapsed.

In addition to tightening monetary policy, the two countries addressed weaknesses in their banking sectors, which made it possible for them to survive a period of tight monetary policy without serious damage to their financial systems. They also tightened fiscal policy to reduce current account deficits, bolster investor confidence, and ensure the availability of funds to cover the costs of restructuring their financial sectors.

In late 1997, Brazil was able to stave off contagion from developments in Asia by acting quickly when it began to have difficulties accessing external financing. First, the central bank doubled interest rates--which were already high. Then, when this move failed to relieve pressures on the real, Brazil moved to reassure investors by addressing weaknesses in its public finances; the real stabilized, despite continuing turbulence in Asian markets. In the short term, this move will depress domestic demand, but it will also help to reduce Brazil's substantial current account deficit.

In contrast with Brazil, the East Asian economies were not experiencing fiscal problems before the crisis of 1997. Nevertheless, a moderate degree of fiscal adjustment was appropriate to contribute to the current account adjustments now needed, restore confidence, and cover the costs of financial sector reforms.

To defend their currencies against further depreciation, the East Asian economies also needed firmer monetary policies than were implemented in the early stages of the crises. Although Indonesia initially increased interest rates substantially, it lowered them quickly when stresses developed in the banking system; this premature easing contributed to the further decline of the rupiah. Korea, Malaysia, and Thailand were slow to raise interest rates and implemented smaller increases than Indonesia.

The Philippines, which took quick action in the face of mounting exchange rate pressures, suffered less of a crisis than its neighbors. The short-term effect of the policy adjustments required in East Asia would normally be to slow the growth of domestic demand and, to a lesser extent, of output, as current account deficits are brought into line with reduced external financing inflows.

Unfortunately, because the crisis has been prolonged, the slowdown is likely to be greater than it would have been had monetary policy been tightened more forcefully early on. This is the result not of the recommended policy measures, as some critics believe, but rather of the loss of confidence reflecting policymakers' failure to take swift and effective action at an earlier stage, as well as of the unreasoned panic in financial markets.

REACTION TO TAX CUTS-RATIONAL EXPECTATIONS

According to a school of economic thought that believes in 'rational expectations', when the government sells debt to fund a tax cut or an increase in expenditure, then a rational individual will realise that at some future date he will face higher tax liabilities to pay for the interest repayments. Thus, he should increase his savings as there has been no increase in his permanent income.

The implications are clear. Any change in fiscal policy will have no impact on the economy if all individuals are rational. Fiscal policy in these circumstances may become impotent. Partly because of the limitations of fiscal policy as a tool of demand management, many governments have switched the focus of fiscal policy towards using it to improve aggregate supply as a means of creating the conditions for sustainable economic growth. This is certainly the case with the current government.

Government Borrowing

The level of government borrowing is an important part of fiscal policy and management of aggregate demand in any economy. When the government is running a budget deficit, it means that in a given year, total government expenditure exceeds total tax revenue. As a result, the government has to borrow through the issue of debt such as Treasury Bills and long-term government Bonds. The issue of debt is done by the central bank and involves selling debt to the bond and bill markets.

Does a Budget Deficit Matter?

There is a consensus that a persistently large budget deficit can be a problem for the government and the economy. Three of the reasons for this are as follows:

- Financing a deficit: A budget deficit has to be financed and day-today, the issue of new government debt to domestic or overseas investors can do this. In a world where financial capital flows freely between countries, it can be relatively easy to finance a deficit. But it may be that if the budget deficit rises to a high level, in the medium term the government may have to offer higher interest rates to attract sufficient buyers of government debt. This in turn will have a negative effect on economic growth
- A government debt mountain? In the long run, government borrowing adds to the accumulated National Debt. This means that the Government has to spend more each year in debt-interest payments to holders of government bonds and other securities. There is an opportunity cost involved here because this money might be used in more productive ways, for example an increase in spending on health services or extra investment in

education. It also represents a transfer of income from people and businesses that pay taxes to those who hold government debt and cause a redistribution of income and wealth in the economy

- Crowding-out-the need for higher interest rates and higher taxes. Eventually the budget deficit has to be reduced. This can be achieved by either by cutting back on public sector spending or by raising the burden of taxation. If a larger budget deficit leads to higher interest rates and taxation in the medium term and thereby has a negative effect on growth in consumption and investment spending, then a process of 'fiscal crowding-out' is said to be occurring.
- Wasteful public spending: Neo-liberal economists are naturally opposed to a high level of government spending. They believe that a rising share of GDP taken by the state sector has a negative effect on the growth of the private sector of the economy. They are sceptical about the benefits of higher spending believing that the scale of waste in the public sector is high-money that would be better off being used by the private sector.

Potential Benefits of a Budget Deficit

What are the main economic and social justifications for a higher level of government spending and borrowing? Two main arguments stand out

1. Government borrowing can benefit economic growth: A budget deficit can have positive macroeconomic effects in the long run if it is used to finance extra capital spending that leads to an increase in the stock of national assets. For example, spending on the transport infrastructure improves the supply-side capacity of the economy. And increased investment in health and education can bring positive effects on productivity and employment.
2. The budget deficit as a tool of demand management: Keynesian economists would support the use of changing the level of government borrowing as a legitimate

instrument of managing aggregate demand. An increase in borrowing can be a useful stimulus to demand when other sectors of the economy are suffering from weak or falling spending. The fiscal stimulus given to the British economy during 2002-2004 has been important in stabilizing demand and output at a time of global economic uncertainty. Perhaps Keynesian fiscal demand management has once more come back into fashion! The argument is that the government can and should use fiscal policy to keep real national output closer to potential GDP so that we avoid a large negative output gap.

Bibliography

Ariel Buira: *Challenges to the World Bank and IMF: Developing Country Perspectives*, London, Anthem Press, 2003.

Cavanagh, John, and Mander, Jerry: *Alternatives to Economic Globalization : A Better World Is Possible,* San Francisco, CA : Berrett-Koehler, 2004.

Cook, T.: *Making Laws & Making News*, Washington, DC: Brookings, 1989.

Crigler, Ann N.: *The Psychology of Political Communication,* Ann Arbor, MI: U. Michigan Press, 1996.

Deresky, Helen: *International Management: Managing Across Borders and Cultures,* New York, Harper Collins, 1994.

Dragoljub Najman and Hans d'Orville: *Towards a New Multilateralism: for Internationally Agreed Programs*", Paris, New York, 1995.

Edelman, Murray: *The Symbolic Uses of Politics,* Urbana IL: University of Illinois Press, 1985.

Fernandes, Tony: *Global Interface Design: A Guide to Designing International User Interfaces,* Boston, Academic Press, 1995.

Golding, P. and Harris, P.: *Beyond Cultural Imperialism: Globalization, Communication and the New International Order,* London, Sage Publications, 1997.

Hoft, Nancy L.: *International Technical Communication: How to Export Information about High Technology,* New York, John Wiley & Sons, 1995.

James, Harold: *International Monetary Cooperation Since Bretton Woods,* Washington, International Monetary Fund and Oxford University Press, 1996.

Jan Tinbergen, Antony J. Dolman: *Reshaping the International Order: A Report to the Club of Rome,* New York: E.P. Dutton & Co., 1976.

Le Prestre, Philippe: *The World Bank and the Environmental Challenge*, London, Associated University Presses, 1989.

Lee, C. C.: *The Challenge and Future of International Communication*, Taipei, China Times Publishing Co. Ltd., 1983.

Martin, L. J. and Hiebert, R. E.: *Current Issues in International Communication*, White Plains, NY: Longman, 1990.

Mole, John: *Mind Your Manners: Managing Business Cultures in Europe*, London, Nicholas Brealey, 1996.

Mosco, V.: *The Political Economy of Communication: Rethinking and Renewal*, London, Sage Publications, 1996.

Peet, Richard, Born, Beate: *Unholy Trinity: The IMF, World Bank, and WTO*, New York, Zed Books, 2003.

Peng, B.: *International Communication and Technology*, Taipei, San Min Book Store, 1986.

Reinard, J. C.: *Introduction to Communication Research*, Dubuque, IA: Wm. C. Brown Communications, 1994.

Stiglitz, Joseph: *The Development Round of Trade Negotiations in the Aftermath of Cancun*, London, Commonwealth Secretariat, 2004.

Taylor, P. M.: *Global Communications, International Affairs and the Media since 1945*, London, Routledge, 1997.

Usunier, Jean-Claude: *International Marketing: A Cultural Approach*, New York, Prentice Hall, 1993.

Victor, David A.: *International Business Communication*, New York, Harper Collins Publishers, 1992.

Vines, David and Christopher Gilbert: *The IMF and its Critics: Reform of the Global Financial Architecture*, Cambridge, Cambridge University Press, 2004.

Whetmore, E. J.: *Mediamerica, Mediaworld: Form, Content, and Consequence of Mass Communication*, Belmont, CA: Wadsworth Publishing Company, 1995.

Wiseman, Richard and Robert Shuter: *Communicating in Multinational Organizations*, Thousand Oaks, CA: Sage Publications, 1994.

Index

□□□